Gifts From the Celestial Kingdom

Peking

Shanghai

Canton
Macao

China Sea

Philippine Islands

Sea of Japan

Japan

Kurile Islands

Islands

Ladrone Isls

Caroline Islands

Marshall

Islands

Aleutian Islan

Sandwich Is

Hono

P

P

40

20

0

20

40

100   110   120   140   160   180

Map of Pacific Rim, showing the route of the *Frolic*'s final voyage, June 10–July 25, 1850. Drawn by S. F. Manning.

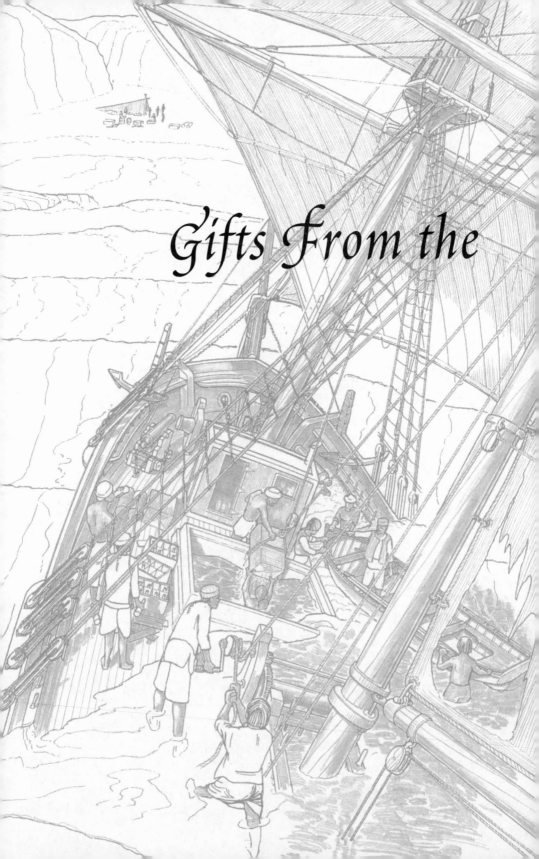

Gifts From the

Celestial Kingdom

A Shipwrecked Cargo
for Gold Rush California

Thomas N. Layton

STANFORD UNIVERSITY PRESS

STANFORD, CALIFORNIA 2002

Stanford University Press
Stanford, California

Printed in the United States of America,
on acid-free, archival-quality paper

Library of Congress Cataloging-in-Publication Data

Layton, Thomas N.
  Gifts from the Celestial Kingdom : a shipwrecked cargo for
Gold Rush California / Thomas N. Layton
      p.   cm.
  Includes bibliographical references (p.) and index.
  ISBN 0-8047-4175-1 (acid-free paper)
    1. Shipwrecks—California—Mendocino County—History—19th century.
2. Frolic (Brig).   3. Ships—Cargo—California—Mendocino County—
History—19th century.   4. Mendocino County (Calif.)—Antiquities.
5. Excavations (Archaeology)—California—Mendocino County.
6. United States—Commerce—China.   7. China—Commerce—
United States.   8. California—Commerce—California.   9. China—
Commerce—California   I. Title.
F868.M5 L385   2002
979.4'1501—dc21   2001049733

Original Printing 2002

Last figure below indicates year of this printing:
11   10   09   08   07   06   05   04   03   02

Typeset by James P. Brommer in 10/13 Sabon
and Poetica display

To
H. A. Crosby Forbes
and
Jacques M. Downs

Contents

List of Illustrations   x
Acknowledgments   xiii

	Prologue	1
CHAPTER 1	The Archaeologist	9
CHAPTER 2	Alta California, República Mexicana, 1844	28
CHAPTER 3	The *Eveline*: Canton, China, 1849	52
CHAPTER 4	The *Frolic*: Canton, China, 1850	74
CHAPTER 5	Point Cabrillo, California, 1850	102
CHAPTER 6	The Wreck Divers	126
CHAPTER 7	The Cargo	149
	Epilogue	197
APPENDIX A	The Cargo of the *Eveline* as Sold in San Francisco	209
APPENDIX B	Invoices for Purchase of the Cargo of the *Eveline* in China	223
APPENDIX C	Bill of Lading for the Final Cargo of the *Frolic*, Canton, May 30, 1850	230

Notes   237
Bibliography   253
Index   259

Illustrations

Flyleaf. Map of Pacific Rim, showing the route of the
         Frolic's final voyage, June 10–July 25, 1850

1.   Map of Northern California and the *Frolic*
     wreck site   2

2.   The *Frolic* struck stern-on against offshore rocks   3

3.   San Jose State University anthropology students
     excavate House 1 at Three Chop Village   10

4.   Fragment of a ginger jar recovered at the *Frolic*
     wreck site and matching sherds excavated at
     Three Chop Village   11

5.   Itemized account for the sale of the *Eveline*'s cargo
     in San Francisco   18

6.   Parasol arm assembly of brass from the *Frolic*,
     with enlarged fragments of ivory from handle   20

7.   Sherds from *Frolic* dragon jar(s) and modern
     dragon jar   24

8.   John H. Everett   29

9.   Monterey in 1842   30

10. Thomas O. Larkin   31

11. Rachel Hobson Holmes Larkin   32

12. Yerba Buena (later San Francisco), circa 1846   33

13. Jacob Primer Leese, Rosalía Vallejo Leese, and their
     six children   35
14. Captain Edward Horatio Faucon   47
15. Richard Henry Dana, Jr.   48
16. John H. Everett's hand-written commentary on the
     first edition of Richard Henry Dana, Jr.'s, *Two Years
     Before the Mast*   49
17. An 1805 Carolus eight-real coin bearing Chinese
     chopmarks, and an 1837 Mexican eight-real coin   50
18. Tingqua's studio in Canton   57
19. Canton factories   59
20. Interior of a Cantonese furniture maker's shop
     showing carpenters crafting Western-style furniture   65
21. John Heard   71
22. Map of South and East Asia, showing the route
     of the *Frolic* in the opium trade   75
23. Map of the Gulf of Canton   76
24. Payment chit with English and Chinese notation   78
25. The brig *Frolic* delivers a cargo of opium to the
     Heards' receiving vessel *Lady Hayes* moored at
     Cumsingmun   80
26. Freight list of the *Frolic*'s final cargo of opium from
     Bombay to China   82
27. Loading the *Frolic* with her cargo for San Francisco   90
28. The brig *Frolic* approaches the Mendocino Coast   103
29. On the night of July 25, 1850, the *Frolic* struck
     offshore rocks stern-on   105
30. Mariano Rosales and his Panaji boys salvage
     supplies from the *Frolic*   112
31. The *Frolic* wreck site, August 1850   115
32. Keetana's band of Mitom Pomo salvage the *Frolic*'s
     cargo of China trade goods   118
33. Caspar Mill circa 1870s   129
34. Louie Fratis   131
35. Don Pifer   133

36.   Jim Kennon   135

37.   Larry Pierson   140

38.   Artifacts from the *Frolic* wreck site displayed on a
      Los Angeles driveway prior to division among the divers   143

39.   Dave and Steve Buller   145

40.   Gold-filigree pendant recovered by Steve Buller from
      the *Frolic* wreck site   147

41.   Payment chit initialed by John H. Everett   153

42.   Bowls carried in stacked rolls aboard the *Frolic*   154

43.   Fragments of long dish and lid from a dinner set of
      Canton pattern from the *Frolic*, shown next to a
      Canton-pattern heirloom piece   156

44.   False pearls from the *Frolic*   158

45.   Typical China-export leather-covered camphor trunks
      in graduated sizes, and trunk hardware from the *Frolic*   161

46.   China-export portable writing desk, and desk hardware
      from the *Frolic*   165

47.   Nine nesting brass weight cups from the *Frolic*   169

48.   "Plain fiddle"–pattern spoons from the *Frolic*   171

49.   Two identical silver tinderboxes from the *Frolic*   174

50.   Gold jewelry from the *Frolic*   176

51.   Wooden window sash (or mullion) with capiz-shell
      pane from Chinese-manufactured prefabricated house
      carried aboard the *Frolic*   181

52.   The China house at Double Springs Ranch, and
      Chinese character on rafter of China house   183

53.   Architect's rendering of the China house at Double
      Springs Ranch   185

54.   Mother-of-pearl gaming piece from the *Frolic*   187

55.   Ivory artifacts from the *Frolic*   189

56.   The "mystery object": an ivory side-panel of a game
      recovered from the *Frolic*   191

57.   Horn and bone artifacts from the *Frolic*   193

58.   Thomas Layton, Charlene Duval, and Edna Kimbro
      sorting potsherds from the Castro adobe   199

Acknowledgments

One of the most important things we archaeologists do is to transport artifacts from their resting places—their archaeological context—back to the behavioral contexts in which they once functioned. My attempt to accomplish that task with the *Frolic*'s cargo required that I investigate many fields beyond my own. For this reason I have many people to thank for their help; though, for my imperfect use of their information and counsel, only I am to blame.

I dedicate this volume in appreciation to two scholars whose research and writings, conducted independently, encompass most aspects of American commerce with China during the eighteenth and nineteenth centuries: Dr. H. A. Crosby Forbes and Dr. Jacques M. Downs.

Crosby's lifetime of rigorous research has defined the study of China export goods, while Jack has brought the same scrutiny to the lives of the people who developed and carried out that commerce. My debt to them is immense.

Colleagues who kindly read early drafts of this manuscript and made important suggestions are James P. Delgado, Richard H. Dillon, Dr. Jacques M. Downs, Dr. H. A. Crosby Forbes, Richard Kelton, Glory Anne Laffey, Dr. Kent G. Lightfoot, Samuel F. Manning, Dr. Adrian C. Praetzellis, and Dr. Russell K. Skowronek.

I am grateful to Samuel F. Manning of Camden, Maine, for his creativity in drafting the original illustrations that bring so much life to this book.

All of the artifacts described here are curated in the Frolic Shipwreck Repository at the Mendocino County Museum, Willits, California. I thank museum director Daniel Taylor for his assistance in es-
tablishing that repository.

Throughout this research I have made repeated requests for information from three archives. I am thankful for the assistance of Laura
Linard, Director of Historical Collections, and Timothy J. Mahoney,
Manuscripts Librarian, at the Baker Library of the Harvard Business
School. I also thank Dr. Conrad Edick Wright and Nicholas Graham
of the Massachusetts Historical Society and Dr. William R. Sargent
and Karina Corrigan at the Peabody Essex Museum.

For permission to reproduce art from their private collections I thank
Richard Kelton, founder of the Kelton Foundation Collection, Cora
Ginsburg, and Francis D. Everett, Jr.

For artifact photography and assistance with the computer software
used to print the images I thank Carlos Araya, Tom Liden, Romaldo
Lopez, and Jean Shiota.

The following scholars provided invaluable information and assis-
tance: Dr. Rebecca Allen, Terese Tse Bartholomew, Dorothy Bear, Rich-
ard Carlson, Dr. Paul G. Chace, Marcus De Chevrieux, Philip P. Choy,
Dr. Julia G. Costello, Nicholas Dean, Jack Douglas, Patricia Dunning,
Charlene Duval, Robert L. Edwards, Amelie Elkinton, Dr. Jan English-
Lueck, William S. Evans, Jr., Richard O. Everett, Salvatore J. Falcone,
Dr. Glenn J. Farris, David L. Felton, Daniel G. Foster, John W. Foster,
Margaret Fratis, Dr. Jay Reynolds Freeman, Peter Gallagher, Jr., Dr.
Brian Gilmour, Patricia M. Grove, R. Paul Hampson, Dr. Vida C. Kenk,
Edna E. Kimbro, Karl Kortum, Dr. Stephen K. Kwan, Dr. Kai-Cheong
Leung, Karl Lueck, Michelle Majer, Deborah McLear, Dr. Victoria Pat-
terson, Mary Praetzellis, Mark Rawitsch, Robert Schwemmer, Dr. Peter
D. Schultz, Dwight D. Simons, Marianne Simoulin, Mark Simpson,
Edith Smith, Patrick B. Smith, Dr. Randall Stross, Dr. George L. Vas-
quez, Christine Crossman Vining, Edward Von der Porten, Dr. Eldon
Worrall, and Kathleen Zaretsky.

Fifteen California sport divers generously allowed me to study their
collections from the *Frolic* shipwreck, and most of them have since -
donated those collections to the *Frolic* repository at the Mendocino
County Museum; they are David Buller, Steven Buller, Cliff Craft,
Louie Fratis, Patrick Gibson, Dale Hartesveldt, James Kennon, Vilho

Kosonen, Vic LaFountaine, Bruce Lanham, Richard Lanham, Patrick Philpott, Larry J. Pierson, Dr. Kenneth Prewitt, and Dr. Paul Selchau.

One of the joys of this project has been meeting descendants of families closely associated with the historical characters in this book. Information relating to the Faucon family came from Morris Earle and Louise Earle Loomis. Family information about the Everetts was graciously given by Francis D. Everett, Jr., Marion Everett Gallagher, Peter Gallagher, Jr., Richard O. Everett, and Cecily M. Johnson. For Dixwell family information I thank Bazil S. Dixwell, Marcia Dixwell DiMambro, Lauren Dixwell Rayfield, Leslie Dixwell, Stephanie Dixwell Quigley, Epes Dixwell Chase, Eleanor Dixwell Morrison, and Douglas Dixwell Morrison.

For emotional and financial support during the writing of this book I am grateful to my extended family—my father, Dr. Laurence L. Layton, who lived to see the final draft, Annalisa Layton Valentine, Dr. David Layton Valentine, Deborah J. Layton, Larry J. Layton, Terrance Lim, Mabel Miyasaki, and Michael Cartmell.

Finally, I thank my editors: Muriel Bell, Executive Editor at Stanford University Press, who has encouraged me in this transgression from archaeological convention, and Ruhama Veltfort, who has improved my prose and my thinking at every stage of the writing process.

Gifts From the Celestial Kingdom

Prologue

Swimming along the tape line, clenching the regulator in my teeth, I felt a slow stab of cold water run down my neck and between my shoulder blades. The yellow tape ahead disappeared into a haze of pale green. I hung motionless in the water. The ocean floor seemed to be moving beneath me, four feet forward and four feet back with each surge of the tidal current.

My partner and I had laid the measuring tape along our best estimate of where the keel line of the remains of the brig *Frolic* would be. We'd wired the shoreward end of the tape to the eye of a massive coraline-encrusted anchor that lay in ten feet of water. Slowly, we had unreeled the tape through a forest of kelp stems, over a congealed mound of anchor chain, and along a two-foot exposure of hand-hewn timber that I thought might be the *Frolic*'s keel. The tape line continued past a pile of cast-iron ballast blocks, eventually stretching along the entire ninety-nine-foot length of the vessel's hull and a little beyond. There, at a depth of twenty-five feet, I had wound the reel end of the tape around the steel spike we'd placed on the bottom to provide a permanent anchor for the other end of our baseline. In my thirty-five years of archaeological field work I had laid out scores of sites in grids with stakes and string, but the inquisitive harbor seal swimming above me reminded me that all of my previous experience had been on dry land.

I had spent thirteen years researching and writing the *Frolic*'s story,[1] but now, in the summer of 1997, I was actually seeing the wreck itself

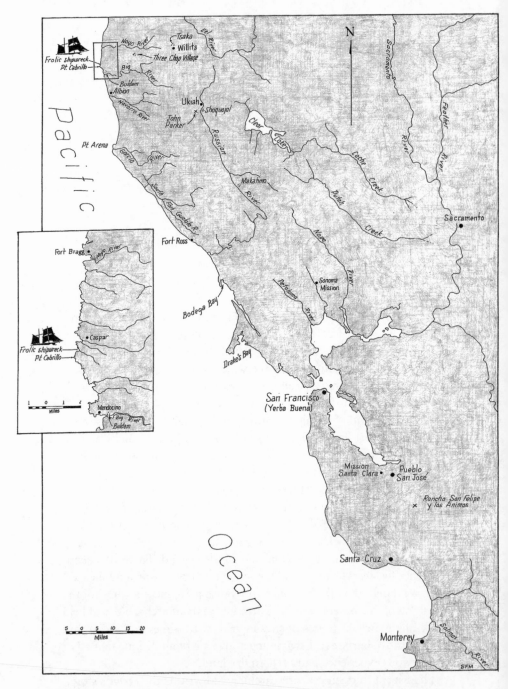

Figure 1. Map of Northern California and the *Frolic* wreck site. Drawn by
S. F. Manning.

for the first time. Although I had completed a course in scuba diving almost a year earlier, we had waited ten months for the water to become "flat" enough for us to begin mapping what remained of the vessel. Diving conditions in the turbulent water along California's Mendocino Coast have little relation to the weather. Even on a clear, windless day, gigantic waves generated by storms far across the North Pacific crash against the jagged rocks. Here, less than a hundred feet from the shore, waves broke directly above the wreck, rendering diving difficult and scientific recording virtually impossible.

As I finned along the baseline about thirty feet from the spike, I began to see an increasing number of blue-and-white potsherds scattered across the bottom. The coarse porcelain bowls that had been among the least valuable of the China trade goods the *Frolic* carried had been crushed as the vessel broke up during the winter of 1850, but the fragments themselves were virtually indestructible. The far more valuable cargo of silks—what had not been salvaged by the Indians and treasure hunters—had quickly decomposed in the salty ocean water.

The bulk of the *Frolic*'s cargo had consisted of perishable items: fabrics, furniture, lacquered ware, and even an entire prefabricated house.

Figure 2. The *Frolic* struck stern-on against offshore rocks marked by the breaking waves at upper left. She eventually lodged near the large rocks in the lower right. Photo by Thomas Layton.

Besides the broken pottery, the only part of the cargo that still remained were items that had been collected by sport divers—some brass hardware (mostly handles, hinges, and screws), a few pieces of gold-filigree jewelry, some silver forks and spoons, and a small, motley collection of bone, ivory, horn, and tortoiseshell articles. With so little to work with, how could I write a meaningful description of the cargo that had been almost completely lost just hours before it would have reached Gold Rush San Francisco?

I had already written a scientific monograph describing our archaeological excavation at Three Chop Village.[2] At that ancient Pomo Indian hamlet, fifteen miles inland from the coast, we had been surprised to recover bits of Chinese porcelain ground into beads and green bottle glass flaked into arrowheads. Painstaking investigation of the historical record had connected those pieces of porcelain and bottle glass to an 1850 shipwreck just north of Point Cabrillo. I had written the story of the brig *Frolic*: her construction in Baltimore, her life as an opium clipper, and her sudden obsolescence. When steam vessels were introduced along the opium route between Bombay and China in 1848, the *Frolic*'s owners, Augustine Heard & Company, had decided to fill her with a cargo of China trade goods to sell in California.

Now that the *Frolic*'s story had been told, the time had come for me to write about her cargo. But I did not want to write a typical archaeological report—a meticulously detailed inventory of thousands of items, of interest only to other scholars. I thought the *Frolic*'s story was exciting, and that a more general audience would be curious about the cargo she had carried. I could imagine a reader, anticipating a tale of a shipwreck and sunken treasure, pulling a book from the shelf, flipping through pages of scholarly tables, specimen numbers, and measurements, and then snapping it shut in disappointment. I wanted to write a different kind of report, a book that would be accessible to ordinary people who wanted to know about the past. I had followed a trail of clues to unravel the story of the *Frolic*, and I would have to do the same now to discover the secrets of her cargo. And below me, on the ocean floor, was the trail of blue-and-white porcelain sherds that I hoped would lead me to that end.

As I swam around the low stack of cast-iron ballast blocks, I could see more and more tiny blue-and-white sherds. They were spread out across the bottom, a confusion of pieces in no coherent pattern, scattered by 147 years of storms and 40 years of pillage. Twelve wreck divers had been persuaded to donate the tangled brass, jagged sherds, and crushed bottle glass they had gathered from the wreck over years of sport diving and treasure hunting. Those artifacts—over two thousand of them—now sat in my lab at San Jose State University waiting to be described.

I was accustomed to working with artifacts excavated from precisely annotated sites by carefully supervised anthropology students, but the pieces I had to report on now had been ripped willy-nilly from their contexts. None of the divers who recovered them had bothered to take notes that might help me reconstruct their interrelationships. Now, underwater, I looked at the only intact remains of the wreck—the vessel's anchors, the corrosion-melded mound of anchor chain, a large windlass, or winch, one small stack of undisturbed ballast blocks, and the exposed keel timber. The random scatter of pottery sherds was the only evidence that the *Frolic* had carried any cargo at all.

As I swam up to the baseline's halfway point, the sherds became more abundant, forming a chaotic jumble of broken bowls and saucers. One of my students had written a thesis describing the design patterns on the sherds donated by the divers, and I recognized the figures she had described: "snail," "peach and fungus," and "bamboo."[3]

To my left, comprising all that was left of the *Frolic*'s hull, was a two-foot exposure of timber with two inch-thick brass bolts protruding from it. I'd seen bolts like these in the divers' collections, many a foot and a half or more in length. Their heads had been flattened by the sledgehammer blows of African-American slaves at the Gardner Brothers shipyard in Baltimore during the summer of 1844. George Gardner himself had inspected the placement of these bolts, confident that their barbed tips would bind the *Frolic*'s white oak frames to her keel forever.

I checked my regulator console. The digital clock told me I had fifteen minutes of bottom time remaining. I swam back about eight feet seaward and turned to get a broader view. But the tape disappeared into masses of kelp in both directions, and I couldn't see more than ten feet of bottom. This was hardly the wider perspective I'd wanted. I focused my eyes on a rock covered with sea anemones waving right and left in ten-second cycles in perfect rhythm with the surge. As I turned away, something caught my eye. At the base of the rock I saw a zebra pattern of parallel horizontal white lines. It reminded me of what one diver, Jim Kennon, had said about his discovery of the wreck in 1965: "The bottom looked unnatural—man-made." I swam closer to the zebra pattern and saw the snapped-off edges of five porcelain bowls, one nested inside another, just as they had been packed in China almost 150 years ago.

I could imagine a pair of Chinese hands holding a stack of twenty bowls, wrapping them in coarse matting, and tying off the roll with a hemp cord. The *Frolic*'s bill of lading listed 676 such rolls of ceramics, and I could picture a line of stevedores tossing them one to the next, up the gangplank and down into her main hatch, as the brig lay at anchor at Whampoa. There, under the vigilant eye of Mr. Deutcher, the first mate, the rolls had been tightly packed in the soggy bottom of the hold.

I could imagine how Captain Edward Horatio Faucon[4] would have observed the diminishing stack of porcelain rolls and considered whether their weight, together with the hundreds of crates still to be loaded and the blocks of cast-iron kentledge at the bottom of the hold, would provide sufficient ballast to keep his vessel from heeling over in a stiff breeze. In 1846, Faucon had lost part of an opium cargo when Bombay port officials had underballasted the *Frolic*. In the Strait of Malacca, the vessel had laid over so far that her pumps couldn't reach the accumulating bilge water and some of the opium had been ruined.[5] Faucon would not have wanted to chance that happening with 243 cases of silks aboard. As I imagined the scene on the *Frolic*'s deck—the stevedores, Captain Faucon, a pet monkey perched high in the rigging— I could see someone talking animatedly to the captain. It was his closest friend, the Heard's accountant John Hurd Everett,[6] the man who had personally purchased the articles for this cargo.

I tied a strip of red plastic flagging to a kelp stem to mark the location of the nest of broken bowls and continued swimming down the baseline. I was thinking about John Everett and his friends, Thomas Larkin[7] and Jacob Leese,[8] in Gold Rush San Francisco. In the spring of 1849, a year before the *Frolic* had been loaded at Whampoa, these longtime California merchants had dispatched the brig *Eveline* to China with three thousand ounces of placer gold dust to buy a cargo of China trade goods. Leese had arrived in Canton as supercargo aboard the *Eveline*, but having no experience in the Chinese marketplace, he had immediately sought out his old friend John Everett for help. A year later, when Everett and the Heards made plans to purchase a cargo for the

Frolic, they studied the *Eveline*'s accounts as a guide, choosing for the *Frolic* only those items that had garnered at least a 75 percent profit for the *Eveline*.

John Everett had spent thirteen years aboard Boston brigs, traveling up and down the California coast from San Diego to San Francisco Bay, peddling manufactured goods at missions, ranchos, and sleepy pueblos in exchange for "California banknotes"—dried cowhides destined for the tanneries of Massachusetts. Five years later, when that trade had played out, Everett was in China struggling to collect a cargo suited to the needs of newer Californians who were arriving by the thousands in wagon trains rolling across the country and aboard ships sailing around the Horn.

I glanced at my console readout. In the twenty-eight minutes I had been on the bottom, I had traced the entire baseline of the wreck. As I flagged a large sherd that had once formed part of the bottom of a china jar, it reminded me of the portrait of John Everett painted on ivory by a Chinese artist—the only surviving image of him. Everett had posed next to a jar much like this one. I had taped a copy of that portrait to the wall above my desk to remind me that there was more to the *Frolic*'s cargo than a collection of broken pieces. The two thousand objects lying in my lab were material remnants of a commercial enterprise that had once spanned the Pacific, a venture engaged in by living people. Now I had the opportunity—and the responsibility—to tell their story.

I was more than a little far afield from the usual activities of my profession. Usually, what we archaeologists do is dig things up. We uncover features—immovable things like house foundations, fire pits, and posthole impressions; "ecofacts"—botanical and faunal remains, such as seeds and animal bones; and artifacts—movable things made or modified by people. Features usually cannot be removed without destroying them, so they are carefully documented as they are excavated. The locations of artifacts and ecofacts are precisely recorded, both in relation to these features and within a three-dimensional grid.

Ecofacts are usually sent off to be studied by specialists in botany or zoology. The artifacts are taken to the archaeological lab to be cleaned, catalogued, dated, and described. Finally, the data from the features, the artifacts, and the ecofacts are combined to reconstruct an account of the past. Descriptions of a past culture at different points in time can then be used to explain how cultures change. This last task—interpreting and explaining the past—is, of course, the ultimate goal that justifies the sweaty excavations and the mind-numbing tedium of cleaning, cataloguing, and describing the physical properties of the things recovered.

But the *Frolic* shipwreck was not a normal archaeological site. Although my students had carefully excavated the few Chinese potsherds and pieces of green bottle glass found at Three Chop Village, the two thousand artifacts from the *Frolic* wreck site had been removed by sport divers who had not recorded their positions in relation to each other or to the parts of the vessel. No ecofacts had been collected. And the divers had destroyed virtually all that remained of the vessel in order to remove the artifacts.

The loss of this data was a tragedy, yet somehow it was strangely liberating. It meant that I could no longer be a purist, studying perfectly documented artifacts. If I wanted to describe the *Frolic*'s final cargo and explain a set of commercial relationships that had ended almost a century and a half before, I was at once condemned to deal with data far more messy than I was accustomed to, and blessed with the opportunity to trace less-traveled pathways.

The study of the *Frolic*'s cargo took me to antique stores, museums, and auction houses; to business archives, probate courts, and genealogical societies. It led me to interviews with wreck divers and—eventually—to fifth-generation descendants of John Everett, Captain Edward Faucon, Thomas Larkin, and other principals of the *Frolic* adventure. And to tell the story, I have taken yet another step away from traditional archaeological respectability. I have interpolated between the facts to create vignettes of John Everett in San Jose, California, and Canton, China; and of the *Frolic*'s sailors at Point Cabrillo in 1850. These intimate glimpses of humanity do not come easily to an artifacts-based materialist. Throughout the text I have attempted to make clear which information is firmly documented and which is my attempt to imagine what might have happened.

What follows, then, is the story of a China cargo—from John Everett sitting on a rented horse in the town square of Pueblo San José de Guadalupe, Alta California, in July 1844, to an archaeologist sitting in his lab at San Jose State University, just six city blocks away, trying to bridge the intervening 153 years.

CHAPTER I

The Archaeologist

I had begun my research on the Mendocino Coast in 1979, shortly after I joined the faculty at San Jose State University. The Anthropology Department wanted me to develop an archaeological research program to teach students proper field and laboratory techniques. We spent our first four field seasons excavating three coastal shell middens, and by the end of that time I had developed a cultural chronology that spanned 4,000 years. All of the sites we had dug, however, represented short-term, seasonal occupations by Indian people—Mitom Pomo—whose permanent villages were elsewhere. Not only did the middens reveal only a narrow range of food-gathering activities, but their deposits were shallow and had been badly jumbled by burrowing rodents. In order to investigate the home territories of these people, in the summer of 1984 I moved my field work inland, where I expected to discover a more complete record of Pomo lifeways in sites representing their permanent homes.

Instead, my students found small pieces of porcelain and green bottle glass in what we had expected to be a late prehistoric Mitom Pomo house pit. The small fragments of blue-and-white porcelain looked vaguely Asian, and we argued over their meaning. Since I believed the house to be prehistoric, dating from before European-Americans settled the area in the mid–nineteenth century, I had to think that the tiny fragments of porcelain and bottle glass had been dumped onto the site more recently—perhaps by people from a nearby logging camp. Never-

Figure 3. San Jose State University anthropology students excavate House 1 at Three Chop Village in July 1984. Photo by Thomas Layton.

theless, as we continued our excavations, each screen load of deposit revealed more fragments of coarse white porcelain, some bearing bits of blue oriental design.

I knew virtually nothing about ceramics. The California and Great Basin sites that I had spent most of my career excavating had been occupied by basketmakers, not potters, and my particular specialty was the analysis of chipped stone tools. To me, the presence of historic porcelain and bottle glass meant an unfortunate contamination of an otherwise pristine late prehistoric archaeological site, and I needed to explain it away. I had wanted to excavate a purely Pomoan assemblage from a site "uncontaminated" by European-American contact, and now Three Chop Village didn't look like that kind of site. Still, I hardly expected that I would spend the next fourteen years of my life following the trail of those potsherds.

The next morning, we excavated a fragment of bottle glass clearly flaked along one edge to form an arrow tip and a piece of porcelain carefully ground into a disk-like bead. Apparently, the Indians living at Three Chop Village had possessed Asian ceramics and green bottle glass. By the end of our two-and-a-half week field season we had excavated three house depressions and recovered 50 fragments of porcelain and 150 fragments of green bottle glass.

I was a California Indian specialist with no particular interest in Asian ceramics. Still, I could see that these sherds provided a unique key to precise information about the Indians, if I could only find out where the pottery had come from. A ranger visiting the site had remarked that the pieces looked like ones on the "pottery beach" near Caspar, where they were believed to have washed in from an offshore shipwreck. If we could identify the ship and prove that the ceramics we had found at Three Chop Village came from it, we would not only know what part of the coast the Indians had visited, but we would also have an exact date for the occupation of the houses.

I found out that sherds of Ming period Chinese porcelain, similarly ground into beads, had been excavated from Coast Miwok archaeological sites along Drake's Bay, seventy miles to the south, and attributed to visits by Sir Francis Drake in 1579 and Sebastián Cermeño in 1595.[1] Perhaps the wreck at Caspar was a sixteenth-century Manila galleon. Eager to date the ceramics, I began to contact local museums and historical societies for any information they might have on a shipwreck near Caspar. I struck pay dirt at the Kelley House Museum in Mendocino. Dorothy Bear, the museum historian, told me that in the spring of

Figure 4. Fragment of a ginger jar (*left*) recovered at the *Frolic* wreck site bearing cobalt-blue design elements exactly matching those on sherds (*right*) excavated at Three Chop Village. Note that the lowermost sherd is chipped and ground into a bead blank. Height of ginger jar is 16.6 cm; diameter of bead blank, 15 mm.

1851, J. B. Ford had recorded in a diary his trip up the coast from Bodega to salvage a shipwreck. Instead of sunken treasure, he had found Pomo women wearing silk shawls.[2] Dorothy proceeded to show me a small collection of sherds and a shoe from a wreck near Caspar. The donor had requested anonymity, but she gave me the telephone number of Richard Tooker, the intermediary who had arranged the donation.

Richard told me the wreck was probably that of the *Frolic*, which had sunk on July 25, 1850. I hoped the diver he knew would have additional sherds from the wreck that might match ours, so I asked Richard for the man's name. Eventually, I was able to talk with fifteen divers and examine their collections, most of which were later donated to the Frolic Shipwreck Repository I established at the Mendocino County Museum.

As I looked over the divers' collections, I realized that the remains of a shipwreck comprised a complex assemblage, including not only the cargo but the outfits and equipment necessary to the vessel's operation, the personal belongings of the officers and the men, and the pieces of the vessel itself. Besides the ceramics, jewelry, and hardware that appeared to have been part of the *Frolic*'s cargo, I had seen navigation tools: parallel rules, dividers, and telescope tubes. One diver, Larry Pierson, had recovered pump valves, pulley blocks, oil lamps, and pieces of pine planking with copper sheathing nails still attached. His collection, languishing in his San Diego garage, included beautifully preserved wooden pistol handles and musket stocks, moist from years of soaking in polyethylene glycol; a hinged "brass hand" paper holder that might have graced the captain's desk; Chinese coins with square holes; and an 1845 British East India Company half-cent piece bearing the image of Queen Victoria. In order to distinguish the cargo of the *Frolic* from the various parts of the vessel, its outfits, and the personal belongings of the officers and men, I would need to research the history of the ship, from her construction through her disastrous final voyage.

In *Western Pomo Prehistory*, a 1990 monograph describing my American Indian researches, I had included, as chapter 4, my description of our excavation of the houses at Three Chop Village and a brief discussion of the connection between the porcelain and bottle glass and the *Frolic* shipwreck. But I was still a long way from analyzing the *Frolic* and her cargo.

I had expected to complete my research and writing on the cargo of the *Frolic* during a sabbatical leave in 1989, but my research at the Baker Library of the Harvard Graduate School of Business led me instead to the story of Augustine Heard & Company and that firm's involvement in the opium trade. The Heard firm had been the one to commission the construction of the *Frolic* as an opium clipper to transport up to 103,000 pounds of narcotic, three times a year, from Bombay to Canton for sale in China.

In the end, the product of my sabbatical was not a description of the *Frolic*'s last cargo, but *The Voyage of the Frolic: New England Merchants and the Opium Trade*, which described the life of the vessel herself: her conception in Boston, her birth in Baltimore, and her active life traversing the China Sea in the service of the opium trade. One chapter briefly described the *Frolic*'s final voyage to California and her wreck on the Mendocino Coast, but I had yet to analyze the China trade goods she had carried on that last voyage. I would have to write another book.

Among the documents I had seen in Boston was the *Frolic*'s final bill of lading, so I knew what her hold had contained when she sailed for California. But I had only a tiny fraction of the original cargo itself to study. Not only had sailors, Indians, and ranchers salvaged most of the *Frolic*'s goods from the wreck, but what remained on board had decomposed in the sea for over a century. I didn't have complete camphor trunks—only handles, hinges, and locks. I didn't have cases of furniture—only one tiny fragment of white marble from an inset table top. All that was left of a Chinese-manufactured prefabricated house was one piece of a wooden window frame, a few fragments of oystershell pane, and a ceramic doorknob assembly. The artifacts I had to describe only suggested a cargo—they hardly represented one. I had only the nonperishable residue: crushed ceramics, nonferrous metals, and a few odd pieces of horn and bone.

The students were gone and I was alone in the archaeology lab with the artifacts I had borrowed from the *Frolic* repository. The fourteen cabinet drawers and eight archival boxes contained over two thousand things—or, to be more precise, pieces of things. Of the twenty-one thousand porcelain bowls that had been loaded aboard the *Frolic* in May of 1850, only one had survived intact.

The *Frolic*'s three-page bill of lading had listed a total of 1,602 cases, packages, rolls, and boxes,[3] but unfortunately, the individual items they had contained were only summarized in general categories:

243 cases Silks	3 cases Silverware
18 cases Grass cloth	30 cases Camphor trunks
101 packages comprising 1 House	54 cases Furniture
4 cases Paintings	100 boxes Sweetmeats
30 cases Lacquered ware	174 packages Sundries
9 cases Scales & weights	84 cases Beer
676 rolls Chinaware	23 cases Merchandise
20 cases Chinaware	33 packages Merchandise

I wanted to describe the cargo in the same terms that nineteenth-century merchants engaged in the China trade had used, but I would need to find out what specific articles were included within such generalities as "174 packages Sundries," "23 cases Merchandise," or "243 cases Silks." In addition to the *Frolic*'s bill of lading (Appendix C), I also had twenty-one payment chits documenting purchases from various Chinese merchants. On one side of each three-by-eight-inch sheet, the payment was recorded in English and initialed by John H. Everett, the Heards' accountant. On the back side, the Heards' comprador had reproduced the record in Chinese.[4] But although these documents provided the name of each Chinese merchant and the total cost of the goods supplied, the merchandise was still not itemized. Only three chits—for beads, matting, and writing desks—gave more specific information than the generic descriptions found on the bill of lading. It was good to know that Laoqua supplied the lacquered ware and was paid $1,005.80, but none of the individual pieces, or even types of ware, was listed.

Comprador

> *Pay Laoqua for Lacq'd Ware*
> *pr Frolic less 31.10*   *$1005.80*
> *One Thousand & five 80/100 Dollars*
> *3 June 1850*   *AH&Co*
>   *pJHE*

I did have an eyewitness description of one very small part of the cargo, but it was no more specific. In 1851, George Gibbs, on a U.S. Army expedition to make treaties with the Indians of Northern California, had visited John Parker's hut in the Russian River Valley.[5] In his diary, Gibbs wrote that he had seen "huge china jars, camphor trunks, and lacquered ware in abundance, the relics of some vessel that had been wrecked on the coast."[6] But Gibbs was no archaeologist, and he, too, had neglected to describe the lacquered ware in detail. And not one piece of it that might have remained on the *Frolic* had been preserved to be collected by wreck divers after a century and a third under water. While I could guess that the *Frolic*'s lacquered ware had included tea caddies, chess tables, shaving boxes, and a host of other items commonly manufactured in China at that time, my documents provided no evidence.

There was, however, another important clue. Ten months before the *Frolic* embarked on her final voyage, the Heards had assembled a cargo for another vessel, the brig *Eveline*. The *Frolic*'s cargo had been patterned on the *Eveline*'s: the Heards had purchased for the *Frolic* only those items that had brought over 75 percent profit for the *Eveline* in San Francisco.[7] The *Eveline*'s bill of lading listed 1,351 cases, packages, bales, rolls, and kegs of cargo. But, like the *Frolic*'s, the list was like an intriguing table of contents ripped from the face of a now lost book.[8] The merchandise was listed only as twenty-five very general categories:

100 cases Sweetmeats	1 case Raisins
2 bales Blankets	1 case Silver Ware
25 cases Trunks	1 case Measuring Rods
100 rolls Matting	2 cases Scales & Weights
57 cases Furniture	7 cases Gutta Percha Buckets
1 case Pearl Buttons	689 packages China Ware
7 cases Clothing	6 packages Rattan Chairs
45 cases Lacquered Ware	12 packages Rattan Baskets
11 cases Sundries	3 packages Umbrellas
6 cases Boots & Shoes	92 packages Tea
14 cases Grass Cloth	55 kegs White Lead
8 cases Nankeens	2 cases Merchandise
106 cases Silks	

I thought perhaps I might find a more detailed description of the *Eveline*'s cargo among the papers of Thomas Larkin and Jacob Leese, the California entrepreneurs who had owned the vessel and sent her to China. Scattered among ten published volumes of Larkin papers, I found documents that described the purchase of the 197-ton brig *Eveline* in January 1849, and her dispatch to China with three thousand ounces of placer gold dust to buy a China cargo.[9] Letters from Leese in China to Larkin in Monterey expressed his chagrin on discovering that stocks of merchandise in Canton had been depleted by a recent spate of purchases by other vessels, and his impatience as he waited through the hot, humid summer for more cargo goods to be manufactured.

Larkin's papers also included a personal shopping list for the Larkin family, including "one set of drawers . . . 3 to 4 feet high having the top turn over for a writing desk," two portable writing desks, a set of chocolate-colored camphor-wood trunks, fine matting for three rooms, shawls and clothing for his wife Rachel and daughter Caroline, a "full tea sett and dinner sett of best Chinaware [with] large pieces marked Rachel Larkin—small pieces marked R.L.," and finally, "some few choice light filagree articles for table and sideboard display." Larkin had given this list to Leese along with $31\frac{1}{4}$ ounces of gold (worth $500) of his personal funds for their purchase.[10]

Leese had managed to buy nearly everything on the list—my first glimpse of the incredible variety of export items for sale in China[11]:

2 writing desks	6 pearl seals
1 silver card case	1 tea & dinner sett (crockery)
1 silver card tray	1 ivory Mandarin boat
1 silver fan	1 ivory flower boat
1 silver cup	1 sett silver ware
1 gold watch chain	1 leather trunk
1 silver fan handle	1 silver basket
6 feather fans	

I went back to the *Frolic*'s bill of lading for a clue to the next step in my research. The three cases of silverware on the *Frolic* had presumably contained at least as great a variety of items as were listed on the Larkin invoice from the *Eveline*. The contents of the rest of the *Frolic*'s cargo categories must have been just as diverse. Somehow I would have to penetrate those vague categories and discover the wonderful items hidden inside the cases and packages.

I had extracted all the information I could from the Larkin papers, and so I turned to Jacob Leese. Perhaps, somewhere, there was a collection of his papers. Jacob Leese had been a brother-in-law of John B. R. Cooper, the captain of the *Eveline* (who was also half-brother to Thomas Larkin). After an active life as an entrepreneur in early California, Leese had become vice-president of the Society of California Pioneers in 1855. Ten years later he had lost his fortune in a Baja California land speculation scheme and had lived the next twenty-five years in poverty and obscurity in Texas. In 1890, at the age of 81, he had returned to San Francisco, where he was struck by a wagon while crossing a busy street. Members of the Society arranged hospital care for the destitute old man and he had donated his treasured scrapbook to the Society library.[12]

I was the only person sitting in the reading room of the Society of California Pioneers in San Francisco. The collection, I had been informed, was not open to the public. It was for the exclusive use of Society members—all of whom were direct descendants of European-Americans who had arrived in California before January 1, 1850. Properly humbled, I held my breath for a moment as the librarian disappeared behind the stacks to search for the Leese scrapbook—my last hope for a clue that might lead me to a detailed description of the *Frolic*'s cargo. As I waited, I found myself nervously counting books on shelves, counting shelves per bookcase, and trying to do the multiplication in my head.

The librarian returned with the scrapbook and several folders full of documents that had been carefully removed from it. The top folder held an application for a cattle brand, dated 1842, complete with Leese's sketch of a cow's head with ear markings. There were letters dating from the 1830s from merchants aboard trading vessels lying off the California coast. There was a long letter from Thomas Larkin regretting Leese's imprisonment during the 1846 Bear Flag Revolt, and another, announcing Larkin's appointment as Naval Agent for the United States and asking Leese to be one of four guarantors of his $30,000 bond.

I opened the second folder and saw a stack of fifteen ledger sheets. The first was headed in a bookkeeper's bold script. My heart pounded: I was looking at the itemized account for the sale of the *Eveline*'s cargo in San Francisco. The sale had been held November 20–24, 1849, by Lovering & Gay auctioneers at Mellus & Company's warehouse, Central Wharf. Each nine-column page listed not only the names of the customers, but the articles purchased and the price paid per item. The first page detailed gold shirt studs, silver needle cases, lacquered shaving boxes, and Chinese lanterns. I flipped ahead to page fifteen and read the

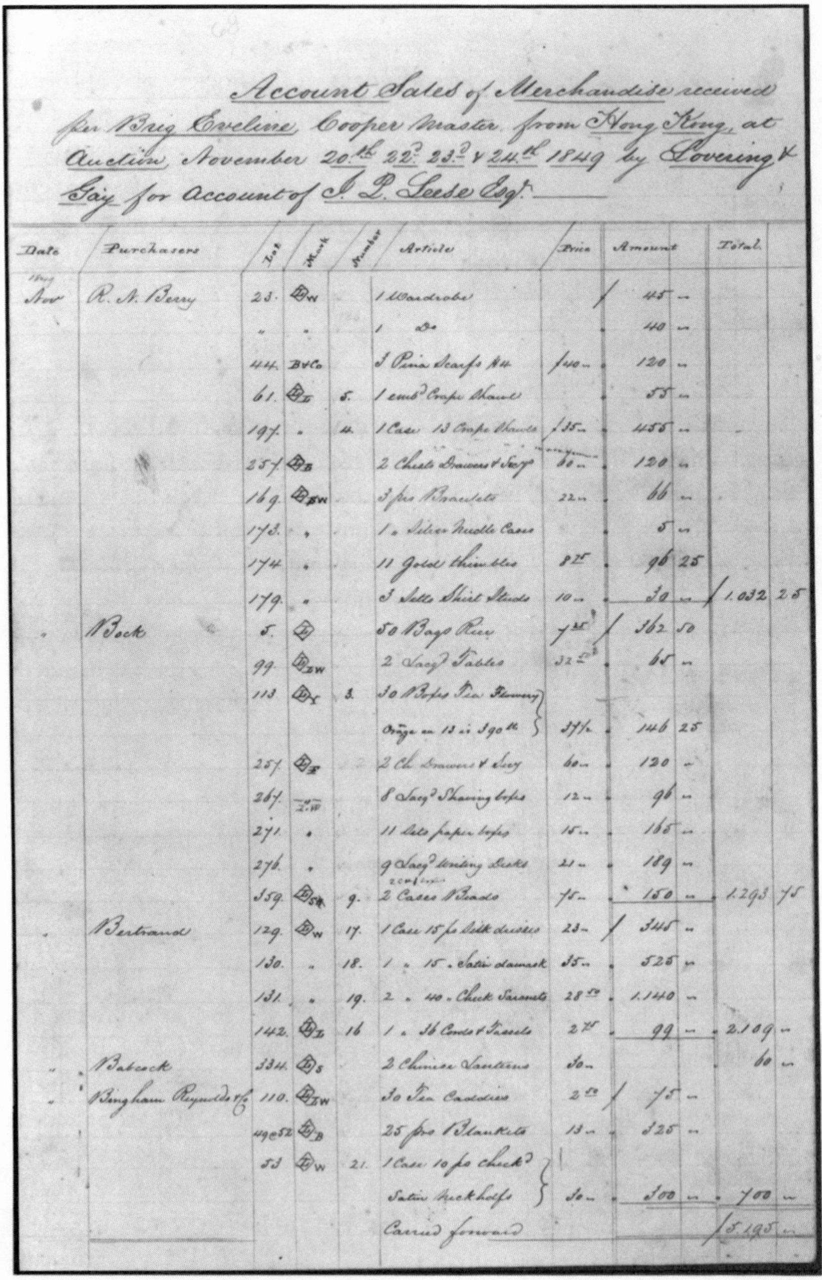

Account Sales of Merchandise received per Brig Eveline, Cooper Master from Hong Kong, at Auction, November 20th 22d 23d & 24th 1849 by Lovering & Gay for account of J. L. Leese Esqr.

Date	Purchasers	Lot	Mark	Number	Article	Price	Amount		Total	
1849 Nov	R. N. Berry	23.	◊W		1 Wardrobe		45	–		
		"	"		1 Do		40	–		
		44.	B&Co		3 Pina Scarfs #4	40 –	120	–		
		61.	◊	5.	1 embd Crape Shawl		55	–		
		197.	"	4.	1 Case 13 Crape Shawls	35 –	455	–		
		257.	◊B		2 Chests Drawers & Secy	60 –	120	–		
		169.	◊SW		3 prs Bracelets	22 –	66	–		
		173.	"		1 " Silver Needle Cases		5	–		
		174	"		11 Gold thimbles	8.75	96	25		
		179.	"		3 Setts Shirt Studs	10 –	30	–	1.032	25
"	Bock	5.	◊		50 Bags Rice	7.25	362	50		
		99.	◊SW		2 Lacq Tables	32.50	65	–		
		113.	◊	3.	30 Boxes Tea Flowery Orange ea 13 " 390 lb	37½	146	25		
		257.	◊		2 Ch Drawers & Secy	60 –	120	–		
		267.	ZW		8 Lacqd Shaving boxes	12 –	96	–		
		271.	"		11 Sets paper boxes	15 –	165	–		
		276.	"		9 Lacqd Writing Desks	21 –	189	–		
		359.	◊SR	9.	2 Cases Beads	75 –	150	–	1.293	75
"	Bertrand	129.	◊W	17.	1 Case 15 ps Silk dresses	23 –	345	–		
		130.	"	18.	1 " 15 " Satin damask	35 –	525	–		
		131.	"	19.	2 " 40 " Check Sarsnets	28.50	1.140	–		
		142.	◊	16	1 " 36 Cords & Tassels	2.75	99	–	2.109	–
"	Babcock	334.	◊S		2 Chinese Lanterns	30 –			60	–
"	Bingham Reynolds & Co	110.	◊ZW		30 Tea Caddies	2.50	75	–		
		49 & 52	◊B		25 prs Blankets	13 –	325	–		
		53	◊W	21.	1 Case 10 ps Check Satin Neckhdfs	30 –	300	–	700	–
					Carried forward				5.195	–

Figure 5. Itemized account for the sale of the *Eveline*'s cargo in San Francisco, November 20–24, 1849 (page 1 of 15). Courtesy Society of California Pioneers.

final entry: twelve ivory back-scratchers at $1.10 each. It could have been an invoice for a tourist shop on Fisherman's Wharf.

The hundreds of individual sales totaled $78,155.67. The last page itemized commissions and sales charges—$9,673.90, including $184.50 for the champagne, cheese, and crackers served to the buyers. I could hardly believe my eyes. In an instant, I had gone from rags to riches— from the meager listing of general categories on a bill of lading to the most richly detailed listing of a China cargo I had ever seen.

In the next folder I found five invoices documenting the purchase of the *Eveline*'s cargo items in Canton. Incredibly, the detail was even greater than on the auction listing. Not only did I find the name of each Chinese supplier, with the name of each article and its unit price, but design features and colors were also catalogued.[13] Years before, one of the *Frolic* wreck divers had retrieved the crumpled brass arms of a folding umbrella and some tiny fragments of tortoiseshell and ivory that appeared to fit together. Now I spotted an invoice entry that explained all of the pieces—seventy-two silk parasols supplied by Wongshing at $2.25 each, with "tortoise sh'l staff, ivory handles & lots of chowchow fringe." Not only that, but the bookkeeper had listed all six color combinations, from "pink & white" to "light blue & lilac."

Back at my lab, I considered the strange patchwork of data I had to work with. On the one hand, I had what remained of some *Frolic* artifacts, after over a century of pilferage and decomposition. On the other hand, I had a virtually complete listing of the *Eveline*'s cargo, the model for the *Frolic*'s. Now, I needed to fit those pieces together.

I had met Dr. H. A. Crosby Forbes in the summer of 1989, when he was Curator of Chinese Export Arts at the Peabody Museum (now the Peabody Essex Museum) in Salem, Massachusetts. I had arrived at his office with viewing sheets filled with color slides of *Frolic* artifacts. Crosby was a historian of the China trade—he knew material culture, but only as complete objects, and I was about to drag him into the piecemeal world of archaeology. He was amazed to see the fragments of "oyster"-shell (actually capiz-shell) windows from the Chinese-manufactured prefabricated house. He was mystified by the pieces of hardware—latches, locks, and handles. I had brought along sherds of the most abundant ceramic styles, but he had difficulty visualizing whole jars and bowls from the tiny jagged fragments. Although he was firm in his conviction that the *Frolic*'s cargo was uniquely important

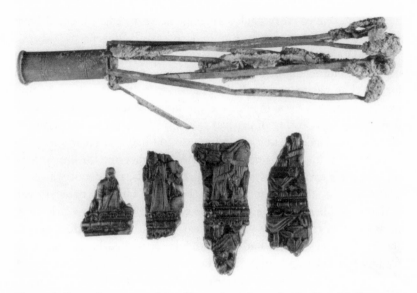

Figure 6. Parasol arm assembly of brass (*top*) from the *Frolic*, with (*bottom*) enlarged fragments of ivory from handle. Length of arm assembly, 18 cm; height of lower-right ivory fragment, 3 cm.

and needed to be studied, Crosby was not able to identify many of the fragments I showed him. He did, however, recognize some of the pot-sherds as coming from "ginger jars," which, he told me, had recently become popular as decorator lamp bases.

Most of the artifacts in the Peabody's China trade collection were well documented, objects purchased by New England families during the last years of the eighteenth and the first third of the nineteenth centuries—the halcyon days of the China trade. They had been expensive; many were custom-manufactured souvenirs meant for display rather than for actual use. But although there were some luxury items aboard the *Frolic*, much of her cargo, especially the ceramics, consisted of inexpensive domestic goods for sale to ordinary California consumers—laborers in mining camps as well as nouveaux-riches merchants in growing towns and cities.

Moreover, the *Frolic*, firmly dated to 1850, had contained a cargo manufactured and dispatched much later than most of the China trade luxury goods at the Peabody. By 1850, Chinese merchandise was no longer high fashion, and the China trade was already in decline. As

Crosby and I walked through the collections' storage areas, past shelf after shelf of polychrome pots, grotesque animal figurines, and sets of fine dishes bearing family coats of arms, I could appreciate his enthusiasm. The *Frolic*'s domestic wares documented a very different China trade.

I had noticed another discrepancy between what I had learned of American merchants in China and the museum's representation of that history. I had spent most of a month at Harvard's Business Library reading the Augustine Heard Company papers, which detailed that firm's participation in the opium trade. "Crosby," I said one day, "your own great-grandfather, Robert Bennet Forbes, was a senior partner in Russell & Company, the Heards' major American competitor in the opium trade. Why is there no mention of opium anywhere among these exhibits?" Crosby grinned—the answer was obvious. The Boston and Salem bluebloods who had created the museum and funded it for generations preferred that there be no mention of the more lurid aspects of their history—even a century and a half later.

The next morning, deep in the bowels of the collections' storage area, I tried to match my twisted and corroded chunks of hardware with the gleaming brass fixtures that adorned the museum's complete pieces of furniture. The large brass handles that most of the wreck divers had collected were relatively easy to match to the hardware on the Peabody's camphor-wood trunks. The rest of the *Frolic* artifacts, however, presented more of a problem.

I had been struggling for some time to interpret eight strap-shaped brass pieces, each joined by a riveted, hinge-like elbow. In 1986, I had brought them to the meetings of the Society for Historical Archaeology in Sacramento, hoping that these experts would know what the hinged straps might have been used for. I thought they might have formed parts of some navigational apparatus used to measure distances, plot courses, or scribe circles; but while these historical archaeologists found my hypothesis unconvincing, none of them could offer any alternative explanation. Now, as I opened a camphor trunk in the basement of the Peabody Museum, the puzzle was solved in an instant! The trunk's lid was held upright by a brass elbow brace identical to my mystery artifacts. That identification gave me confidence that with persistence I might be able to make some sense of the rest of the collection.

Now I needed to learn more about China trade commodities. Most of the relevant publications were either museum exhibit catalogues or sales brochures for the major auction houses—Christie's, Sotheby's, and Martyn Gregory. The most important exceptions were Crosby's own books on China trade silver,[14] and a magnificent volume, *The Decorative Arts of the China Trade*, by his colleague, Carl Crossman. These references, however, only confirmed what Crosby had told me, that while luxury items were well known, there was virtually no information available about ordinary, inexpensive trade goods. I hoped my own efforts would result in a useful contribution.

⚜

One afternoon, back in San Jose, as I was writing up my research at my favorite coffeehouse, I felt a need for a break. I walked up Lincoln Avenue and wandered into an antique shop. I scanned the shelves for blue-on-white Chinese ceramics, but when I didn't see any, I started toward the door. Stacked on a chair was a pile of free circulars advertising San Francisco Bay Area antique shops. What caught my eye was a headline: "Great Wall, Chinese Antique Furniture, wholesale and retail. Visit our 10,000 square foot warehouse."

The following morning I drove up the Eastshore Freeway to San Leandro. The Great Wall was a warehouse divided into two parts, one filled with antiques, the other with contemporary merchandise, and I headed for the antiques. Stacked from floor to ceiling along two walls were heavy black tables, leather-covered trunks, and apothecary cabinets with rows of square drawers, each with a tiny brass pull-ring. The old furniture gleamed under fresh coats of lacquer and furniture oil. The back wall was hung with long wooden signs bearing carved characters in red and gold. I had seen similar signs in photographs of nineteenth-century Chinese street scenes.

I peeked into the adjacent storeroom and saw other old pieces in their original, unrestored condition—stacks of scratched and worn cabinets caked with ancient dirt, showing the wear patterns of everyday use. Mr. Shing, the Great Wall's proprietor, told me that he had just received two more container loads from China. I felt the same queasiness as when I had handled my first wreck-diver artifacts from the *Frolic*. The things in The Great Wall had been looted, too, but on a far larger scale—here, I was seeing the cultural patrimony of China being shipped out by the ton.

I was looking for a set of trunks similar to those that the *Frolic* had carried. Mr. Shing had twelve antique leather-covered camphor trunks on display, but their brass handles and latches were quite different from the trunk hardware in the *Frolic* collection. I showed him photographs of complete camphor trunks from the Peabody Essex Museum's China trade collection, but Mr. Shing had never seen ones like them. As I pointed out details of handles, corner garnishes, and the hundreds of brass tacks decorating edges, faces, and lids, it suddenly dawned on me that the camphor trunks at the Peabody—and those aboard the *Frolic* —had been made expressly for export to the West, with decorative elements familiar to Westerners. The *Frolic*'s trunks were not, then, purely "Chinese"—they were European-American trunks, made in China. Incredibly, I had never before considered the full meaning of the term "China export goods."

I tried to see how the Chinese who manufactured the *Frolic*'s trunks might have viewed them. Mr. Shing had been tactful, saying only that he did not recognize the designs, but those nineteenth-century artisans might have judged the *Frolic* trunks to be garish monstrosities manufactured for tasteless barbarians. I wondered whether trunks made for export to Africa or Southeast Asia had borne special designs suited to those markets, too.

That morning, I had laid several blue-and-white sherds from the *Frolic*'s cargo onto the Anthropology Department's photocopy machine. I now carried these dark, blurry images in my notebook, hoping to find some comparable blue-and-white porcelains among Mr. Shing's antiques, but there were no matches. One of my prints showed a large basal sherd recovered from the *Frolic* during a recent dive. The curvature suggested a jar that expanded upward from a bottom about a foot wide. The eight-inch band of design showed a pattern of stylized waves breaking around the base of the jar. The sherd was similar in curvature and thickness to several other sherds from wreck divers' collections, two of which bore what looked like fish scales, and another, a long, billowy blob.

At The Great Wall, I looked at a display of modern blue-and-white ceramics and saw a stack of flowerpots on the floor. There, extending around the base of one, was the familiar pattern of breaking waves. I pulled out my photocopies and laid them out on the floor in front of the pot. The "fish scales" in the photocopy were replicated on the side

Figure 7. Sherds from *Frolic*
dragon jar(s) (*left*), and
modern dragon jar (*right*).
Lower sherd, 18.9 cm
horizontal; dragon jar,
14 cm vertical.

of the pot, but now I could see they were dragon scales. And above
and below the dragon were the same billowy blobs, representing stylized clouds. Were these pots truly Chinese, or, like the *Frolic*'s camphor trunks, were they simply Chinese-manufactured? The designs, in-
corporating dragons, waves, and clouds, were Chinese in origin. But
the vessel forms—flowerpots with holes in the bottom for water to
drain out—were obviously made for suburban backyard patios and
the California lifestyle.

Stacked on the floor and on the shelves I found dragon flowerpots
ranging from eight inches to over three feet in height. I picked one up
and found another packed inside. As I carried my two dragon pots to
the checkout stand I marveled at the efficiency of shipping them in
graduated sizes, nested one inside another. I remembered the wood furniture I had seen at the Peabody Essex Museum: sets of tables, one fitting beneath the next, and camphor trunks, likewise designed to fit in-

side each other in nests of five. Not only had the Chinese produced export goods to meet Western tastes, but, where possible, they had manufactured them in size increments so they could be nested to efficiently fill every bit of expensive cargo space aboard vessels bound for Boston, London, and San Francisco. The woman at the register ran her sensor wand across the bar codes. My dragon pots and matching dishes were on sale for $19.95 each.

As I drove home, I thought about Canton in 1850 and the strange, artificial world of shops clustered around the "factories"—offices—of Western merchants. These shops had specialized in objects produced only for export rather than for the domestic market in China. The closest approximation of that marketplace today would be the tourist shops of San Francisco's Chinatown, where souvenirs are sold to visitors from Nebraska and Berlin. The next morning, I drove to San Francisco.

The historic Chinatown district in San Francisco actually embraces two distinct purlieus. One is the home of a dynamic Chinese-American community, the other the Chinatown of tourist shops and restaurants. I passed the shops that served the residents of the neighborhood—grocery stores with bok choy and bitter melon stacked in crates along the sidewalk, butcher shops with whole pigs and ducks hanging in the window, and herbalists with dishes of shriveled ginseng root and dried sea horses, all with signs written in Chinese characters. But the China trade had never been a commerce among Chinese. Rather, it had been a business of Chinese merchants supplying goods and services to a Western market, and that was the Chinatown I needed to see now. I turned onto Grant Avenue and looked for the largest tourist shop I could find.

China Bazaar was crowded with tourists. At the cash register sat a bored-looking Asian-American girl wearing a Cal Berkeley sweatshirt. Next to a large rack of postcards was a bucket crammed with long-handled wooden implements—"Backscratchers, 99¢." I remembered the ledger entry from the sale of the *Eveline*'s cargo: her ivory backscratchers had sold here in San Francisco for $1.10 in November of 1850. I walked down an aisle past bins of garishly colored rubber snakes and lizards.

I passed a row of obese, red-and-gold plaster Buddha figures. There were ceramic angels with gold-edged wings playing lyres and lutes, and potholders with pictures of cable cars and the Golden Gate Bridge. There were ceramic toothpick dispensers depicting convicts in black striped suits, with "Alcatraz" written across their chests and sharp wooden toothpick tips emerging from the open tops of their heads to represent their bristly hair. I thought of the figurines I had seen on the shelves of the Peabody Essex Museum—porcelain Buddhas, Chinese tradesmen, and costumed Mandarins designed for display on sideboards and buffets. Those statuettes and the Alcatraz toothpick dispenser seemed to me to be of the same mercantile tradition. I wondered if my friend, Crosby Forbes, would wince—or laugh—at such a comparison.

I began to look more carefully for articles that would resemble more closely those shipped aboard the *Frolic* and the *Eveline*. I saw tables with inset stone tops, of the same white marble as the fragment recovered from the *Frolic*. There were lacquered chessboards with jade-green plastic chessmen. The cow-horn checkers from the *Frolic* had probably been made to accompany similar game boards. The Chinese boats reminded me of the ivory Mandarin boat and a flower boat Jacob Leese had purchased for Thomas Larkin. But it was illegal now to import elephant ivory, and the boats I saw on display were made of finely grained ivoroid plastic.

In the back of the room I saw a matching set of three carved wooden chests in graduated sizes. When I opened the top chest, the rich, medicinal scent of camphor wafted forth. A Chinese Commercial Guide published in 1863 had warned that some cheaply made China trunks were actually made of pine and merely rubbed with camphor oil.[15] I looked at these chests and wondered.

I walked around the corner to Washington Street and into Sam Wo Restaurant—ten feet wide and three stories tall. I remembered how during the 1970s, the now-deceased waiter, Edsel Ford Fong, had harangued me and other bemused patrons in a mélange of Spanish, English, and Chinese. I was reminded of the China trade pidgin, a mixture of Portuguese, English, and Chinese, that John Everett must have spoken in Canton as he went from shop to shop assembling the *Frolic*'s cargo. I ordered a bowl of *juk*—thick rice soup with roast pork. On the worn Formica table were two bottles, one of soy sauce and one of Louisiana hot sauce. Both Edsel Fong and John Everett would have approved.

As I sipped tea, my thoughts returned to John Everett. Before he went to China, Everett had been engaged in the hide-and-tallow trade for over a decade, traveling up and down the California coast peddling Boston-manufactured goods for dusty cowhides. His friendship with Jacob Leese and Thomas Larkin and his knowledge of the California market had brought Leese to him in Canton in 1849 to purchase the *Eveline*'s cargo—and that, in turn, had led to his purchase of the *Frolic*'s cargo in 1850.[16]

Everett had spent many nights at the home of Jacob Leese, not far from the spot I sat in now. Early in July 1844, here in Yerba Buena— later to be named San Francisco—Everett had planned his trip down the Peninsula to collect from his defaulting debtors in Pueblo San José. One of the key figures in the *Frolic*'s last voyage, he had been a California businessman in the years before the discovery of gold brought consumer culture to the new state. His story was part of the broader context I wanted to provide for the story of the *Frolic*'s cargo.

Here in Yerba Buena, 150 years ago, Everett would have read the most recent newspapers from New York and Boston—four months old—and worried about how the rumored annexation of Texas to the United States might affect business here in Mexican California. Over brandy, he and Leese might have spoken of their old friend Captain Edward Faucon, now completing his third voyage to China. In his letters, Everett had written of waiting impatiently for Thomas Larkin to send his holsters up from Monterey.[17] He would need visible weapons to discourage thieves as he rode south to Pueblo San José along the road that Californians still call El Camino Real.

CHAPTER 2

Alta California, República Mexicana, 1844

*F*rom my third-floor office window, looking beyond the Bank of America building, I could almost see where San Jose's first plaza had once been. All week I had been reading descriptions of Alta California during the Mexican period. John Hurd Everett was an inveterate letter writer, and I had discovered a series of his letters to his friend Thomas Oliver Larkin, written between 1844 and 1850. I looked down at the three letters lying on my desk—one dated July 13, 1844, posted from Yerba Buena, and two posted on July 21 and 26 of the same year from Pueblo San José.[1]

In these letters, Everett described his last trip to California before he left it for the China trade. The commerce in hides and tallow that had been the mainstay of the economy of Mexican California had become unprofitable. Cheaper hides were now being shipped to New England tanneries from Argentina. Not only that, but it was Everett's misfortune to be employed by Eaton & Company, whose inexperience in the trade had greatly undermined his best efforts as supercargo of the brig *Tasso*. Everett's letters reeked of his frustration in trying to collect overdue notes from his debtors, and his doubts that the *Tasso* would earn even enough to cover the costs of the venture.

I tried to imagine Everett in Alta California. Taped to the wall above my desk was a color laser print of a portrait of a blue-eyed John Everett painted in watercolor on ivory in China. His starched white collar accentuated an incipient double chin, while beneath his open jacket

Figure 8. John H. Everett
(1810–89) in China circa
1850. Watercolor on ivory.
Courtesy Francis D. Everett, Jr.

his five-button vest struggled to restrain a developing "corporation."
Thinning, reddish-brown hair framed a still-youthful face. His parted
lips suggested he might have been interrupted while relating a risqué
anecdote.

Everett had sailed up the California coast in July of 1844, stopping
at Monterey to see Larkin and at Yerba Buena to visit Jacob Leese before riding down the peninsula to Pueblo San José. I closed my eyes
and imagined him stepping ashore in Monterey on an early morning
153 years ago, emerging from the fog with his valise on his shoulder,
and walking up from the beach toward Thomas Larkin's house.[2]

"Smallpox—Stay back!"

Thomas Oliver Larkin, reputedly the richest man in Alta California,
seemed strangely small standing on the upstairs balcony of his house,
a bulky blanket draped over his shoulders. Everett dropped his valise

HARBOUR and CITY of MONTEREY, California 1842.

Figure 9. Monterey in 1842. Larkin's house and store, somewhat inflated by the artist (hired by Larkin), is the two-story building with full-length balcony at far left. Lithograph. Courtesy Oakland Museum.

to the ground. It held his soiled clothing and a ledger crammed with overdue notes. He rubbed his shoulder where the weight of the two pistols at the bottom of the bag had dug into it as he walked. As the oarsmen had pulled toward the beach, Everett had dreamed of the familiar guest room in Larkin's luxurious upstairs quarters above his store. His stomach had growled as he anticipated a breakfast of frijoles on hot tortillas, and coffee. Rachel Larkin would give his dirty laundry to her Indian washerwoman. Over cigars, he and Tom would trade the most recent news from their correspondents in Boston, New York, and Honolulu in the Sandwich Islands. And he could retrieve the holsters he had left on his last visit, before the winter rains. It wouldn't hurt to look well-armed as he traveled around collecting debts.

"Rachel's got the pox," shouted Larkin.

Larkin had recently returned from Mazatlán, where smallpox had broken out. Word had spread up the coast like wildfire. Had Larkin brought the pox to Monterey? Everett had received an inoculation just weeks ago at Abel Stearns' house in Pueblo de los Angeles—pus taken from a woman recovering from smallpox, rubbed into a small incision in his arm. He massaged his arm, still sore from the inflammation. That was supposed to prove the vaccination had "taken." But who would be fool enough to enter a house visited by that scourge?

"How is she?" asked Everett.

"I think she's improving," said Larkin, raising his eyes skyward.

Everett stood immobile on the street. He had been so certain of Tom Larkin's hospitality that he had made no alternative plan.

"Get back on the schooner," shouted Larkin. "Take my overdue notes and collect down the Bay. Stay with Leese. I'll find your money down here."

Everett opened his valise, untied the black ribbon that secured his bulging ledger, and flipped through the pages. He pulled out five notes, each bearing the signature and the flamboyant flourish of a merchant or ranchero living within a morning's ride of Monterey.

Regaining his composure, Everett shouted instructions. "Go after

Figure 10. Thomas O. Larkin (1802–58), circa 1846. Courtesy Society of California Pioneers.

Figure 11. Rachel Hobson
Holmes Larkin, age 42, in
1849. Oil portrait by Joseph
Knapp. Courtesy Society of
California Pioneers.

Riós and Dye. If they don't pay, get a lien on their houses." He stopped
short. His words were echoing down the street. Everyone would know
his business. He walked closer to the balcony.

"Get what hides Riós has," he whispered. "And get a note legalized
by the *juzgado* for the rest—due next year at 2 percent, and no discount for cash."

Tibercio, Larkin's *majordomo*, brought out a small packet of papers and placed them on the ground. Everett hesitated. No one knew
exactly how smallpox was transmitted. He rubbed his vaccinated arm
again, like a talisman. Pulling a dirty handkerchief from his pocket, he
wrapped it around the papers and shoved them into the ledger. Hoist-
ing the valise back onto his shoulder, Everett retraced his steps toward
the beach.

The sun had already dropped below the hills when they anchored off
Yerba Buena. They had been delayed in Monterey because the customs

officer could not be found. Then they had waited outside the narrow entrance to the bay of San Francisco for the incoming tide. Someday, thought Everett, one of the new steam vessels plying the Atlantic routes might enter the bay against the current of the outgoing tide, but no one would dare try it on a sailing vessel. The captain would remain aboard till morning, when the high tide would facilitate an easy landing, but Everett, impatient for a clean bed and a hot meal, paid a sailor to row him to the beach.

The oars creaked as they pulled around the stern cable of an oil-stained Russian whaler, the only other vessel anchored in the shallow cove.

"She smells like the State Street fish market," said the sailor, a Boston man.

Everett smelled the sweetly rancid odor and grunted agreement. He stared up at the massive hulk, her port riding-light flickering in the dusk.

The rising tide had not yet covered the glistening expanse of mud and sea grass that stretched out from the landing platform. The sailor poled the boat until it would go no further. Everett considered his pre-

Figure 12. Yerba Buena (later San Francisco), circa 1846, by Tingqua. Gouache on paper. Courtesy The Kelton Foundation Collection.

dicament. He took off his shoes, placed them inside his valise, rolled up his trouser legs, and stepped into the cold sticky muck.

"Sweet Jesus," he exclaimed as one trouser leg slipped down into the mud. Wisps of fog were blowing in, partly obscuring the whaler.

"Damn Eaton & Company," he muttered under his breath. They had ignored his recommendations—based on his ten years of experience in the trade—and dispatched the *Tasso* to California without cash to pay her duties. Most Boston firms covered their customs fees in Monterey by canceling overdue notes owed them by the governor for supplies advanced during previous voyages. Since the governor of Alta California rarely got funds from Mexico City, he was constantly in debt to the firms that supplied what he needed to feed and support his retinue of administrators, servants, and soldiers. But this was Eaton's first venture in California, and since the company had no notes on the government and no cash for duties, Everett had been forced to surrender a third of the *Tasso*'s cargo to Micheltorena's port warden at a hefty discount.

Everett readjusted the weight of the valise on his shoulder and began walking barefoot up the slope to the frame house Leese used as both a residence and a store. He felt winded and sore, and all of his forty-one years.

"Señor Everett!" A tall, sandy-haired man—Jacob Leese—emerged from the doorway and lifted the valise from Everett's shoulder. He looked down at Everett's wet trouser legs and mud-caked feet. "Did you swim ashore?" he asked.

Everett was staring at four open barrels with blocky Cyrillic lettering, lined up against the wall. He glanced back toward the Russian whaler still lying in the bay.

"Oui, Monsieur," he replied, placing his right hand between the buttons of his shirt and striking a Napoleonic pose. "Just like those barrels did."

Leese smiled sheepishly.

The whaler was no longer visible, the last of its rigging enveloped by the fog. Everett wondered what had been in Leese's barrels when they came ashore. As a courtesy, whalers were allowed to put in for firewood, food, and water without inspection by the customs officer. But their water casks rarely came ashore empty, and the contraband merchandise they contained paid no duties. It wasn't fair, Everett thought.

Figure 13. Jacob Primer Leese (1809–92), Rosalía Vallejo Leese, and their seven children, circa 1861. Courtesy Society of California Pioneers.

The whalers were taking little risk even if they were caught smuggling. As they had no real need to stop in California, banishment would do them no harm. But for Boston brigs, making the four-month voyage around the Horn year after year to ply the coast, smuggling was out of the question—one seized load would mean being barred from the California trade forever.

"I figured you wouldn't stay long in Monterey," said Leese. "It's a shame about Mrs. Larkin—how is she?"

"Tom thinks she's improving," Everett nodded, "and how is Doña Rosalía?"

"She's up visiting the General," Leese sighed. "She got tired of shivering here in the fog. She'll be back, in two weeks."

Leese had grown prosperous after his marriage to María Paula Rosalía Vallejo—her brother was General Mariano Guadalupe Vallejo, *co-mandante* of Alta California. He had come far since Everett first met him ten years earlier, when he and Faucon had anchored the *Alert* at San Pedro. Leese had been virtually destitute then. The year before, he had collected 450 mules from Missions San Miguel and San Luis Obispo to sell in Santa Fe, but had lost all of them to Indians on the Mojave River. Hoping to make himself useful enough to justify a small commission, Leese had taken Everett to be introduced at nearby ranchos. Even then, flat broke, Leese had been full of schemes to make his money back.

Then, as Everett and Faucon were sailing back to Boston aboard the *Pilgrim*—having exchanged vessels, as planned, with Captain Thomp-son—Leese had somehow arranged to accompany the newly appointed Governor Mariano Chico on the long ride from Pueblo de los Angeles up to Monterey. By the time they had reached the presidio, the ambi-tious Ohioan had a signed authorization in his pocket to proceed north to Yerba Buena and take a town lot of his choice. Within a year he had built a store, converted to Catholicism, married Rosalía, and acquired a launch, the *Isabella*, to deliver merchandise around the bay and up the rivers into the interior. And very little of that merchandise, Everett re-flected, had ever paid duties. Now Leese divided his time between Yerba Buena and the town of Sonoma, where he served as *alcalde*, or mayor.

"Come on in," said Leese with a chuckle. "I reckon a hot meal is what you want to see first."

The glowing ship's lamp dangling from a rafter revealed that Leese's shirt was as dirty as Everett's own. A half-finished cup of coffee stood on the table. Leese poured a fresh cup for Everett and disappeared into the back room that served as his store. Everett scanned the shelves along the far wall. A stack of blue-and-white Chinese platters stood on the bottom shelf. He wondered if they had come from the whaler. He pic-tured the open barrels outside the door. It wouldn't have been necessary to pry off the tops just to fill them with water.

Leese returned with a bottle. "They come from the Islands," he said, gesturing toward the platters. He poured a slug of brandy into each cup.

That was another thing that was making it more difficult to sell Boston goods, Everett thought. "Warm-water Yankees"—Boston men based in the Sandwich Islands—were assembling cargoes of Chinese silks and other goods dumped in Honolulu by vessels from a score of ports. They could have their ships off the California coast in less than a month, ready to smuggle merchandise ashore at night. They never even revealed their presence in California waters, so, like the Russians, they paid no duties on their goods. Both Leese and Larkin did a good business buying such merchandise without inquiring into its provenance.

Everett drank deeply. The sweet *aguardiente* tasted better than the sour Mission wine he'd had at Monterey. Now *californios* were bartering it for imported goods.

"Things ain't been so good," said Leese as he recorked the bottle. "Hides are scarce, and hard money's scarcer."

"What about the *matanzas?*" asked Everett.

"Nobody's skinning cows. They're scared about Texas—afraid Don Manuel's gonna call 'em all up for service. You seen any papers?"

Larkin had included a newspaper with the packet of notes. It was a Boston paper, four months old, carried overland to Mazatlán and then up the coast in a Chilean barkentine. It was filled with the bluster of Southern senators demanding annexation of Texas. Talk like that would only delay the *matanzas* further, threatening the entire Yankee trade in California.

"I hear Larkin still holds notes for the good Commodore's stay in Monterey," said Leese.

Everett nodded. Two years before, the "courageous" Commodore Jones of the American squadron had "captured" the town of Monterey while it slept. His apology and retreat two days later had done little to appease the Mexican authorities. Now John Charles Frémont, that primping banty rooster, was traveling down the valley of the San Joaquin, "exploring" the territory of the Mexican Republic. These belligerent gestures from the United States were hardly improving the climate for trade.

The mission bell sounded faintly in the distance. A dog's bark echoed against the bare hillside above Leese's house. Everett considered the best route for his trip down the peninsula to Pueblo de San José. Perhaps, first, he should cross the bay on Leese's launch and collect from the Peraltas and their neighbors along the eastern shore. Then, after Larkin sent up his holsters, he would be ready to ride south.

❊

Don Antonio María Pico, first *alcalde* of San José de Guadalupe, sat behind a massive oak table. Everett stared at the scuffed green tendrils of a painted floral design that seemed to crawl up its legs. Probably manufactured at Mission Santa Clara, he thought, as he waited for the *alcalde*'s dispensation to take the one empty chair. With regal formality Don Antonio held Everett's passport up to the leftmost stream of light passing through the barred window, scrutinizing the blue seal pasted at the bottom by the *alcalde* of Yerba Buena. Turning, he pulled his chair forward to a loud squawk. A chicken emerged from under the table, fluffed its feathers, and disappeared out the doorway.

Leaning back in his chair, Don Antonio pulled his stained jacket around his girth. The brass buttons fell short of the holes, and two were missing. Eagle pattern, thought Everett. Tom Larkin had a gross of them in his store at Monterey—an unsold remainder of the *Tasso*'s cargo. The frayed gold braid on Don Antonio's cuffs needed replacing, too. Everett noted each item and mentally wrote out an invoice for the goods.

"Cattle stealing is rampant," said Don Antonio, ignoring the chicken and fixing his eye on Everett's account book. "I urge you to be most vigilant in your dealings. We will have to seize any hide without a brand and a bill of sale at the *embarcadero*." He had, he added, just sent two hide thieves in chains with the last mule train to Monterey.

"*¿Indios?*" asked Everett.

"*No, Mexicanos—¡Gente de razón!*" answered Don Antonio, rolling his eyes in disgust.

Everett handed the stack of overdue notes to Don Antonio.

The *alcalde* leafed through the unpaid bills of the citizens of the pueblo with far less attention than he'd given to the passport. Placing the wrinkled papers on the table, he absently slid them a few inches toward Everett—not so far as to reject the validity of the countersignatures of the former *alcalde* of El Pueblo de San José, but far enough to distance himself from their cumulative culpability. Eight notes were for goods sold from the *Tasso*; four were debts owed Larkin. Everett had held back the delinquent note bearing Don Antonio's own signature and looped flourish, preferring to discuss it later in the privacy of his garden. There, he would offer to discount the note if the *alcalde* would force the others to pay.

"And, of course, you will allow me to procure a horse for you," said Don Antonio, leaning back in his chair.

Everett nodded. A horse hired through the good offices of the *alcalde* would probably cost more than one obtained elsewhere, but it was a small price to ensure the good will of the supreme municipal officer of the pueblo. Everett mentally calculated the likely overcharge for horse hire and added it to what Don Antonio owed.

"Come to my stable on the plaza in the morning," said Don Antonio.

Lunging toward its tormentors, the bear fell sprawled on its belly, its left rear leg pointing awkwardly toward a post set in a circle of clawed earth. The bear limped back to the post, dragging its chain, and crouched behind it. Everett stared at the blood-caked manacle bolted around the beast's ankle. It looked familiar to him. A small boy began to cry as an older boy twisted a wooden cattle prod from his grip. Taking aim, the older boy thrust the sharpened end into the bear's ear. The bear uttered a sharp bark, then a whimper. Everett's horse, suddenly identifying the species of the dust-covered beast, whinnied and danced backward.

"*Buenos días, Señor Caballero*," said the older boy, bringing his wooden lance to a soldierly vertical.

Everett reached forward to calm the horse. The iron manacle that held the bear looked like the ones on the earthen floor of the *juzgado* where he had presented his papers to Don Antonio.

The two boys resumed their struggle for the cattle prod. Digging his heels into the flanks of the horse, Everett pulled the reins to the right. The animal, once again oblivious of the cowering bear, turned slowly to face south down the empty plaza toward the Monterey road. The morning sun cast the ribs of the horse in relief. A rooster, perched atop the firewood beside the whiskey shop, answered a distant braying donkey. Everett could see rude benches and tables through the open door, where, the night before, hardened vaqueros had spread cards, hurled dice, and wagered on the forthcoming combat between the bear and Don Pedro's bull. Glancing back at his saddlebags, Everett surveyed the maze of thick black scars, the tracks of Spanish spurs, extending from the horse's belly to his loin. He hoped he would have better luck collecting here than he had the week before on the east shore of the bay. Half of those notes still remained outstanding.

It had been three and a half years since Everett had come out on the *Tasso*. He had visited the pueblo with his case of fabric swatches and sketches of dress patterns—the latest fashions in Boston, Paris, and Mexico City. Don Antonio's wife and daughters and their neighbors had chattered with excitement as he displayed his samples of Boston gingham and French lace, dainty shoes of patent leather, thimbles, needles, pots, and pans. Their husbands had sipped *aguardiente* at the far corner of Don Antonio's shaded patio, and one by one each had succumbed to the entreaties of the women, none wishing to be outdone by the liberality of another. As usual, Everett had left the gathering with long lists of the families' orders, each one bearing the flowing signature of its patriarch.

Everett had arranged to meet each man at his house, his store, or at one of the many ranchos within a morning's ride of the pueblo. His experienced eye had noted every possible need—every broken pane of glass, the want of iron bars to fortify a window opening, missing hinges and locks for doors on a partially constructed addition—and compared it with the *Tasso*'s cargo. As he scanned the empty shelves, he proposed Boston goods to fill them. Aboard the *Tasso*, he had had plows for planting, scythes for harvesting—all the hardware needed to farm, hunt, build, or cook, and all the fashionable soft goods necessary to turn eyes at a fiesta. His saddlebags had been filled with knives for the spring *matanza*, their blades razor-sharp to flay the hundreds of cattle whose hides and tallow would be the currency to pay for the goods he sold.

In January, Everett had dispatched the *Tasso* for Boston crammed with eighteen thousand hides and thousands of bags of sticky yellow fat.[3] J. B. Eaton & Company, his employer, would profit twice: once on the New England goods he had peddled up and down the coast, and again on the sale of the hides and tallow in Boston. But not all the merchandise Everett had sold had been paid for yet. So, though he had already been on the coast for thirty-nine months, he had decided to remain behind through the winter rains until after the spring *matanzas*. Then, once again, the mud-bound trails would turn to ribbons of dust as wooden-wheeled *carretas* bearing another year's harvest of cowhides creaked their way toward harbors and *embarcaderos*. Those hides, Everett hoped, would pay off the last of his outstanding notes.

Everett slapped his reins against the horse's skinny rump. Legs splayed outward, eyes closed, the animal's head drooped nearly to the ground. The vaquero had demanded twelve reales per day, saddle included, but had settled for eight—in silver. Most of that money, Everett suspected, would find its way back to Don Antonio. It was not Everett's practice to pay hard money when a bag of tobacco or a card of buttons would have yielded a discount to match whatever craving he could read in the vaquero's eyes. He cursed his lack of inventory. The senescent horse stumbled forward into a measured walk. It would be a long day, thought Everett.

The Monterey Road led south beside the willow-lined *acequia*, with its fresh water flowing toward the pueblo. Farther to the east, rounded, stubble-covered foothills glowed golden between brush-filled canyons. Everett directed his horse away from the choking dust of the roadway to the thin band of greenery adjoining the irrigation ditch. Beyond the willows, a brush fence surrounded a vineyard heavy with purple grapes. In the middle of the field, an Indian boy stood on a rickety wooden platform with a stack of pebbles at his feet to pelt marauding birds. The boy waved at Everett and shouted something at two Indian women standing barefoot in the water among willows draped with shirts, pants, and striped blankets.

Former neophytes, thought Everett. The cash-starved administrators of Alta California, at the outer frontier of the República Mexicana, had carved the missions into ranchos and granted them in place of salary to soldiers, clerks, and sundry purveyors who had advanced food and supplies to the provincial government. Ownership of the Indians had passed along with the land they stood on. And, for a while, secularization had been good for business. More ranchos meant more people who needed goods and had hides to sell. But as Boston brigs had crowded the coast, the profits had diminished, and now there were intimations from the East that this year's shipments were glutting the market. If hides fell below ten cents a pound, there would be no profit at all, much less simple interest on the cost of the trade goods.

And there were problems with the Indians, too. The efforts of the Mission fathers to "civilize" them had produced a skilled workforce of farmers and herdsmen, but it had also fostered a taste for horsemeat. Now, from San José to San Luis Obispo, whole herds of horses were being driven off to the *tulares* of the San Joaquin Valley. Indeed, Don Antonio had warned Everett to be watchful even with this poor specimen of a horse and keep it corralled at night, guarded by dogs who would bark a warning should rustlers slip in.

Everett's horse stopped, waited as a brown sow emerged from the ditch, then drank deeply, sucking water in great gulps. Everett felt the shrunken animal expand beneath him. The double slap of wet cloth against flat rocks and the soft laughter of the Indian women provided rhythm and melody as he meditated on the *Tasso*. The horse snorted, shook the water from its snout, and resumed walking.

The *acequia* curved eastward toward a spring at the mouth of a ravine. The Monterey Road continued straight, shimmering in the heat. Everett turned left at the solitary oak Don Antonio had described and rode past a brush corral onto Rancho Cañada de San Felipe y las Animas—"The Glen of Saint Philip and the Souls." Everett thought of the apostle Philip, the loaves and fishes, and the Reverend Dr. Channing's Sunday School lesson in Boston, long ago. The ground was littered with disarticulated bones.

Señor Thomas Bowen owed $140—eighty hides at current prices. Everett surveyed the sun-bleached scatter of bones. Not one held even a dried morsel of meat. They were from last year's *matanza*, maybe the year before, he thought. Weathered skulls were stacked four deep against the corral. He felt as if their sightless sockets followed him up the path.

Everett's horse plodded along the track past Bowen's cornfield, the stalks freshly stripped of their ears. "Five barley loaves and two small fishes!" Everett repeated the words from the parable. He was hungry. As he emerged from the chaparral-choked arroyo, he saw Bowen's long, low adobe with four doors and four windows. Two barking dogs loped toward him. A barefoot Indian ran to take his reins as a tall, blond, red-complexioned man wearing a brightly colored serape emerged from the farthest doorway. Bowing theatrically, Thomas Bowen led Everett around the corner of the house and past a row of oak barrels, their newly charred interiors still acrid. One still bore the Cyrillic lettering of its earlier life, like the barrels at Leese's.

Bowen gestured toward a chair at the shady corner of the veranda. He placed two tumblers on a bench, uncorked a bottle, and poured a clear liquid into them. Everett took a sip as Bowen leaned forward expectantly.

The whiskey was raw and burned his throat. Everett wondered if it had experienced any contact at all with oak charcoal.

"The true essence of Scotland!" he rasped, struggling not to choke.

Bowen smiled, raising his brows to reveal bloodshot eyes. Nearby, a young Indian woman, her hair tied with a red ribbon, patted out pale white tortillas—wheat flour, noted Everett. Clearly, Don Tomás had better use for his corn.

Everett knew he would need all the leverage he could muster to extract payment from Bowen. He had heard that the man was deeply in
debt. Many merchants in town were said to hold notes against Rancho
San Felipe, but Everett knew well how to get his note paid off first. He
had already called on Bowen's wife in town to ask what her husband
might need at the rancho. He handed Bowen an axe head and a bundle of nails that had been delivered to her, just after Bowen's departure. Everett's sharp eye noted an almost imperceptible hesitation as
Bowen reached to take the package.

Years of visiting remote ranchos had taught Everett how to guarantee a warm welcome, a hot meal, and a night's lodging. He always had
with him some item that needed to be delivered—a package or a long-
awaited letter. Any simple errand required an equal act of reciprocity,
and Everett knew his stock-in-trade was more than fabrics and hardware. His most important commodity was news from the outside world,
and the gossip he'd heard at every rancho from San Diego to Yerba
Buena. He corresponded with Boston, Mazatlán, and the Sandwich Islands. He received papers from New York and Canton, and he knew
how to embroider his anecdotes with enough scandal to entertain any
host for a week—and longer, if necessary.

Everett actually kept two ledgers. The official one was a detailed
written account of sales and payments. The other was a record he kept
in his head, its unwritten pages tallying favors and obligations. For
most of his customers, the contents of the second ledger were more important than the contents of the "real" one. As Bowen opened Everett's
bundle, he knew he had incurred a new debt, guaranteed not by his
signature or another note against his property, but by a lien on his reputation as a gracious host.

Everett bided his time, sipping whiskey and enjoying his advantage.
He wanted Bowen to be at least two favors in arrears before they discussed payment for the goods he had bought almost two years ago
from the *Tasso*. Bowen knew he was digging himself into a deeper hole
with Everett, but his rancho was isolated and he had had no news for
weeks. The ranchero snuck a glance at Everett; then, staring intently
up the arroyo, he mumbled, "Any news from the coast?"

Everett uncrossed his legs, straightened in his chair, cleared his throat,
and began a formal recitation. Bowen squirmed. He had hoped the
news might dribble out informally, in conversation, without Everett
even being conscious that he was giving away anything of value. He

nodded as Everett described the vessels anchored off Santa Barbara and Monterey and the gossip passed on by their officers. Everett spoke of the smallpox, Larkin's petition to start a school in Monterey, the Southern senators' campaign to annex Texas, and recent prices paid for hides and tallow in Boston. Finally, pausing for dramatic effect, he announced Governor Micheltorena's plan to collect a dollar-per-gallon tax on locally distilled beverages.

Bowen grimaced. "*¡Díos y Libertad!*" he said, lifting his almost empty glass in the direction of Monterey.

Gradually approaching the object of his visit, Everett inquired about the health of Bowen's mother-in-law, Doña Estancia Pacheco. Like Leese, Bowen had arrived in Mexican California penniless, embraced Catholicism, and married a citizen of the República. He had then filed for some of the land being stripped from the missions. Rancho San Felipe had probably come through Juan Bautista Alvarado, the previous governor. Everett wondered what connections Bowen might have with Micheltorena, Alvarado's successor.

Everett's nose caught the odor of stewing beef and his stomach growled.

"I have a few hides now to go toward that note," Bowen volunteered, swirling his glass, "but by November, I could pay the whole amount in silver."

Everett did not answer. That money, if it ever materialized, might be seized by Bowen's other creditors. He took another sip of his drink and winced—a mere four months of aging would not help this whiskey. The girl who had been making tortillas brought a porcelain platter for Bowen's inspection, then placed it on the bench. It held a long tortilla with a steaming pile of stringy beef piled along its full length, surmounted with four fried eggs. Bowen wiped his knife against his knee and drew it across the tortilla. Folding his half of the tortilla around the meat, he took a bite. A droplet of egg yolk slid down his chin. Everett copied Bowen's motions with the remaining half. As the two men ate, Everett planned his itinerary. Tomorrow he would visit Rancho Los Coches, and then Mission Santa Clara. Perhaps Father Mercado would have a better horse for him to rent for the ride back up the peninsula to Yerba Buena.

Gulping the last of his whiskey, Bowen brought his tumbler to the bench with a crash. Rising, he gestured toward an adobe outbuilding.

A small cowhide was staked out on the ground outside for drying, hair side down. Everett surreptitiously eyed the left rear quarter to see if a brand showed through. Inside the shed was a stack of twenty-seven hides, each with legs and neck folded inward, then doubled over, hair side out. One by one, Bowen flipped the hides onto the floor. Everett sorted them by brand. Eight bore Bowen's uppercase "B," the brands on four hides were mutilated beyond recognition, and fifteen had no brands at all.

"Your cattle had admirable success in eluding the iron," said Everett.

Bowen shrugged. "My Indians did a bad job finding the calves."

"Don Antonio's lieutenants will have most of these locked in the *juzgado* before they even smell the bay," said Everett. He imagined the *alcalde* scrutinizing a bill of sale for unbranded cowhides. Don Antonio would probably try to negotiate yet another discount on his own debt. And if the remaining fifty-three hides yet to be delivered had equally dubious provenance, it would only prolong Everett's association with the *Tasso* and with Eaton.

Everett looked at the three piles. "I'll give you a 5 percent discount for good silver."

"Make it 15 percent," said Bowen, "Forty dollars now, the balance in November."

The men shook hands.

Back at the veranda Bowen cheerfully refilled the tumblers—too cheerfully, thought Everett. He wondered if Bowen had suckered him. Did Bowen have hides with good brands stored elsewhere? Did he have more cash? Bowen disappeared into the house and returned with a canvas bag. He dumped twenty-five, eight-real pieces on the bench and arranged them in five stacks of five.

"I'll send another fifteen in the morning," said Bowen.

Everett sorted through the coins, separating out four of them worn so thin that their dates could not be read. An eight-real coin was supposed to weigh one ounce, the equivalent of an American dollar. Back at the pueblo, he would weigh and discount them for underweight. Extracting hard money from Bowen had been like squeezing blood from a turnip.

Now Everett felt a gnawing apprehension. He did not want to tempt fate by carrying a bag of silver back to Pueblo San José. No vessel from Monterey had arrived at Yerba Buena during his stay with Leese, and

against his better judgement, he had finally set off for San José still without his holsters. What if Bowen's Indians were to follow and rob him as
he rode toward the pueblo?

Everett opened his saddlebag. Slowly and deliberately he removed
the two unholstered cap-and-ball pistols. Holding them up and examining them carefully for maximum dramatic effect, he placed one into
each side pocket of his jacket. Then, opening a small monogrammed
box, he removed a quill and a bottle of ink and amended Bowen's note.

⚜

Everett's horse picked up speed as they retraced the road to the pueblo.
The sun beat down with deadly intensity. Everett could see a thin
stream of fog passing through a low spot in the coastal mountains, dis-
sipating into nothing as it flowed down the slope into the crucible of
the Santa Clara Valley—just like his own efforts, he thought. Forty-
three months out of Boston, thirty-nine on the Coast, and if the *Tasso*
lost money he would earn nothing but a commission on sales. He
could have done better staying at home in Boston, tending a shop.

It hadn't begun this way. He had first come to the Coast thirteen
years before, aboard the *Chalcedony* with Captain Steele. Mrs. Steele
had been aboard and had given birth to two children during the two-
year voyage. Although the distracted captain had officially served as
both master and supercargo, Everett, the clerk, and Edward Faucon,
the first mate, had been the real managers of the operation. Everett recalled Abel Stearns' isolated hide house on the beach at San Pedro,
twelve miles from the merchant's home in the Pueblo de los Angeles.
"*Pueblo de los Puercos,*" Faucon had called it. Everett recalled the
loads of hides they had ferried out to the *Chalcedony* under cover of
night. In those days, little attention was paid to brands and all manner
of cargo had been stealthily off-loaded.

He and Faucon had proven themselves on their next trip, coming
out in 1834 on the *Alert* and returning on the *Pilgrim*. That two-and-
a-half-year venture had been Everett's first as supercargo, and Faucon's
first as captain. He remembered scheming with Faucon to help young
Richard Dana, the Harvard sophomore who wanted so desperately to
return to Boston. Their action had not won them the admiration of
Dana's captain, Francis Thompson, but it had established a friendship
with the young man. Back in Boston, Faucon had decided not to re-

Figure 14. A pencil sketch of Captain Edward Horatio Faucon (1806–94) in China circa mid-1840s. Courtesy Massachusetts Historical Society.

turn to California. In his opinion, there were already too many Boston brigs on the Coast. He had instead gone to China to make his fortune.

I should have gone there with him, thought Everett. Dana's new book, *Two Years Before the Mast*, correctly depicted Faucon as the model of a good captain and Faucon's career now seemed assured. But that was the only saving grace of Dana's book. Most of it was rife with errors and outright lies, each of which Everett had dutifully marked on the margins of its offending pages. But indicting Dana had not freed him from the growing melancholy that crowded in when he was alone with his thoughts. Faucon's last letter from Boston had reported on his negotiations with Augustine Heard & Company. He was buying a one-fifth share in a new clipper, *Frolic*, now being built in Baltimore for commerce on the coast of China. Faucon's news had only compounded Everett's sense of his own failure.

Everett thought of Ysidora Bandini and the playful glint in her dark eyes. She had come to Abel Stearns' house when the old man had mar-

Figure 15. Richard Henry Dana, Jr. (1815–82), at age 25, from an 1840 daguerreotype. Courtesy National Park Service, Longfellow National Historic Site.

ried her sister, Arcadia. Don Abel had built his adobe "*palacio,*" with its grand ballroom, for Arcadia. The two sisters were barely of age, but they supervised a workforce of Indians and hosted fiestas, balls, and banquets. Arcadia had come to love the horse-faced Don Abel, and every man—merchant, ship's officer, or soldier—fell for Ysidora.

No, collecting on overdue bills was not the only reason Everett had decided to allow the *Tasso* to sail for Boston without him. He had wanted to speak to Ysidora's father, Don Juan Bandini, and had even made an appointment with the old man at his home in Santa Barbara. Now, he didn't think he could go through with it. What if Don Juan were not to encourage the union? After all, what did Everett have to offer her? And what would his own father think if he were to leave the Reverend Dr. Channing's staid Unitarianism and embrace papal idolatry? And his brother a minister!

Everett's hand ached from clenching the reins. He tried to banish Ysidora from his thoughts. He had always been able to quell loneliness with hard work, and on this trip he had stayed in a frenzy of activity. Still, the emptiness persisted. He had felt it as he watched Don Abel and Arcadia in Los Angeles, and again as Larkin expressed his concern for Rachel. It had overcome him in Yerba Buena, hearing Leese speak of Rosalía. And he did not have anyone waiting for him in Boston.

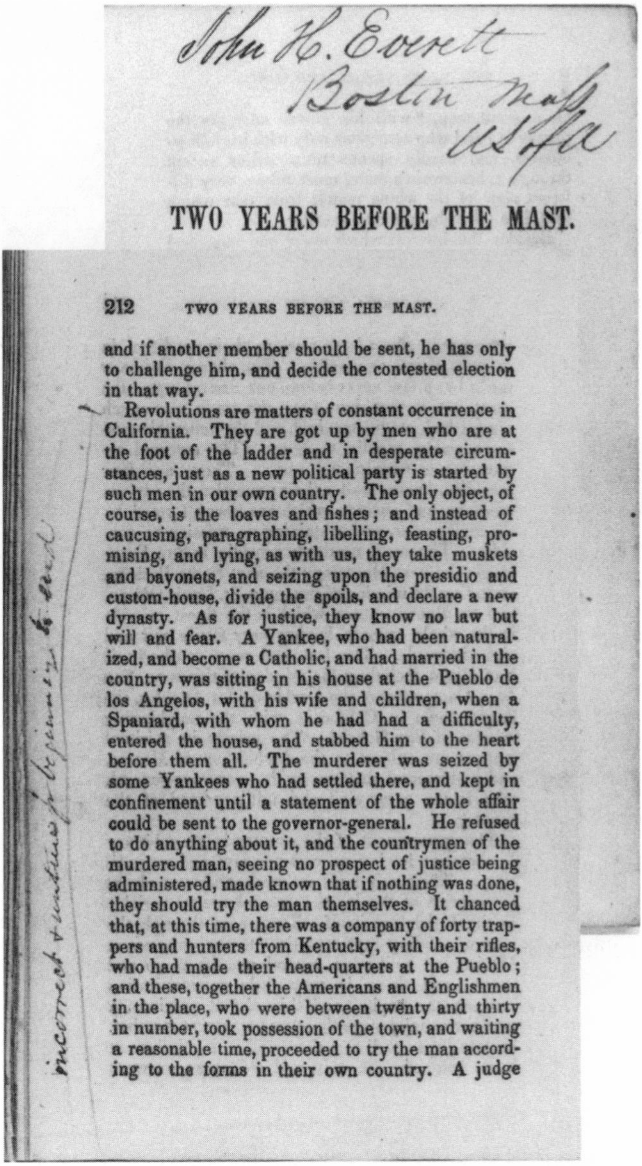
John H. Everett
Boston Mass
US of A

TWO YEARS BEFORE THE MAST.

212 TWO YEARS BEFORE THE MAST.

and if another member should be sent, he has only to challenge him, and decide the contested election in that way.

Revolutions are matters of constant occurrence in California. They are got up by men who are at the foot of the ladder and in desperate circumstances, just as a new political party is started by such men in our own country. The only object, of course, is the loaves and fishes; and instead of caucusing, paragraphing, libelling, feasting, promising, and lying, as with us, they take muskets and bayonets, and seizing upon the presidio and custom-house, divide the spoils, and declare a new dynasty. As for justice, they know no law but will and fear. A Yankee, who had been naturalized, and become a Catholic, and had married in the country, was sitting in his house at the Pueblo de los Angelos, with his wife and children, when a Spaniard, with whom he had had a difficulty, entered the house, and stabbed him to the heart before them all. The murderer was seized by some Yankees who had settled there, and kept in confinement until a statement of the whole affair could be sent to the governor-general. He refused to do anything about it, and the countrymen of the murdered man, seeing no prospect of justice being administered, made known that if nothing was done, they should try the man themselves. It chanced that, at this time, there was a company of forty trappers and hunters from Kentucky, with their rifles, who had made their head-quarters at the Pueblo; and these, together the Americans and Englishmen in the place, who were between twenty and thirty in number, took possession of the town, and waiting a reasonable time, proceeded to try the man according to the forms in their own country. A judge

incorrect + untrue fr beginning to end

Figure 16. John H. Everett's hand-written commentary on the first edition of Richard Henry Dana, Jr.'s, *Two Years Before the Mast* (1840). Courtesy Bancroft Library, University of California, Berkeley.

Figure 17. An 1805 Carolus eight-real coin (*left*) bearing Chinese chop-marks, minted by Spain in Mexico City; and (*right*) an 1837 Mexican eight-real coin.

The horse walked across the plaza of the pueblo toward the corral. Don Antonio's vaquero stepped from the cantina and took his reins. Everett dismounted and slid his saddlebags over his shoulder. The vaquero waited expectantly for the payment of two days' horse hire. Everett pulled four silver coins from his pocket and inspected them before handing the man the two most worn ones.

The plaza was empty except for scores of ground squirrels, each sitting sentinel atop its mound of dirt. Everett looked at the coins in his hand. A "República Mexicana" bore the image of an eagle perched on a cactus, a skinny snake in its beak. And that's what it's come to, he thought. Almost four years with the *Tasso* and he had done no better than that eagle. He shuffled the coins. The other was a Carolus dollar bearing the imprint of Spain and the Indies. Its surface was covered with chop marks, tiny Chinese characters, each placed by a shroff in Canton or Shanghai as a personal guarantee of silver content, and each one signifying a transaction. He thought again of Faucon sailing his own vessel in the China Sea.

Everett walked across the plaza, threading his way among the little mounds of dirt. One after another the squirrels disappeared into their holes—just like his California debtors, he thought. He glanced again at the Carolus dollar with its exquisitely chiseled Chinese glyphs. He was sick to death of dusty cowhides and stinking tallow. He would never get rich like this. It was time for him to seek his fortune elsewhere.

CHAPTER 3

The 'Eveline'

Canton, China, 1849

The *Tasso*'s cargo had arrived in Boston to a glutted market, and John Everett wrote to Larkin that, as he had feared, it hadn't paid simple interest on the investment—or even the cost of the insurance. And in the spring of 1845, Everett returned to Boston, too. After staying on in California to collect his notes, he had gone home by the overland route—across Mexico by stage, up the Mississippi and Ohio Rivers from New Orleans by steamboat to Wheeling, then across the mountains to Baltimore and home.[1]

Boston had changed so much during his absence that Everett could hardly find his way around town. With nothing to do, in a few months he was bored and looking for work. He wrote to Larkin in September 1845 that he was ready to embrace the first good offer to once again become a "commerciante"—if he couldn't find a rich wife first![2] In April of 1846 he received a letter from his old friend, Captain Edward Faucon, in China. Faucon's letter made the "land of the Celestials" sound like a fountain of opportunity.[3]

Everett arrived in Canton that fall, and on January 1, 1847, began working as a bookkeeper at Augustine Heard & Company. Of course, a bookkeeper's small salary had not been enough reason to sail halfway around the world. Everett was looking for a sinecure, a vantage point from which he could speculate in whatever business prospects might come his way.

In May of 1849, most unexpectedly, Thomas Larkin's friend and partner Jacob Leese arrived in Canton from California aboard the *Eveline*, seeking to purchase a China cargo. Everett had already written to Larkin in Monterey, suggesting that he buy a cargo of China goods to sell in California.[4] But Larkin's answer had been delayed and the *Eveline*'s arrival, with her 3,000 ounces of placer gold dust (worth over $50,000), was thus a complete surprise. Leese was eager to return to California with a cargo quickly, while the market for China goods was still lucrative, and he contacted Everett as soon as he arrived in Hong Kong.[5] Within days, Leese and Everett had met in Canton. With the *Eveline* venture, John Everett would introduce Augustine Heard & Company to the burgeoning California market.

The purchase of the *Eveline*'s cargo was Everett's first chance to play an important role in the Heard firm, and it substantially increased his standing. The fact that Leese and Larkin had come directly to him —and that no one else in the Heard firm knew anything about the California market—made him personally responsible for assembling the cargo.

But Everett's task would not be easy to fulfill. Four other vessels— the *Rhone*, the *Emmy*, the *Honolulu*, and the *Corréo de Cobija*—had recently sailed for California with large China cargoes, leaving local stocks of export goods depleted.[6] Everett would have to contract with a number of different silk merchants, porcelain dealers, furniture makers, silver workers, and goldsmiths to manufacture the merchandise he needed. It would be almost three months before the 1,353 cases, packages, bales, rolls, and kegs could be delivered and loaded onto the *Eveline*. In that time, Everett would establish important relationships with the manufacturers and tradesmen, and eight months later, when the Heard firm wanted to purchase a cargo for their own vessel, the brig *Frolic*, they would return to many of the same suppliers.

The affairs of the *Frolic* and the *Eveline* were closely intertwined; the two vessels and their cargoes were part of the same commercial strategy. The *Frolic*'s cargo would be based on the *Eveline*'s; thus, a careful study of the *Eveline*'s cargo, which was fully documented by invoices and auction listings, provided the best opportunity to make sense of the crushed and corroded fragments from the *Frolic* that the divers had collected and the far greater array of perishables that had decomposed without leaving a trace. My first task, then, was to reconstruct the story of the *Eveline*.

❦

"I'll want spring couch bedsteads, chests of drawers with secretary tops, and marble-top tables."

"For heaven's sake, Jacob, tables and secretaries?" John Everett rolled his eyes. "They're much too bulky—they leave too much empty space in a crate—cargo space to San Francisco is too valuable to squander like that."

"He's right," added John Cooper, carefully folding the *China Mail* he had been reading. "The brig is only 196 tons."

Jacob Leese stopped pacing across the floor to listen to his brother-in-law, the *Eveline*'s captain.

"We need to squeeze as much as we can into the hold," Everett explained. "We need to pack it tight, with things that stack; things that nest, one inside another. You don't want big expensive pieces of furniture. A crate with a table rattling around inside it is one sale. That same crate crammed with three hundred cotton shirts is three hundred sales, with every cubic inch paying its way."

John Everett tried to conceal his exasperation with Leese. He could remember when the man had been tough and practical, ready to argue the value of every cowhide, but time and the 250 pounds of gold Leese had brought from California seemed to have softened his business sense. Indeed, the gold had thrown the whole firm into a tizzy. For the nine years of its existence, Augustine Heard & Company had ignored California, for good reason. There had never been a market for California cowhides in the Celestial Kingdom. It was true that twenty-five years earlier, Captain Cooper's cargo of sea otter pelts, aboard the *Rover*, had bought a China cargo. But the otters had long since been over-hunted to annihilation, and in any case, clothing styles in China had changed. Now, suddenly, there was gold, plenty of it, and the demand for rich China cargoes to fill the holds of California-bound vessels was so great that the shops along Old and New China Streets were completely depleted of inventory.

"Damn! It is essential that we get the brig filled and back to California without delay," said Leese resuming his pacing back and forth across the room.

Everett could understand his friend's frenzy of frustration. Leese had spent the two months of enforced idleness on the voyage to China thinking about the cargo he would purchase, and now there was nothing to buy. A carefully planned trip—two months over and two months back—would be stalled for unknown numbers of months while he waited for cargo goods to be manufactured from scratch. Meanwhile, what if the California market were to change? Worse still, what if the miners came down from the mountains and spent all their gold before the *Eveline* could return?

"Now, Jacob," Everett teased, "surely being held hostage in Canton—even for a year—is better than being incarcerated at Captain Sutter's fort."

"That rabble!" Leese exploded in fury. "That odious, pompous backstabber Frémont and his pack of thieving Judas Iscariots!"

Everett instantly regretted his jibe. Now he would have to hear Leese's tirade about the Bear Flag Revolt yet again. Leese and his brother-in-law, General Vallejo, had always supported California's independence from Mexico, but three years ago they had been kidnapped by Frémont's thugs and locked for days in a filthy cell at Sutter's Fort. Then, that same landless rabble, self-styled as patriots, had robbed Don Guadalupe of six hundred horses and a thousand head of cattle. It had taken all of Tom Larkin's influence as American Consul to force the *californios* to release Leese and Vallejo. The livestock were gone forever.

"Jacob, Jacob!" interrupted Captain Cooper. "Your *californios* treated Tom Larkin no better. They descended on him as he slept! Men who had been his neighbors—men to whom he had provided the credit to build houses and farms. Of course," Cooper added with mock sympathy, "once they had captured him, they had to suffer his company."

Leese stopped pacing. The picture of the eminent Tom Larkin as a hostage was too incongruous to contemplate. His captors had not anticipated how difficult the prickly merchant would make their lives. Leese and Cooper had both married sisters of General Vallejo, and as Larkin was Cooper's half-brother, he, too, was family. Everyone knew better than to cross Tom Larkin—"the Baron Rothschild of California"—the man who held mortgages on everybody, and whose money could extract favors anywhere in the República.

The unfortunate *californios* had forced Larkin to ride three hundred miles from Monterey to Pueblo de los Angeles as their captive.

They had hoped to exchange him for one hundred Mexican prisoners-of-war captured by the Americans. How could they have known how completely the fortunes of war—and the balance of power between captors and prisoner—would shift during the long ride south? For as they rode along the Camino Real through San Luis Obispo and Santa Barbara, they received word of the victories of the American forces, and their treatment of Larkin improved correspondingly, from the abuse due a loathsome enemy prisoner to the hospitality accorded an honored guest. The changing tides of the war forced them to realize that it was impolitic to offend the richest American merchant in California—the Consul of the United States of America. Larkin was the one man whose influence might protect them should the Americanos ultimately prevail. Before they reached Pueblo de los Angeles, the "captive" was sleeping in the best bed, while his "captors" spread their blankets on dirt floors. Indeed, even before Larkin was released in the City of the Angels, Mexican officials were already visiting him to importune for favors in the new California Republic.

Everett watched with relief as Cooper skillfully distracted Leese from his anger at being delayed in Canton. He, too, would have to find a way to manage Leese when it finally came time to purchase a cargo for the brig *Eveline*.[7]

I got out my books on the China trade and looked at the illustrations: paintings of the Canton waterfront, sailing vessels, and Chinese storefronts. One particular illustration caught my eye—a watercolor by an artist/merchant named Tingqua, showing his own shop.[8] I looked up at the photocopy of John Everett's unsigned, undated portrait taped to my wall. Perhaps Tingqua had painted it. I imagined Everett sitting for the portrait in Tingqua's studio. I could see him shift in his chair, straighten his back, and place his elbow on the large blue-and-white China jar next to his stool. I watched him shift his gaze to the upper left-hand corner of an unfinished miniature portrait hanging on the far wall of the studio—a sleeping child with rosy cheeks.

"Mr. Everett, why you move all the time? You want bad picture?" Tingqua stepped from behind a massive easel and glared disapprovingly over his black-framed spectacles.

Figure 18. Tingqua's studio in Canton, China, circa 1850, by Tingqua. Gouache on paper. Courtesy The Kelton Foundation Collection.

"Mr. Tingqua," Everett retorted, "why should sit still? Señor Sunqua say you paint everybody face on same body!"[9]

Tingqua sputtered. Sunqua was the better-known portraitist, and Everett knew that Tingqua was sensitive to the fact that the older artist still dominated that business. Smirking at his own repartee, Everett tried to reassume his pose. He averted his eyes from the disturbing daguerreotype hanging just to the right of the sleeping child—the same little girl lying dead, hands folded across her chest. Hoping Tingqua would not notice, he moved his gaze slightly to the left, fixing on the portrait of an elderly mustachioed Parsee merchant with a white silk cape over his shoulders and a turban on his head.

Tingqua's portraits hung in two rows on the wall, most of them watercolors on thin slabs of ivory. Some were merely inked outlines, while others glowed with warm flesh tones. Larger portraits, painted in oil on canvas or glass, stood at the foot of the wall. Everett squinted. The morning sun streaming through the skylight hurt his eyes. He stared at a framed panorama of the thirteen Canton factories. By Imperial edict, virtually all European and American activities, residential and commercial, were confined to these buildings.[10] Near Hog Lane, toward the right side of the illustration, stood his own current residence, the building occupied by Augustine Heard & Company, on the site of the old Dutch factory. Bulky cargo junks and sampans crowded the broad river that ran in front of the factories. In the foreground, Tingqua had painted a Mandarin's patrol boat with twenty-six oars in the air and an ornate pennant flying from her stern.[11]

Everett had arrived early for his sitting. Leese would be meeting him at eleven. Then, once again, they would visit shops along Old and New China Streets to select goods for the *Eveline*. Everett dreaded these shopping appointments with Leese, with their interminable discussions and delays as the inexperienced Californian tried to make decisions. Throughout the past week, Everett had met alone with each supplier to make his selections before returning with Leese. It took all the tact he could muster to lead the unsuspecting Leese to choose the same items he had already decided on. The charade was exhausting—how much simpler it would have been for him just to purchase the cargo himself!

Tingqua emerged again from behind his easel, loudly clearing his throat. He signaled Everett to come and inspect the portrait. Everett struggled to his feet. One leg was asleep. He limped to join Tingqua behind the easel.

"All finish. No touch," said Tingqua.

Everett stared at the glistening wet paint, carefully studying the picture.

"No, not finish yet," he said. Somehow it still needed something, but what? Pulling a large white handkerchief from his side pocket, he fluffed it and stuffed it part way into his breast pocket. Satisfied with the effect he returned to his perch and resumed his pose. Tingqua grumbled from behind the easel.

"Too much trouble. . . . Charge three dollar more."

"I give you two," said Everett. Nine dollars, for a masterpiece! He would give it to Oliver and Betsey, his brother and sister-in-law. And he would buy the most elaborate carved-ebony frame he could find.

Everett descended the stairs from the studio, pausing to watch Tingqua's assistants as they inked and hand-colored China scenes onto broad

Figure 19. The Canton factories, circa 1850, by Tingqua. The building occupied by Augustine Heard & Company, on the site of the old Dutch Factory, is shown directly behind the side-wheel steamer. Enlarged portion of a panorama. Gouache on paper. Courtesy The Kelton Foundation Collection.

sheets of paper. Bound albums of pictures lay open on a display table. The images were familiar. Here were the thirteen steps of tea production, from tree to table; and the thirteen steps in making porcelain, from digging clay to packing china sets in boxes. There were the usual panoramas of the Hong Kong and Macao waterfronts and Whampoa anchorage. One album caught his eye—the six stages of opium addiction. He flipped through the pages. The first panel showed a happy, richly attired young man; the last showed the same man gaunt-eyed, in rags, sitting on a tattered mattress. Everett would order it for sister-in-law Betsey.

Betsey—Mrs. Oliver Everett, a minister's wife—disapproved of Everett's employment at Augustine Heard & Company. It was well known in Boston that the firm did a large business transporting opium from

India and taking commissions on its sale in China. Betsey, however, worked tirelessly raising funds to support missionary work in China, and she believed opium to be the primary cause of moral degradation among its idolatrous pagans. She had begged John to seek employment with Mr. King and the "true Christians" at Olyphant & Company, who steadfastly refused to trade in the drug. Betsey's husband, the Reverend, would commend the moral message of the opium pictures, depicting the inexorable consequences of a dissolute life—a Chinese version of Hogarth's "The Rake's Progress." Betsey, however, would be outraged at John's hypocrisy.

John Everett smiled. Betsey would not like this portrait of him any better. He had posed with jacket unbuttoned and his thumbs in his lapels, like a pompous, self-satisfied merchant, with his eyes slightly raised as if toward eternity. It was an expression similar to that of the divine, Reverend Mr. Pierpoint, in the portrait that hung in Oliver and Betsey's parlor. Oliver would hang the offending portrait of Brother John at the foot of the stairs, next to the oils of their mother and father.

⁂

That same portrait had been passed down to five generations of Everetts. Even though the modern descendants had no memories of John Everett himself, they all knew the story of Betsey's response to his painted likeness. Oliver had indeed hung the picture in the family gallery at the foot of the stairs, and for the remaining twenty-five years of their marriage, each time Betsey turned the image she detested to the wall, Oliver would dutifully turn it back.

The albums of pictures in Tingqua's shop interested me because I knew similar ones had been aboard both the *Eveline* and the *Frolic*. Although the *Frolic*'s had been destroyed by sea water within minutes of her collision with an offshore rock, their loss did not absolve me as an archaeologist from a good-faith effort to describe them. The *Eveline* invoices listed twelve books, each containing twelve rice-paper paintings, purchased for $1.50 per book from Fockhing. They had sold in San Francisco at $6.00 each—300 percent over invoice. Fockhing had also supplied toys, tortoiseshell combs, and pearl beads for the *Eveline*. However, as his name did not appear in any listings of Chinese artists, I assumed he had dealt in general merchandise and the picture books were included in his stock.

Eight months after the *Eveline* sailed for California, Everett and the Heards would buy four cases of paintings directly from Tingqua to send to San Francisco aboard the *Frolic*. I had found the payment chit for $87.50, bearing Everett's flowing initials at the Baker Library at Harvard.[12] Although I could never know exactly what the *Frolic*'s paintings had depicted, I suspected that they might have included copies of a panorama of the San Francisco waterfront as it had appeared in 1846, three years before the Gold Rush—a scene so outlandishly pastoral that San Franciscans would have snapped up the pictures as curiosities. I had discovered such a picture by Tingqua, copied from a now lost sketch made by an early visitor to San Francisco, in an auction catalogue. It was apparently the only copy in existence.[13] I wondered if others had been lost aboard the *Frolic*.

"Ai-ya!" John Everett froze for an instant at the warning and jumped quickly back into Tingqua's shop. He felt a rush of air as a massive crate, hanging from a pole between two coolies, passed only inches from his chest. Without breaking stride, the barefoot men continued loping down Old China Street toward the waterfront. Everett steadied himself and stepped again onto the cobbled pavement. Stacks of produce, awning supports, and signboards blocked the narrow passageway. A barber trotted down the street toward him. From one end of a pole across his shoulders hung a pot of steaming water atop a smoking charcoal brazier; from the other, a stool with drawers for his razors and tweezers. Everett had to turn sideways to avoid being hit by the assemblage. The street seethed with humanity—white-gowned Parsees, turbaned Hindus, a rich Chinese merchant surrounded by his retinue, a sedan chair with drawn curtains shielding a haughty Mandarin from violation by plebian eyes.

Everett checked his watch. He still had over an hour before his appointment with Leese. He started down the street, dodging men bearing loads of various shapes and sizes. Mindful of the ever-present pickpockets, Everett buttoned his jacket across his watch and chain. On the streets of Canton, he never carried more money than he needed, for a beggar or to tip a porter. When he made a purchase, he signed a chit to be presented to Achen, the Heard's comprador, for payment. A loud wail broke his thoughts. He drew back from a commotion outside Pohing's porcelain shop. A blind man and a child with a distended stomach stood banging gongs and shrieking. An exasperated clerk threw the child a square-holed copper coin and the noise stopped immediately. Leading the blind man by a string, the child moved two shops down, where the pair resumed their performance.

Spotting Everett outside his shop, Pohing came to the doorway, bowed deeply, and invited the American inside. He gestured toward the marble-topped ebony table reserved for special customers. A servant brought a pot of tea and two small cups, their glaze cracked and crazed. They were delicate and beautiful, unlike anything for sale in the shop. Everett recognized Pohing's subtle compliment.

"Where Mr. Leese?" asked Pohing, suppressing a smile. "Maybe him want to change order again?"

Everett grimaced. He and Pohing had spent a very long afternoon with Leese looking at display samples. Leese had wanted to order matched sets of fine china. Everett and Pohing had argued for coarse stoneware bowls more suitable for miners at the diggings. They were cheap and could be stacked at the bottom of the *Eveline*'s hold in place of ballast. Finally, they had settled on four sizes of shallow bowls, two sizes of rice bowls, and cups and saucers—21,000 pieces to be delivered in 680 nested stacks, each wrapped in rice grass or old matting. Over Everett's protestations that they were too dainty for the rough men in the gold fields, Leese had also ordered fifteen giant porcelain sugar jars, each containing a tea-setting for twelve complete with pitchers for coffee, tea, and cream.

"You have Mrs. Larkin name paper?" asked Pohing. The old man jiggled his cup and stole a furtive glance at the few stray tea leaves.

Everett reached into his pocket.

"Here, full name on big dishes," he said, pointing as he handed the templates to Pohing. "But just first initial on cups and saucers." He pointed to the letters.

Larkin had asked Leese to buy a complete tea set and matching dinner service for twelve, to be made of the best porcelain and marked with Rachel's name. Everett had seen the egregious misspellings that Chinese artists painstakingly applied to exquisitely fashioned sets of porcelain, and he didn't want that for Mrs. Larkin's set. He watched as Pohing moved his finger from right to left, scrutinizing the printed letters.

Everett swallowed the last dregs of his tea and returned the ancient cup to the table. The tea he had been served at ranchos up and down the mission trail had been absolutely dreadful. To correct that deficiency in California hospitality, the *Eveline* would carry two thousand pounds of curious oolong, flowery orange pekoe, young hyson, and fine caper. Everett had also bought more stimulating beverages— 288 bottles each of port and sherry and 2,412 tall green bottles of pale ale.[14]

Cheap stoneware bowls had been a good choice—at least from an archaeologist's point of view. After almost 150 years under water, those ceramics were the major part of my sample of the *Frolic*'s cargo. The *Eveline*'s 680 nested rolls had sold so well in California that the Heards returned to Pohing for another 676 rolls to ship aboard the *Frolic*. In addition to the rolls of stoneware, the *Frolic*'s bill of lading listed twenty cases of porcelain. These had probably contained finer items that could not be stacked in rolls. The fragments of a "Canton"-pattern serving dish with a matching lid that a wreck diver had brought up indicated at least one matched dinner set. Fragments of a large jar and a teapot spout suggested that the *Frolic*, like the *Eveline*, had carried sugar jars with tea sets packed inside. The *Eveline*'s pale ale had sold so profitably that the Heards nearly tripled the order for the *Frolic*, loading 6,009 corked bottles aboard.[15]

Everett rose from his chair, thanked Pohing, and stepped gingerly into the street. As he passed Woushing's silk shop, his stomach tightened into a knot. Only a week ago he and Leese had met with Woushing to negotiate most of the *Eveline*'s massive order of silks. He recalled how the embarrassed merchant had tried to explain his inability to give a firm delivery date for the order. All of the silks in his warehouse had just been sold and dispatched aboard a spate of vessels, and all he had in the store were display samples. He would have to special order from his supplier in Shanghai, who would in turn have to contract with the local loomsmen.[16]

The news had been upsetting. The silks were the most expensive merchandise the *Eveline* would carry. Leese had fumed and cursed about the new delay, damning all Chinese silk workers to places in hell so horrible that only he, a wedding-bed convert to Roman Catholicism, could imagine them.[17]

Everett crossed the street to Ahoy's clothing shop. He needed to order his own winter wardrobe. He looked down at his shirt. Fortunately, Tingqua had not reproduced its murky color in the portrait. No one in Canton expected white cotton shirts to be returned white from the laundry. Their color varied with the season—a light brown tint in winter, when the river carried mud from flooded rice paddies; a yellow tinge in summer. Even more distressing were the India ink laundry marks placed in the most conspicuous locations. And buttons were a lost cause—the laundry men crushed most of them with their scrub rocks. Some merchants shipped their shirts a hundred miles to Hong Kong to be boiled in clean well-water. Not only were they whiter, but they took longer to sour. Everett resolved to do the same when Ahoy delivered his new clothes.

"How Mr. Leese?" asked Ahoy.

Everett rolled his eyes. "Today Mr. Leese look at furniture."

Ahoy beckoned a clerk to take Everett's measurements. Everett recalled his last visit here with Leese, who expected to select the clothing for the *Eveline* himself. The transaction had started smoothly enough, with the Californian contracting for a hundred dozen cotton shirts.

"But," Ahoy had suggested, "every shirt need a vest."

Leese had become more and more confused as Ahoy proceeded to describe the array of available vests, with fabrics, colors, sizes, and styling options in all combinations. Throwing up his hands, Leese had sheepishly asked Everett to decide.

Everett had quickly ordered 202 vests in sizes 1, 2, and 3, half double-breasted, half single-breasted, and with equal numbers of straight and rolling collars. Examining the book of fabric swatches, he had decisively chosen a black satin figured with green flowers, and two white satins, one figured with brown, the other in blue. He had rounded out the vest order with figured velvets and Scotch plaid.

Then, before Leese could interrupt, Everett had rattled off an order for uncut bolts of plain and figured silks, velvets, satins, crepes, sarsnets, camlets, and damasks in a full spectrum of colors and patterns. He carefully limited his purchase of ready-to-wear garments to be sure they would sell, choosing only those that did not require a tailored fit: handkerchiefs, aprons, shawls, loose jackets, and dressing gowns. At Leese's

Figure 20. Interior of a Cantonese furniture maker's shop circa 1820s showing carpenters crafting Western-style furniture. Gouache on paper. Collection of Cora Ginsburg.

insistence, though, he had ordered four fancy silk ball dresses in coffee, cinnamon, strawberry, and lilac.

"How many shirt you want this time?" asked Ahoy. "You want baker's dozen like before?"

Everett nodded. "No button," he cautioned, "just make holes for studs."

Ahoy's clerk was writing down the last of the measurements as Everett stepped out into the street.

It was time to meet Leese. Everett could hear the pounding of hammers as he turned into Carpenters' Square. He smelled the rich medicinal odor of camphor. Yesterday, they had visited the furniture shops of Hecheong, Yenchong, and Ushing. He had yet again advised Leese against buying large pieces, since their crates would take up too much space in the *Eveline*'s hold. He suggested they buy instead portable writing desks of mahogany and rosewood with small compartments for pens and paper—like the one on his own work table. But Leese had been adamant about ordering blackwood tables with marble tops, couches, bedsteads, wardrobes, and chests of drawers with secretary tops.

Today they would order trunks. Everett spotted Leese standing in the open room that served as Ashoe's workshop and display area. He was watching a workman cane the rolled foot of a chaise lounge.

"Señor Leese," greeted Everett, gesturing toward the chaise lounge. "Indeed, a most sensible and practical piece of furniture for a gentleman of your stature—but first, one ought to make sure one's coat and trousers are not consumed by moths. Would not such a gentleman first purchase a good set of camphor trunks?"

It was a sore topic. Everett had once left a pair of pants and a jacket with Leese at Yerba Buena, and returned to find the wool garments riddled with moth holes.

"Your bugs won't much like these," Everett continued, pointing to a stack of leather-covered camphorwood trunks, their brass tacks glistening in the sun.

"How many do you think we need?" asked Leese.

Everett paused to pretend to calculate a sum he had already figured out. Trunks nested one inside another were a good value, as they wasted little cargo space.

"Twenty-five sets in sizes 2, 3, 4, and 5—in blue, green, red, and brown," said Everett. He paused for a moment, but to his relief Leese wasn't adding any complicating details.

Ashoe scribbled a quick record of the order.

"When can deliver?" asked Everett. "Our boat at Whampoa now."

"Maybe two, three week," said Ashoe.

Leese was examining a mahogany drop-leaf table that stood against the far wall. A porter entered the shop and dumped a basket of hardware onto the floor with a loud clatter. The pile of brass trunk handles, fresh from the foundry, glistened gold where the mold seams had been filed away. Everett glanced toward Leese, still inspecting the table. The man had extended the leaves. Everett sensed more complications.

He shook his head. "I fear the *Eveline* will sail with a carnival of couches and tables sliding back and forth across her deck."

"Perhaps not," said Leese, lowering one leaf, "if I can charter another boat."[18]

⚜

Camphor trunks had been a good choice for the California market. They were popular everywhere, since their pungent interiors repelled moths, preventing their larvae from eating expensive silks and woolens. Everett had been wise in selecting leather-covered trunks rather than varnished ones for the *Eveline*. Even decorated with painted flowers, they were less expensive than the plain varnished-wood versions. The leather had hidden the ugly knotholes and blemishes that riddled the lower-grade camphor boards they were made from. In the course of my visits to museum collections, I had found that the insides of many leather trunks had been covered at the time of manufacture with Chinese wallpaper—effectively hiding their cheap, knotty wood.

And Everett had been smart not to order any size 1 trunks for the *Eveline*. A Massachusetts antique dealer specializing in China trade goods told me that although these—the largest size—were today the rarest of the leather trunks, they were still too large to sell well, even to modern collectors.

The *Eveline*'s twenty-five sets of trunks sold so well in San Francisco that Everett and the Heards increased the order to thirty cases for the *Frolic*. Two distinctive brass corner protectors recovered by wreck divers confirmed that some of these had been of the more expensive varnished-wood type.

Everett had become so impressed with the varnished trunks himself that he bought a set of three for Oliver and Betsey. Like his ivory portrait, I had traced these down through the generations to their current owner in Buffalo, New York, and he had graciously allowed me to photograph them. Captain Faucon had bought both kinds of camphor trunks for himself. A search of the heirlooms passed on by his daughter Catherine revealed a leather-covered trunk in Vermont and two varnished ones in Connecticut.

⚜

"Watch that puddle!" exclaimed Everett. It had rained briefly while they were inside Ashoe's shop.

"I seem to recall you walking right through the mud," said Leese, "before you came here and got so fancy."

Everett blushed, recalling Yerba Buena cove, the Russian whaler, and his muddy pants. It seemed eons ago.

"I think we've spent quite enough of your money for today," he said, changing the subject. He was tired of keeping Leese out of trouble. The *Eveline* was already fully committed, and with so many traders eager to ship their own cargoes to California, he doubted that Leese would be able to find another vessel to charter.

As the two men turned down Old China Street, Everett looked at the shops where they had made their purchases. They had bought lacquered ware from Laoqua—glossy black chess tables painted in gold, writing desks, cabinets, tea caddies and trays, and hundreds of boxes for paper, cards, cigars, and shaving outfits, each packed in its own tiny crate. From Gaoqua, they had bought a hundred rolls of red-checked grass matting, to cover the splintery plank floors in hastily built houses at the California diggings. From Chyloong, they had procured a hundred boxes of preserved fruit, each containing two jars of ginger, two of citron, and two of kumquats. Even if Californians were leery of the unfamiliar confections, they would spend their money just to get the blue-painted jars.

Leese stopped in front of Wongshing's silver shop.

"I need to buy flatware for the family," he said. "Why don't you go ahead—we can talk tonight at dinner."

Everett felt a surge of relief; today's shopping was over, and he had escaped another protracted negotiation. Everett paused outside the shop to look in at the objects on display—a large silver punch bowl and a row of tankards with hinged lids. Here, he and Leese had ordered gold shirt studs, filigree earrings, scent boxes, brooches, thimbles, and bracelets. Leese had been enchanted by the silver tinderboxes shaped like seashells, each containing a flint and a tuft of tinder.

Wongshing's long narrow sign, its gold characters painted on a field of red, was swinging in the breeze. At the bottom, Everett noted a new inscription, painted in shaky, awkward Roman letters: WONG SHING, GOLd & SiLVER. Everett peered in at the counter. Leese was engaged in animated discussion with Wongshing himself—pointing with a silver soup ladle toward some item on a shelf. Everett started for home.[19]

I was on fairly solid ground discussing the *Eveline*'s gold and silver. I knew Leese had carried a shopping list of items for family and friends, and I had the itemized invoices from Wongshing listing six silver flatware settings for twelve. Each of those sets had fifty-four pieces, including a soup ladle and special spoons for sugar, salt, and gravy. California miners would have had little use for these elegant accoutrements; they were special gifts. One set was for Leese's wife, Rosalía, another for Rachel Larkin; two for various Vallejo relations,[20] and the remainder for business colleagues. Apparently, Wongshing's stock had been somewhat depleted too, for Everett and Leese had purchased more gold jewelry and silverware at Cutshing's on New China Street.

The Heards had held Leese's three thousand Troy ounces of placer gold dust until they got the highest possible price for it, and the proceeds would buy more merchandise than the *Eveline* could carry back to California. By the time the vessel departed, she fairly bulged with goods—and people. Both Larkin and Leese had wanted house servants, so the Heards' comprador had indentured nine Chinese, who somehow squeezed aboard the crowded vessel.

Leese had wanted to import skilled Chinese workmen as well. Labor costs in California were high, and he anticipated a tidy profit selling indentures to merchants there. The Heards' comprador had already executed contracts with fifteen men, only to discover there was no space for them left aboard the *Eveline*—and no other vessel available for charter. Leese eventually used his excess capital to buy a 17 percent interest in China goods to be shipped by Bush & Company aboard the *Mariposa* and the *Mary*, and he sent the laborers aboard the *Mary* at a cost of $125 per man.[21]

John Everett quickened his pace and skirted past a drunken English sailor retching after a night of excess. He passed through the China Street gate and turned onto the esplanade fronting the "Thirteen Factories." A file of coolies carried chests of tea from the Spanish factory toward a lighter at the river's edge. By evening the tea would be twelve miles down river at Whampoa anchorage, ready for loading aboard an outgoing vessel.

Everett threaded his way among street vendors crying their wares, their discordant calls layered in strange harmony. He passed fruit stands; a pot mender bored tiny holes through porcelain sherds with a bow drill and bound them together with fine copper wire; a toothless old woman sewed up the tattered shirt of a bare-chested Lascar sailor; a circle of men discussed the salient features of fighting crickets, each for sale in its own tiny cage. He crossed Hog Lane. The new church Mr. Jardine had built sat on the esplanade just beyond the alley's filthy lower entrance, appropriately close to the back rooms where purveyors of arrack, rice wine, opium, and young "virgins" made large profits from the loneliness and moral weaknesses of sailors.

The noonday heat radiated up from the stone pavement. Everett removed his hat, pulled the "immortalized" handkerchief from his inside pocket, and wiped his forehead. The hot sun on the top of his head reminded him of his thinning hair.

Finally, the months of waiting were over. The goods had been delivered and loaded aboard the *Eveline* and the brig would sail in the morning. Tonight, Jacob Leese and Captain John Cooper would be the honored guests at a farewell dinner. Everett hurried downstairs, pausing for a moment to compose himself. From the far side of the dining room, he could hear John Heard's loud voice and a rumble of laughter. John was describing, yet again, how he had beaten a Russell & Company sloop in the Spring Regatta.

Loud squabbling in Chinese erupted from the direction of the table. Each servant had stood behind his master's chair in the usual seating arrangement, but now the comprador was ordering them to different positions. Any change in their distance from the head of the table represented either a promotion or a demotion for both the merchant and his servant. The comprador rang a bell and the room fell silent. John Heard led the men toward the table, seating Leese and Cooper to his left and right. Everett's boy, Ahsing, smirked from his new position near the head of the table, just to the left of Leese.

Everett smirked, too. Two years ago, he had sat far down the table, just ahead of the clerks, but his status had improved markedly over the last three months. The *Eveline* had come to the Heards only because of his correspondence with Thomas Larkin and his long friendship with Leese, cultivated over years of travel up and down the California coast. Now Augustine Heard & Company was earning commissions on the 250 pounds of placer gold Leese had brought to the firm—one commission for selling the gold, another commission for buying and storing the China goods, and yet another commission for arranging the in-

Figure 21. John Heard
(1825–94) in China circa
1850. Watercolor on ivory,
by Sunqua. Courtesy
Carl L. Crossman.

surance. Indeed, John Heard now seemed so completely captivated by
the prospects of commerce with California that he had loaned Brinley,
his senior clerk, $10,000 in house funds to become a junior partner in
the new commercial house planned by Leese and Larkin.

John Heard stood and tapped his spoon against his glass for attention. "I wish to propose a toast to Mr. Jacob Leese, to Captain John
Cooper, and to our own Mr. Brinley, who will embark tomorrow aboard
the good brig *Eveline*. We wish them Godspeed." Then, turning to face
the portrait hanging on the wall behind his chair, he repeated the toast
that he offered at every meal: "And we drink to the continued good
health of the founder of this firm, Mr. Augustine Heard."

Now, Leese stood and proposed a toast, to all his colleagues in California and China, and especially to his old friend, Don Juan Everett,
for his assistance in purchasing the finest China cargo ever dispatched
to San Francisco.

The waiters brought in the first course of the banquet. On each silver platter lay a massive river fish smothered beneath a thick brown sauce of sweetened ginger.

Everett felt a cool breeze from behind. The servants had begun waving their fans.

As Everett finished his fish, Leese stood. The champagne was having an effect on him. His face was flushed, his speech slurred.

"I propose a toast to the United States of America, and to California. May she soon be a state in our fair Union!"

Everett almost choked on his champagne. What a hypocrite! Leese and his Vallejo in-laws wanted an independent Republic of California, not a mere state, subject to the whims of Washington! Still, it was amusing to watch Leese manipulate John Heard's patriotic sentiments.

Heard stood, his glass raised to propose another toast. The servants grabbed for bottles to refill their masters' glasses. Heard cleared his throat and the room fell silent.

"Tonight we celebrate the beginnings of regular commerce between Augustine Heard & Company and our new associates, Jacob Leese and Thomas Larkin, in California. They will soon become the major purveyors of China goods in California, and we will prosper with them. Our Captain Faucon knows the waters of California well, and our clipper brig *Frolic* is admirably suited to carry China goods to any location along that coastline."

"Hear! Hear!" called Jacob Leese, standing to raise his glass.

Everett struggled to his feet, and all down the long table merchants and clerks rose to join the toast. Their crystal goblets shot spears of reflected candlelight across the walls and ceiling. Everett smiled. Regular commerce with California! Because of him, Augustine Heard & Company was better positioned than any other house in China to profit from it.[22]

❧

One hundred and fifty years later, I admired Everett not only for his ability to capitalize on his experience and business connections, but for his knack in assembling such a profitable cargo for the *Eveline*.

Besides the merchandise that he and Leese had purchased from the Canton merchants, Everett had augmented the *Eveline*'s cargo with imported goods that were not Chinese at all. From Singapore had come thirty-six dozen buckets and five dozen bowls molded from rubbery gutta percha sap. And as Californians had to eat, Everett had ordered bulk foods that were unlikely to spoil during a two-month voyage: 1,500 pounds of chocolate, 10,758 pounds of sugar, 148 bags of dried peas, and 50 bags of rice. They had augmented the bulk foods with smaller orders of dates, prunes, Malaga raisins, pickles, soy—and 500 tins of sardines.

As a private speculation, Captain Faucon had asked to send twenty-five kegs of dry white lead. Everett made the purchase in Hong Kong. Faucon imagined that that quantity of lead, when mixed with linseed oil, would be sufficient to paint an entire town of raw-wood houses—at least on the side facing the street.

John Everett started up the stairs. Feeling a bit dizzy from the champagne, he ran his hand along the banister.

"Perhaps we should consider sending a cargo of our own."

Everett turned to face John Heard.

"Why settle for a commission when we might gain all of the profits?" said Heard.

Everett steadied himself. There was a glint in Heard's eye.

"Yes," he replied. "And I would be willing to invest in such a venture."

CHAPTER 4

The 'Frolic'

Canton, China, 1850

The Eveline venture went splendidly. The three-month delay in assembling her cargo had turned out to be a blessing in disguise. By arriving later, she had avoided the glut of China goods brought in on five other ships over the summer. When the *Eveline* anchored at San Francisco on October 24, 1849, the previous cargoes were long gone—auctioned to wholesalers, delivered to retailers in towns scattered throughout the diggings, and sold yet again to comfort-starved miners and merchants outfitting their houses and places of business.

Things were not going so well for the *Frolic*'s career in the opium trade. In the spring of 1848, the introduction of a steamship on the Bombay-to-Canton route had badly undercut her profits. The steamer operated more cheaply than the *Frolic*, even with the extra cost of fuel to heat its massive boilers. It required a smaller crew, and since it could push away from rocks and shoals regardless of the wind, it paid considerably lower insurance premiums.[1]

Captain Faucon looked for ways to cut the *Frolic*'s costs. Though he had always manned her with American and British seamen, he now hired Portuguese-speaking native crews of Malaymen and Lascars from the west coast of India.[2] But even with these economies, Faucon recognized that the *Frolic* was becoming obsolete, and he sold his one-fifth interest in the vessel back to the Heards.[3]

When the *Frolic* was dismasted by a typhoon in September 1849, Faucon must have felt relieved that he was no longer a part-owner of

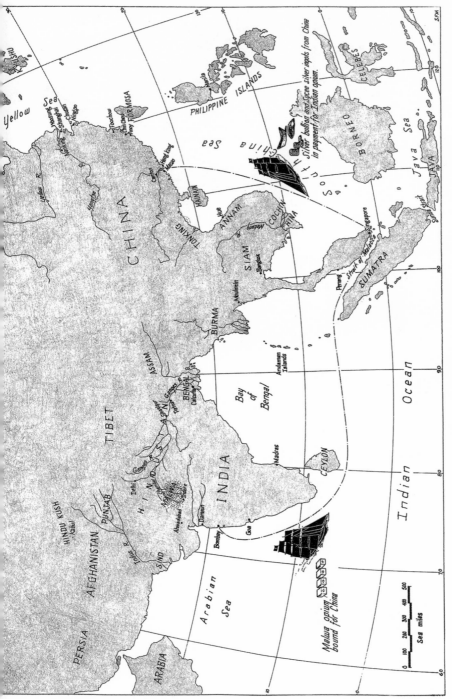

Figure 22. Map of South and East Asia, showing the route of the *Frolic* in the opium trade, 1845–50. Drawn by S. F. Manning.

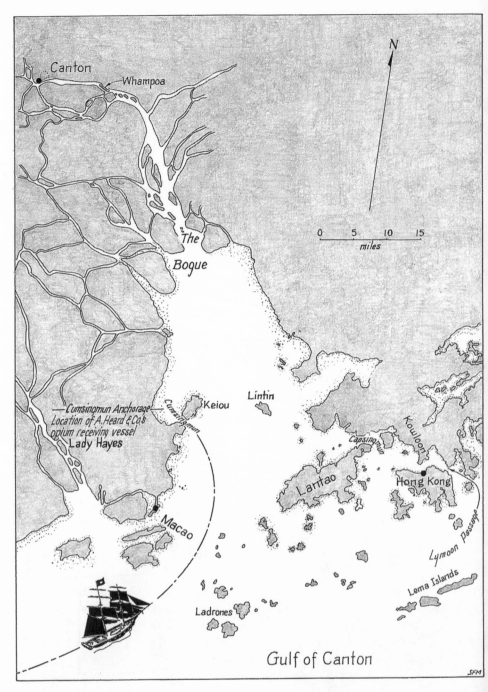

Figure 23. Map of the Gulf of Canton. Drawn by S. F. Manning.

the ship. Once the repairs had been made, John Heard had decided to sell her—but that was before the ledger sheets from California detailing the *Eveline*'s profits gave him a better idea. Rather than sell her, the Heards decided to dispatch the *Frolic* to San Francisco with a cargo like the *Eveline*'s, including only those items that had fetched at least 75 percent profit for Leese and Larkin.[4] During March and April of 1850, John Everett bought much of that cargo from the same merchants who had supplied the *Eveline*. Faucon, far away in India, was, of course, not party to that decision. In May 1850, when the captain was sailing to Cumsingmun to off-load 850 trunks of Malwa opium into the Heards' warehouse vessel, the *Lady Hayes*, he would have been surprised to discover that his next destination would be San Francisco and that his cargo had already been purchased and packed for loading.

Everett leafed through the stack of itemized orders for the *Frolic*. Sixteen hundred crates and packages of China goods, for which the Heards had advanced over $35,000 in company capital, were ready to be loaded onto the *Frolic* at Whampoa and Hong Kong. Tomorrow, as John Heard had requested, Everett would travel to Cumsingmun to personally deliver the news of the *Frolic*'s next undertaking to Faucon. To make it more palatable to the dour Captain, Everett was authorized to offer him a $5,000 interest in the cargo—the same as his own.

Everett rechecked his tally and compared the orders with the invoices from the vendors that had already come in. He would draft the next batch of payment chits as soon as he returned from his meeting with Faucon. As he read the names of the suppliers, their familiar faces came to his mind: Pohing for porcelain, Goqua for matting, Hecheong for furniture. Tingqua had been the first to submit an invoice—you could expect a bill from the artist before the paint was dry. Everett reviewed Tingqua's chit. Back in April, he had drafted, initialed, and transmitted it to the comprador for payment. On the back, Achen had scribed two columns of characters in his distinctive hand, certifying that Tingqua had been paid $87.50.

Everett reached for the *Eveline* folder and pulled out the ledger sheets listing the prices her goods had brought at auction. He flipped through the pages. Total proceeds of $77,685! Leese and Larkin had done well, even after Lovering & Gay's 10 percent commission. The auction fees

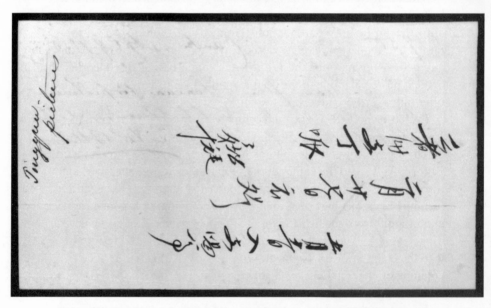

Figure 24. Payment chit, front side requesting the Heards' Chinese comprador to "Please pay Tinqua for pictures a/c *Frolic*," initialed "JHE" by John H. Everett. Reverse side shows comprador's notation in Chinese. Courtesy Baker Library, Harvard Business School.

were standard, but the fees for warehousing had been exorbitant. Waterfront space in San Francisco was so scarce that merchants were roofing over beached ships and painting business names over the barnacle-encrusted hulls.

High warehouse costs were a major concern in planning the *Frolic*'s voyage to San Francisco. Reluctantly, the firm had been ready to capitulate to painful reality, but then Everett had come up with an idea to avoid the costs of storage entirely. Leese had used some of his excess capital to buy prefabricated houses and shipped them aboard the *Mary*, and these had sold quickly in San Francisco. Everett suggested that the Heards send ahead a prefabricated house, together with a crew of Chinese carpenters to assemble it, to serve as both warehouse and emporium. Then, after the *Frolic*'s cargo was sold, they would sell the house itself for an additional profit. Mr. Anthon, who would be supercargo in charge of selling the *Frolic*'s goods, had sailed in April aboard the *Stockholm* with the house and carpenters. He would rent a lot in San Francisco and have the house ready to receive the *Frolic*'s cargo by the middle of July.

Everett read through Lovering & Gay's itemized charges for advertising and selling the *Eveline*'s goods. The agents had billed for printing one thousand catalogues, a hundred posters, a hundred circulars, and the cost for shipping these to Sacramento, Stockton, and San Jose; advertisements in two newspapers; and $11 for men with loud voices to cry the sale on the streets of San Francisco. There were additional charges for receiving, sorting, and displaying the cargo, including 250 feet of boards for display tables, and twine and cards for labels. Lovering & Gay had not cut any corners. For the preview, they had fortified the bidders—and themselves—with champagne, cheese, and crackers, charging that to Leese as well.

Everett leaned back in his chair. The Heards' interests would be well served by Mr. Anthon, and by Captain Faucon who, in addition to his salary as captain, would be offered 2 percent for his services as assistant supercargo. Faucon would be pleased with that, Everett hoped. He put away the pages and went to pack for his trip to meet with the Captain.[5]

The oars stopped creaking and the boat glided to a stop fifty yards from the *Lady Hayes* at Cumsingmun Anchorage, just beyond the

Figure 25. The brig *Frolic* delivers a cargo of opium to the Heards' receiving vessel *Lady Hayes* moored at Cumsingmun, May 1850. A fast crab will speed purchases to Chinese brokers near Canton. Original illustration by S. F. Manning.

jurisdiction, and responsibility, of the American Consul in Canton. The opium trade was illegal in China, and the helmsman knew better than to approach an opium receiving vessel without a signal from her deck officer. John Everett looked up at the massive hulk. Her upper masts had been removed to reduce wind resistance, so that even in a typhoon the vessel could maintain her position at anchor. The brig *Frolic*, tied close to her starboard flank, looked like a whale calf snuggling against its mother.

The oars creaked again, pulling toward the larger vessel's stern. Everett reached for the ladder and stepped onto its lower rung. His foot slipped on the green sea slime, and for an instant he hung by his hands. The Chinese oarsmen snickered as he struggled upward, water sloshing in his left shoe.

"Don Juan!" Faucon's voice pierced the din of activity from across the deck. Everett blushed, hoping Faucon had not seen his gaffe. He was nervous about how the Captain would receive the news of his new assignment.

"Bienvenido, Edward! I presume our letter did not reach you at Singapore." Everett tried to recover a semblance of professional demeanor. The oarsmen were still giggling from below.

"No, but Captain Langley tells me I'll need charts for the North Pacific."

Everett relaxed. Faucon had already received the news, and with good humor.

"Do you have letters from home?" Faucon asked eagerly.

Everett pulled two thin packets from his pocket. The pale blue stationery bore the return address of Daniel Weld, his sister-in-law Betsey's father. Everett knew that Faucon had borrowed $1,000 from John Weld, Betsey's older brother, to help buy his one-fifth share of the *Frolic*, but he had paid that off years ago. Everett waited as Faucon looked intently at the carefully rendered copybook script before he slipped the letters into a coat pocket and snapped to.

"We brought 869 chests," he said to Everett, frowning, "but hardly any are consigned to us." Faucon walked toward a table shaded by a canvas canopy. Everett followed. He was still curious about those letters. The Welds had married Everetts for generations; they were his relations. And he had always shared his personal news with Faucon. How could the man receive two letters from home and simply shove them in his pocket? But Faucon's attention was on business.

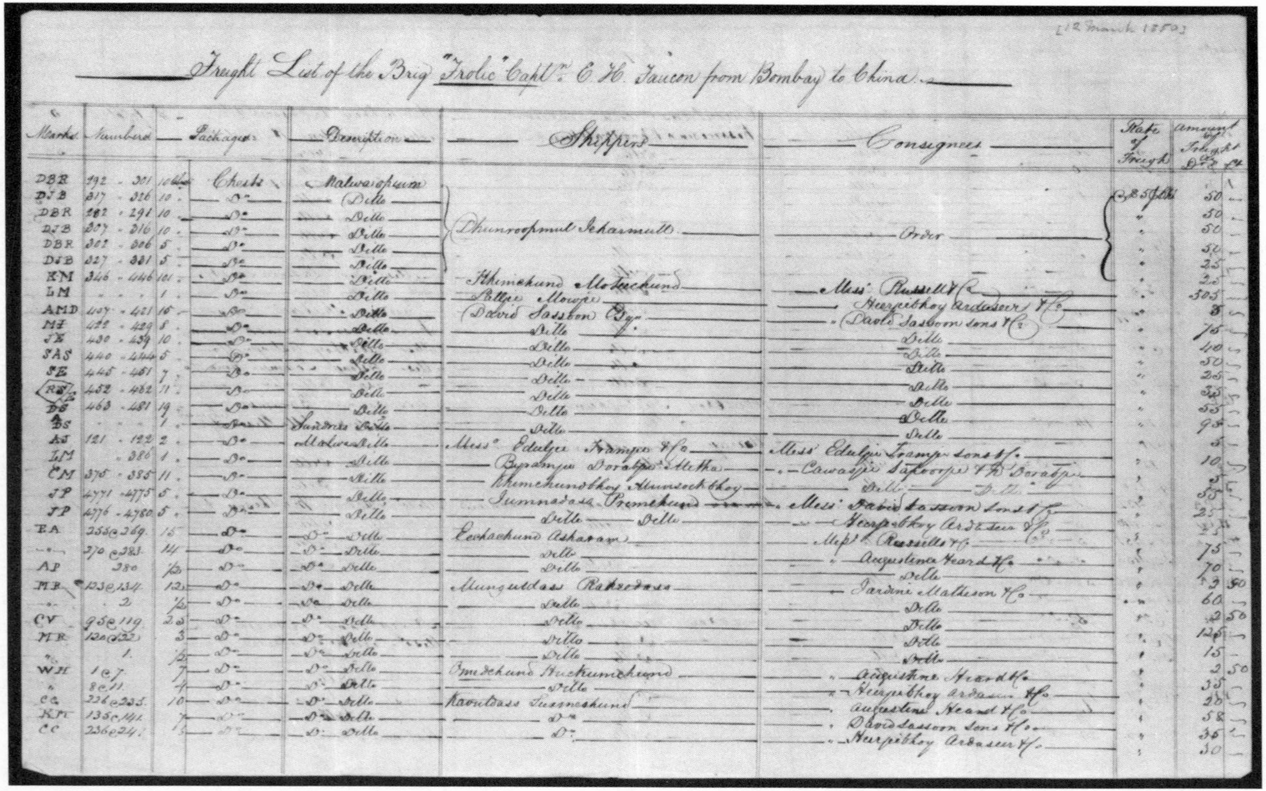

Figure 26. Freight list of the *Frolic*'s final, 869-chest cargo of opium from Bombay to China, March 12, 1850. Courtesy Baker Library, Harvard Business School.

"Mr. Deutcher," he called out, "I need to see the numbers!" Sailors were stacking burlap-covered chests across the deck. The *Frolic*'s first mate turned the offending trunk around to show the label on its side.

Faucon adjusted the two brass weights that held down the corners of the *Frolic*'s bill of lading—still curling upwards from two months rolled inside his map tube. He ran his finger down the second column, matching the numbers on his list to those stenciled in black on the upper right corner of each chest. Beneath its number, each chest bore the initials of its owner in Bombay, and below that, the name of the Canton firm to whom it was consigned for sale.

"I still can't see the numbers." Faucon sounded testy. He walked toward Mr. Deutcher, leaving Everett alone at the table. Everett looked down the list of consignees. Faucon was right. The chests were assigned to Jardine Matheson, David Sassoon, Russell & Company, and an assortment of Hindu and Parsee firms. Only twenty-five were consigned to be sold by the Heards.

Everett frowned. The Heards were not operating the *Frolic* just to earn $5 per trunk for freight. George Dixwell, the recently retired architect of the firm's commerce in opium, had bought the *Frolic* as part of his strategy to influence the Indians to increase the number of chests they consigned to the Heards for sale. He had even convinced Kessressung Khooshalchund & Company to take a 40 percent interest in the vessel. With "number one" opium selling at $800 per chest, a 2 percent commission was worth three times the freight. Under Dixwell's watch, the *Frolic* had more than paid for herself, but now, profits were slipping. As much as John Heard bragged about his recent trip to India, he obviously had not gained any new consignments. What a bust! It was a good thing that the *Frolic* was going to California.

Shouts and a loud clatter from below turned Everett's attention to the rail. A forty-oar fast crab was tying to the *Lady Hayes*. Bare-chested oarsmen, glistening with sweat, were fixing their long wooden blades to the sides of their vessel. Captain Langley was helping a Chinese merchant, dressed in fine black silk, step from the ladder onto the deck. He led the merchant to a chair next to his own. Now the merchant's entourage clambered up the ladder, the last two men struggling to drag up an iron-bound box bearing a large brass padlock.

Everett watched carefully. He knew the procedure for testing and selling opium from the hundreds of invoices he had processed in Canton, but he had never actually witnessed it. Langley sorted through his papers to find the authorization-to-sell that matched the one carried by the Chinese and handed it to his clerk. The thousands of chests stored below were filed numerically by consignee so that any one of them could be quickly found and retrieved.

Suddenly, the deck of the *Lady Hayes* came alive. On the port side, a Lascar fed wood into a cast-iron stove with a loud clanking. From the starboard, Everett heard the clinking of silver. The iron box was open. Sitting beside a pile of shoe-shaped ingots of sycee silver, two Heard company shroffs flipped coins into baskets, sorting Spanish from Mexican and shaved from full weight. They struck one coin against another, listening for the telltale ring that distinguished genuine from bogus. Another man hammered the head shroff's chop mark into each coin that passed inspection, his guarantee that he, personally, would replace it should it later be found counterfeit or underweight.

Langley's clerk emerged from below followed by two Lascars, each carrying a chest of Malwa opium. Everett could make out the familiar "KK" mark of Kessressing Khooshalchund, and beneath that, the mark of Russell & Company, the Heards' major American competitor. Five years ago, when the *Frolic* first began the Bombay–Canton run, Mr. Kessressing had sent out identical consignments aboard her, one to the Heards and the others to the Heards' main competitors. It was a contest to see which firm would earn the highest returns. Only after the Heards had proved themselves had Kessressing agreed to take a 40 percent share of the *Frolic*. Now his firm was again consigning to the competition. John Heard's efforts to secure the Indians' business had obviously failed.

In front of the two testers, one of the Lascars cut away the burlap wrappings, pried loose the lids of the chests, and cleared away the poppy leaf packing. The merchant's opium tester selected three flattened cakes from each chest. Langley's tester slit open the cakes, placed samples of each in brass beakers, and poured boiling water over them. He stirred the mixture and poured the resulting liquid through rice-paper filters.

Everett watched the merchant and his tester examine the residue left on the filters—the tangible evidence of adulteration. Hindus in the Malwa uplands augmented the weight of the opium they sold with a miscellany of cheap substitutes, from river clay to cow dung. Waving his arms, the tester shouted a running commentary as he pointed along the row of soiled filter papers. The merchant bellowed his responses and the interpreter fairly screamed translations above the commotion. Now the filtrates were retrieved from the stove, each boiled down to a black paste. One by one, the tester placed a tiny sample from each into his pipe and inhaled. His commentary, the responses, and the translations continued.

Everett recalled Betsey's horrified look when he had attempted to explain the economic necessity of the opium trade. During his last visit to Boston, Betsey, once again attempting to put an end to his bachelorhood, had called him into her parlor to be inspected by two spinsters and a young widow. They were discussing, Betsey had informed him, the "Opium Question."

Everett squirmed. His performance had not enhanced his romantic prospects. In his enthusiasm to demonstrate his erudition, he had thoroughly offended the ladies' moral sensibilities. Beginning his dissertation on political economy, he had pointed out the obvious—that the silk they wore, the tea they were drinking, and the fine porcelain they were drinking from all came from China. But, he had explained, the Chinese were not good trading partners. They refused to accept good New England manufactures in exchange for their wares. Indeed, in their greed, they would only accept silver, and thus were draining the world's currency into the coffers of their emperor, where it would never be seen again. The ladies had all voiced their indignation toward the wicked emperor, his sinful hoarding, and his base interference with free commerce.

Opium, Everett had continued, was the only product for which the evil Chinese would return *our* silver. To save Christendom from bankruptcy, the British had been forced to grow opium in India and export it to China. Indeed, the sale of opium had averted a financial depression which would have caused the children of honest tradesmen in Boston and London to starve. The silence in the parlor had been palpable when he had finished his discourse. Through clenched teeth, Betsey had uttered a curt, "Thank you, Mr. Everett."[6]

The crash of the shroff's hammer and the ring of silver coins dropping into the basket reminded Everett of the inexorable action of a guillotine. He tried to efface that image, picturing instead the swinging pendulum, the gears, the cogs, and the chime of the grandfather clock that counted out Boston time in Oliver and Betsey's living room. He rubbed his eyes. A harsh cacophony of voices rose and fell as Captain Langley, the merchant, their testers, and their interpreters haggled. Along the railing, sailors fingered swivel guns loaded with lead shot and iron nails. Acrid smoke mixed with the sweet, pungent steam of boiling opium wafted across the deck. A true picture of Hades, Everett thought, at least as that place had been described by the Reverend Mr. Pierpoint back in Boston. But here in China, on the back side of the world, Boston reasoning was turned on its head, and the bubbling cauldrons signified not eternal punishment but earthly reward.

❧

Faucon returned to Canton from Cumsingmun with Everett, and they were guests of honor at a Heard banquet the following night.

"Tonight we celebrate our second commercial venture to California . . . " John Heard paused, waiting for the conversation to stop before he continued, " . . . a speculation already well underway, for even as I speak, Mr. Anthon is overseeing the construction of our emporium in San Francisco. But allow me to first salute Mr. John Everett, who found such an exquisitely simple way to avoid the devilishly expensive costs of a San Francisco warehouse. Our little house will be the perfect place to store and display our cargo in that burgeoning metropolis."

Everett raised his glass of bubbling champagne toward his colleagues. He hesitated for an instant. It was a false show of modesty, he knew, but it would appear unseemly to take the first sip in a toast to one's own health.

"However, tonight," Heard continued, turning to the man sitting at his right, "tonight we offer our prayers to our own captain, Edward Horatio Faucon, to whose able hands we now entrust the success of this venture across the North Pacific."

Faucon sat taller in his chair.

"Captain Faucon is very familiar with the treacherous waters of the California coast, and he has anchored many times at San Francisco. I assure you, however—." John Heard paused for theatrical effect. " . . . I assure you that both Captain Faucon and I are immensely pleased that this voyage has nothing to do with cowhides, nor with tallow."

A clerk tittered from the far end of the table, and then the whole room erupted in laughter. John Heard, pleased with the response to his joke, smiled broadly and continued.

Everett listened to the familiar recital of Faucon's triumphs—how the *Frolic*'s captain had beaten Jardine Matheson's fastest clipper, the *Anonyma*, by more than a week in a race from Bombay to Canton. Everett noted that while John Heard emphasized the *Frolic*'s glorious past, he avoided mentioning that she now cost more to operate than she earned. And even as he praised Faucon's skill, Heard gave no intimation that only a few months ago he had made up his mind to sell the *Frolic*, thus casting doubt on the captain's future with the firm. Only the *Eveline*'s receipts, with their 300 percent profits, had induced John Heard to give the clipper a reprieve.

Everett looked at Faucon. His friend's body was still thin and sinewy, but his black hair had thinned and there were flecks of gray in his beard. Heard had not mentioned that Faucon would carry a power-of-attorney authorizing him to sell the *Frolic* in San Francisco, should an opportunity arise. Everett was hungry, and anxious for the toasting to end. John Heard's testimonials sounded hollow, intended more to glorify himself than to honor his colleagues. Everett suppressed a yawn. He would have to awaken early tomorrow to travel downriver with Faucon to Whampoa and see him off.[7]

"Sweet Jesus!" Everett grabbed the low railing for support. The fast crab rocked violently as two oarsmen attempted to pole its long, narrow hull through the swarm of boats anchored along the shore. The Chinese helmsman cursed the harbormaster—first in Portuguese and then, for the benefit of his two passengers, in English. The harbor authority was supposed to maintain a clear passage from the factories out to open water, but every morning found the port clogged with sampans and an impenetrable web of mooring lines.

"You'll be carrying enough beer to supply San Francisco for most of an evening," said Everett.

Faucon grunted his assent. Never a cheerful sort, he seemed even more taciturn and preoccupied than usual. Everett wondered why: Was it the prospect of a voyage to California, or did Faucon regret selling his share of the vessel on the eve of what might turn out to be her most lucrative venture?

Everett averted his eyes from the bright rising sun and pondered Faucon's bad luck. As captain and one-fifth owner of the *Frolic*, he had been allowed to carry trade goods on his own account. But his timing had been bad, and he'd lost money speculating on his own in opium. Even the twenty-five kegs of white lead he'd sent aboard the *Eveline* had been one of the few items to lose money at the auction. At least, Everett reflected, Faucon had sold his share of the *Frolic* before the dismasting. Maybe he had anticipated the additional expenses for maintaining an aging vessel. Insurance had paid for the masts, yards, and sails, but not for the new copper bottom, nor for replacing the rotted keelson.

Finally clear of the harbor, the fast crab gained speed, her prow slicing through the green water, her sixteen oars creaking as one to the chant of the coxswain. The steersman took a zigzag course, past rice paddies, through narrow openings in fish weirs, skirting the sand bars and snags that prevented most ocean-going vessels from passing above Whampoa. Carried with the ebb tide, they covered the twelve miles in less than an hour. Everett first spotted the pagoda on the hill above Whampoa, and then the *Frolic*, anchored two hundred yards off shore. Four chop boats, their broad decks piled high with numbered crates, were tied to her stern.

As they pulled close to the *Frolic*, Faucon checked the load lines painted on her hull. Two were exposed that had never emerged above water except when the vessel heeled over in a heavy breeze. The captain surveyed the full length of the vessel along the water line.

"We'll have to load heavy to the stern or she won't steer," he said, speaking more to himself than to Everett.

Captain Faucon had been worried all morning about whether he had ordered enough—or too much—ballast removed from the *Frolic*. The clipper carried a massive pile of cast-iron blocks along her keelson, and calculating adjustments to that weight had been easy when she carried opium. A cast-iron ballast block weighed one hundred pounds, and a chest of Bombay Malwa weighed one hundred and forty. And the weight of silver ingots and specie carried back from Canton was known down to the ounce. During his five years carrying opium and treasure, Faucon had been able to make a simple calculation among these three known quantities. A straightforward addition or subtraction of ballast blocks provided the perfect displacement and balance.

But this cargo—1,602 boxes, crates, and rolls—comprised everything from candied ginger to silk parasols, and the sizes of the containers gave little indication of their relative weights. The port warden had estimated the total cargo weight at 135 tons—significantly more than the 60 tons of Malwa Faucon had just brought from Bombay. Accordingly, he had ordered half the *Frolic*'s ballast removed, but now she fairly bobbed in the water and he was concerned.

Faucon boarded first, and by the time Everett reached the deck the captain had undergone a metamorphosis. His usual brooding demeanor had disappeared, and he looked tall and confident as he walked across the *Frolic*'s freshly scraped pine deck. He was at home in his own world where he reigned supreme. He strode briskly toward the main hatch, followed by Mr. Deutcher, the first officer, and a tall, light-skinned Lascar with a head serang's green sash tied round his waist. Everett glanced down at the chop boat tied to the *Frolic*'s port side, its deck piled high with rolls of porcelain from Pohing. A line of Chinese stevedores were pitching wicker-bound packages, one to the next, up over the *Frolic*'s rail and down through the gaping hatch opening.

"Mr. Deutcher, load the porcelain aft until line four is submerged," said Faucon. "And rig the winch for lifting crates."

The head serang, Mariano Rosales, moved closer to hear the captain's orders. He waited for Mr. Deutcher to repeat the commands to him in English before shouting them on to the men in Portuguese. For two years, Everett had seen Rosales' name on the crew lists that Faucon submitted for payment at the beginning and end of each voyage. He had noticed the name, as the man was paid nearly twice the salary of an ordinary native seaman. And Everett had been puzzled at first by the many Hispanic names on the crew lists. They seemed more appropriate to Mexican California than China. But Faucon had explained that Mariano Rosales—though he looked like a Hindu—was a Catholic from Goa, the Portuguese colony two days' sail south of Bombay, and it was Rosales who now supplied most of the *Frolic*'s crew from among his family and neighbors in Panaji town.

Rosales, Mr. Deutcher, and the captain had lowered their voices. The serang was bowing submissively and gesturing toward a cluster of men standing by the port rail. Something was wrong. Everett moved closer.

"Four men! How long will it take to replace them?"

Everett couldn't hear Rosales' mumbled reply.

"I don't want drunks and thieves on my vessel." Faucon sounded angry. "If there are no good seamen here, you damned well better find them in Hong Kong!"

It seemed the four men huddled at the rail were afraid to sail across

Figure 27. Loading the *Frolic* with her cargo for San Francisco, Whampoa Anchorage, May 29, 1850. Original illustration by S. F. Manning.

unfamiliar waters to California. The Lascars and Malaymen were from the tropics, and it was hard enough to get them to sail as far north as Shanghai in winter. They had heard stories about the North Pacific—thick, cold fogs, frigid waters, men shivering for months in soggy clothes that never dried.

Everett leaned against the starboard railing and watched Rosales shout orders. The four deserters were lugging their sea chests toward the ladder. A boy named Juan crawled to the end of the mainsail yard, threaded a line from the deck winch over a pulley block sheave, and ran it down to a stack of crates on the deck of a cargo junk. Dark-skinned Lascars manned cranks at either end of the winch. They grunted in cadence as they hoisted the first crate aboard. Everett recognized the mark of the furniture maker Hecheong. Still to come were the prefabricated house and the two hundred cases of Edinburgh ale waiting to be loaded at Hong Kong. Faucon would have to leave space in the hold for them.

On the forward deck, five pigs stared forlornly at Everett from a cage lashed to eyebolts set through the deck planking. A sixth pig shrieked in terror as Rosales' men dragged it up the side of the vessel in a cargo net. Hundreds of screeching birds—geese, chickens, jungle fowl, and pigeons—fluttered and pecked for position inside stacked coops.

Everett leapt back as a green melon rind splattered onto the deck, splashing a sticky halo of juice across his shoes. He peered upward. From the topsail yard, Mr. Harrison's monkey licked its hands and looked downward, aloof from the activities below. The monkey returned Everett's stare with a look of disdain. Everett had no more real function aboard this vessel than the monkey. The two of them were mere spectators, and the monkey had the better vantage. Feeling humbled, Everett looked aft and saw the Heards' red-and-white diamond flag hanging flaccid in the humid heat. He was sleepy and he needed a quiet place to sit. He started down the companionway.

Ahsig squatted on the floor of Faucon's cabin, surrounded by the parts of two disassembled oil lamps. Everett watched the servant wipe soot from the chimneys, insert new wicks, and return the lamps to their leveling gimbals—one above Faucon's bed, the other above the table. Everett slumped, exhausted, into the chair. Two chronometers ticked side by side on the table, their hands two minutes apart. The invoice for cleaning and adjusting them had just arrived from a clockmaker in Hong Kong. Everett wondered how far apart the clocks would be in two months, when the *Frolic* would be nearing California. Faucon would need to use the faster of the two to figure his longitude with a margin of safety. Of course, if he put in at Honolulu he could reset both clocks for the second half of his voyage.

The thick glass blocks set into the deck above diffracted a rainbow of colors against the pine plank walls. On the table lay Norrie's *General Chart of the North Pacific* and a well-thumbed copy of Caesar's *Bellum Gallicum*. Typically Faucon, thought Everett. He picked up a small leather-covered case, idly opened it, and recognized the younger sister of his own sister-in-law Betsey—a demure, smiling Martha Weld. So that was Faucon's secret! Everett's shame at peeking at the picture mixed with envy and sadness. Faucon had a reason to return to Boston, and he did not. He closed the case and climbed the steep stairs back to the deck.[8]

⚹

In the weeks after the *Frolic* had been safely dispatched, Everett turned his attention to his official function as bookkeeper, reconciling the Heard firm's accounts. It was dull, stultifying work, and in the August heat he found he could not stay awake through the afternoons. It was a long summer, and by the end of September he was eagerly awaiting word of the *Frolic*'s arrival in San Francisco.

Everett took the tray Ahsing offered with a touch of irritation. The boy had taken his own good time bringing the bottle of beer. The Edinburgh ale, bottled in Hong Kong and loaded aboard the *Frolic*, had tasted so good when he sampled it that Everett had ordered a supply for the firm. The cool bottle dripped sweat in the noontime humidity. The second week into October was still beastly hot—so hot that Everett had gone to his room rather than join his colleagues for lunch.

Ahsing pulled the cork and poured the dark amber fluid into a tumbler. A month ago, the firm had bought two full tons of New England ice, and, God willing, it would last till the arrival of the next ice ship. There was talk that this winter the Chinese would start cutting their own ice in the north. Everett shuddered to think of the disgusting surprises to be revealed in ice cut from the duck ponds of Shanghai.

"Mr. Everett, mail come. You got package." Ahsing handed him a ragged roll of newsprint addressed in Jacob Leese's familiar scrawl.

Flattening the *Daily Alta California* on his lap, Everett looked at the date—August 3. It had taken eight weeks from California. Hurriedly, he turned to the "Arrivals" column—still no mention of the *Frolic*. Perhaps Faucon had put in at Honolulu for repairs and been delayed.

Everett had been keeping track of the California market ever since the *Eveline* had arrived in Canton in May of 1849. Now, a year and a half later, his leather-bound journal bulged with clippings from the *Daily Alta* announcing sales and auctions of China goods in San Francisco. There had been five auctions in May, but none during June or July. With luck, China goods would still be scarce when the *Frolic* arrived.

Steeling himself, John Everett opened the newspaper to the sales and auctions. "Blessed Savior," he whispered. "Let there be no China goods on sale in San Francisco." He skimmed down the column.

> *Fresh China goods tomorrow—*
> J. B. Starr & Co. Auctioneers.

No vessel was listed. Perhaps it was only a small consignment of chow-chow items from Singapore or Manila. Everett struggled to his feet, spread out the paper to its full width on the table, and continued skimming down the column.

> *Catalogue sale of extensive and splendid assortment of*
> *China goods ex 'Hugh Walker'*

The *Hugh Walker* had sailed from Hong Kong fifteen days before the *Frolic*. Everett hoped her goods would be sold and gone before the *Frolic*'s were advertised. And if the *Frolic* had put in for repairs at Honolulu, the market would have even more time to recover. He penciled an "X" next to each item to clip after the paper circulated among the rest of the staff.

Everett tried to remember how many China cargoes had competed with the sale of the *Eveline*'s. He flipped back through the pages of his journal—the *Emmy* in May, the *Corréo de Cobija* in June, the *Rhone* in August, and the *Petrel* and *Mariposa* in September—but none in October. If the *Frolic* could have a full month without competing goods, she might do as well. He resumed scanning the newspaper, considering each news item in terms of its benefit or detriment to the *Frolic* venture.

CITY ORDINANCE

*Effective July 28. All tents, houses or other buildings, the exterior
portion of which is constructed in whole or in part of cloth,
within the fire limits of San Francisco, shall be removed or the
cloth replaced by wood or some less flammable material.*

That was certainly good news! Replacing a city of tents with wooden
buildings would increase the value of the house sent with Anthon on
the *Stockholm*, and the *Frolic* carried another, complete with oyster-
shell windows. Reports of San Francisco burning in May and again in
June had brought cheers from the clerks at the dinner table, and even
a toast by John Heard to the health of pyromaniacs and the decrepi-
tude of chimneys. Everett imagined the soft orange glow of San Francisco in flames with only a twinge of guilt, as he pictured crates from
the *Maid of Jalpha* going up in smoke.

The "Importations" column listed thirteen frame houses and two of
iron in stock with various San Francisco merchants—hardly enough to
rebuild a whole city. The port summary listed 467 vessels arrived during
May, June, and July, carrying 14,291 passengers. A letter reprinted from
the *Sacramento Transcript* estimated that fifty to one hundred thousand
emigrants were crossing the Plains, "a quarter of whom would not reach
Eldorado without subsisting on their animals." Everett began to relax.
With so many people, in need of everything, the *Frolic* venture could
not help but be a success.

Everett closed the paper and stepped out onto the balcony. In shirtsleeves, John Heard walked across the esplanade toward the boat shed.
The firm's boatman had commandeered four coolies to lift John's precious racing sloop *Amelia* from her dry berth and carry her down the
ramp to the river. Everett watched Heard scull the sixteen-foot sailboat
out through the sampans into open water. The southwest monsoon was
about played out. Within a month, cool fall air would begin to flow
down the river. But now, afternoon breezes could flow in either direction
and surprise even the most experienced competitor in the Fall Regatta.

John Heard, now the firm's senior partner in Canton, was still green,
thought Everett. Though he was twenty-five years old and had nine
years in Canton, he had only last year made his first business trip, to
Bombay. His youth and inexperience showed in his failure to secure
more opium consignments from the Hindu and Parsee suppliers. Everett
knew that the only way to succeed in business was to invest time and ef-

fort in personal connections, well-seasoned over years of reciprocity, like his relationships with Thomas Larkin and Jacob Leese. Heard had never taken the time to establish links with solid men outside his family's firm. Indeed, he had never worked anywhere else, and his only regular correspondence was with his uncle, old Mr. Heard, in Ipswich, and with the firm's Mr. Dixwell in New York.

Everett resented John Heard. The younger man had been born with a silver spoon in his mouth, and hadn't had to work his way up. Heard had never sold gingham to a señorita or collected cowhides from a ranchero. He hadn't fought fleas in an adobe on the trail of the padres or rode the Monterey Road with pistols loaded for highwaymen, Indians, or grizzly bears. But at Augustine Heard & Company blood ran thicker than water, and John Heard was the protégé of his uncle Augustine, the founder of the firm. "And what can't be cured," mumbled Everett, "must be endured." He took a deep breath and exhaled slowly, resolving not to brood about John Heard. Perhaps he ought to look in on the clerks working in the counting room. He started down the marble steps. From the treasury he heard a familiar clinking sound. A $40,000 shipment of silver had just arrived from the firm's opium station near Shanghai.

Everett saluted Sunkee, the senior shroff, and crossed the hall. A low buzz of laughter and conversation came from the counting room, and the smoke of Manila cheroots hung heavily in the air. Everett cleared his throat to announce his presence. Three clerks on tall stools adjusted their postures in deference to the Heards' senior bookkeeper. Inhaling deeply, Everett walked to his desk. Once again, he reflected on how what was a sin in Boston became a virtue in China. Boston ladies might be appalled at the smoke, but nary a mosquito penetrated the blue haze of his counting room.

"Gentlemen, how goes the *Europa*?"

"We'll be done by supper, Mr. Everett. We've almost finished the oolong."

The bark *Europa* was about to sail, and Everett's boys should have completed the accounting for her 125 tons of tea a week ago. But Mr. Hedrick, the tea-taster, had rejected all of the young hyson. "Wretched sweepings from last year's harvest," he'd sneered. This had resulted in a long delay for more tasting, inspecting, weighing, packing, and arranging bribes for a last-minute "revenue chop," before the *Europa*'s cargo could be completed with forty-six tons of oolong. Now Everett's boys were tired from copying the long, itemized invoice and the ship's manifest in triplicate.

Everett commiserated. "My good fellows, as soon as you finish the job, the rest of the afternoon will belong to you."

The senior clerk beat a drum roll on his desk, whistled a snatch from a polka, and the boys dipped their pens, infused with new urgency. Everett recalled the interminable afternoons he had spent clerking for his uncle on Central Wharf in Boston. Now he was thankful for that apprenticeship, for the Heards' accounting was as complex as anything he had ever encountered.

Since the firm's income came from commissions, a high volume of trade was essential to its success. A tea shipment took four months to reach Boston from China, and payment might not be returned for a year or more. In the firm's early days, the partners had not controlled sufficient capital to advance a year's credit on more than a few cargoes. But George Dixwell, just retired as the firm's senior partner in China, had found the necessary capital for expansion in the profits from the opium trade. Dixwell had cultivated relationships with Hindu and Parsee opium traders, and the firm had reaped the rewards. Everett flipped a page in the ledger and marveled at the investors' exotic names: Pestonjee Framjee, Cowasjee Shapoorjee, Kessressing Khooshalchund. The proceeds from the Indians' opium paid for teas shipped to Boston, with shortages covered by drafts on Baring Brothers bank in London. Everett's ledgers documented the tangled threads of obligation and redemption that stretched around the world.

"Mr. Everett, we're finished!"

The two younger men mock-waltzed toward the granite archway. Everett winked and stepped backward as if to do a pirouette.

"If you boys knew your accounting half as well as your cotillion, you could retire rich at twenty."

Everett was proud of his boys. They were learning to be businessmen. He had trained them to keep books, calculate rates of exchange, and draft business letters. They knew the importance of maintaining regular correspondence. To keep up with world events that would affect the firm's business, he made them read newspapers from San Francisco, London, Bombay, and the Straits. Their success would reflect well on him.

Augustine Heard the younger—Gus—had spent a full year with Everett in the counting room. He had picked up the work quickly—for a Harvard man. Now Gus was junior partner, and in two years, when his older brother John finished his China term and returned to Boston, he would become senior partner in China. Everett approved of Gus. The young man had the good sense to underplay his ability with modesty and charm—unlike his older brother, who masked his incompetence with arrogance and effrontery. With a Harvard education combined with an Everett apprenticeship, young Gus was already a better merchant than John Heard.

Gus reminded Everett of his own nephew, Percival Lowell Everett. In two years, Percy would be seventeen. He would be graduated from Mr. Chauncey's School and have a year of experience clerking on Central Wharf. By then, the Heards would need a new clerk, and Percy could do worse than get his China training under Gus. Everett would broach the subject and, if Gus agreed, he would write to his brother Otis—Percy's father.

Everett listened as the boys' laughter echoed up the stairway. Across the hall, Achen was at work. With his left hand the Heards' comprador worked an abacus, while his right scribed a column of characters on a payment chit. Everett watched as the scholarly Chinese reached for his teapot, splashed a few drops of tea into the depression in his inkstone, and with a quick stirring motion ground and mixed a block of black pigment into the liquid. He dipped his brush and continued writing.

Everett returned to his desk and began proofing the senior clerk's draft invoice for freight and commissions on thirty-three chests of Malwa, consigned by a Hindu in Ahmadabad. He could still hear the faint clicking of the abacus as Achen threw ebony discs left and right along the rods. He looked up to find John Heard standing beside him.

"We lost the *Frolic*," said Heard abruptly.

Everett's stomach knotted. He felt an ache across his shoulders. He stared dumbly, unable to ask the question. The picture of Martha Weld and her copybook handwriting flashed through his mind.

"Oh," said Heard, "Faucon is all right. You can read his letter. We won't lose any money," he continued. "The cargo was fully insured, and we'll probably get more for the vessel than she was worth."

Everett stared at Faucon's flowing script. In an instant his closest friend had been lost, and then restored, but he still felt the loss. He tried to read but his eyes wouldn't focus. When he looked up again, Heard was gone.

Everett left the counting room, walking down the granite-walled hallway through the arched entry and out into the stifling heat of mid-afternoon. He stopped at the water's edge. A black cormorant, a brass ring round its neck, surfaced and fluttered onto the stern of a sampan. The fisherman seized the bird by its legs and jerked its neck until a small fish fell into the boat. Then he pitched the bird back into the water. Everett felt like he was strangling. He and Faucon were no better than cormorants working for the Heards. He walked to the new American garden and sat alone on the bench.

The trees were still hardly more than spindly sticks. The "red, white, and blue" waved feebly from its pole, a three-piece ship's mast complete with shrouds which guyed it upright. Everett stared up at the field of white stars—twenty-six of them. California would make it twenty-seven, if Thomas Larkin had his way. Everett could just picture "Governor" Larkin, assisted by "Senators" Leese and Vallejo, auctioning city lots from the steps of a gold-domed statehouse in Benicia.

He opened Faucon's letter and began to read.[9]

> E. H. Faucon
> St. Francisco
> Aug. 5, 1850

> Messrs Augustine Heard & Co.
> Canton

> Dear Sirs
>   It is my painful duty to communicate to you unwelcome news—as unwelcome for you to read as for me to write. The *Frolic*, on the night of July 25, was totally lost on a reef about 60 miles NW of Fort Ross—formerly a Russian settlement—in about the latitude of 38.25 and longitude of 123.20.
>   The particulars are as follows. The 25th was a fine clear day, with a fresh NNW wind, which at 4 P.M. had increased so much that I deemed it prudent to close reef the topsails, and furl the jib, mainsail and t'ry sail. The wind was not so strong—had we been in mid ocean—to make it necessary to come under such snug canvas, but we were rapidly running in towards the coast, and—judging from my former experience in this quarter, that a NW gale of some duration had set in—I wished to reduce her rate of sailing to be prepared to haul either way should it be necessary during the night. At sunset

(7 P.M.) the wind had moderated very much and (as was expected) the faint outline of high land was seen at a very great distance—at least 50 to 60 miles. I pointed the land out to both officers who happened to be standing near the wheel and directed the chief officer, Mr. Deutcher, to make the following entries in the log: "7:15 land seen NE & E 50 to 60 miles distant. St. Francisco bears SE true 100 miles." Course & distance run from noon to 7 P.M. ESE 65 miles. From 7 to 8 P.M. the vessel went 4 to 5 knots, the wind moderating fast, but thinking it might soon freshen up, only one reef was shaken out, at 8 P.M., and the jib and mainsail set.

At 9 P.M. the wind was faint from north, reefs were let out and top gallantsails set. At 9:30, after the top glt. sails had been set, the chief officer came below and said, "I see something to windward which looks like breakers." I had just finished some writing, and not doubting but what we were at least 60 miles [from the coast] from the direction of our course ESE, I replied, "Breakers! its impossible. How do they bear?" "North sir." "There can be no breakers in that direction at all events," was my answer. This conversation took place as we were passing out of the cabin and up the companionway. I will here state that the chart I had was a Chinese copy of Norrie's General Chart of the North Pacific taken, I think, from Vancouver's Survey.

The longitude at noon was determined by sights from chronometers taken both forenoon & afternoon. There were two good instruments on board, and, as they differed 16 miles, the position was determined from the one farthest East (which I considered the best of the two timekeepers). Owing to thick weather and fogs, not a single opportunity [had] offered for lunars [during] the whole passage. I will also add that the whole day had been very clear and the moon was up about 8 P.M. It was my intention to run in towards the land under snug sail, and— as the weather appeared perfectly clear and the coast a bold one—to approach, make the land, and run down towards St. Francisco.

As soon as I reached the deck I saw instantly the breakers. The helm was put to port and the vessel hauled off SW/W. The wind was light from N-NNE and directly from the line of breakers, and the swell was setting SE. The reef appeared to extend 1 1/2 miles in an ESE and WNW direction. No land was to be seen although the breakers were close to. To my consternation I saw that by the influence of a tide or current, the vessel was rapidly approaching the reef although what light air there was (about a 3 knot breeze) came directly from the same quarter as the reef bore and the swell was setting us S.E. When 50 feet from the breakers we got soundings 10 fathoms. A moment after, she struck stern on with 8 fathoms under her counter.

The rudder went immediately and the water was soon up to within a few inches of the cabin floor. A moment after she struck she swung round hard against the swell alongside of the rock over which the sea broke furiously. I then for the first time saw land, apparently at a very short distance, and between the reef and the shore two or three islets or large rocks. The brig struck on the Eastern extremity of the breakers. Inshore from the point near it the coast curved in to the Eastward.

As soon as my position was clearly seen to be hopeless, the quarter boats were lowered and—as it afterwards seemed at a most providential moment and with a couple of men in each under the direction of the two officers—were kept clear from the vessel in case her spars should fall or the breakers fill them. The boats were kept off with some difficulty as the tide or a current appeared to be sweeping them in all the time. As the vessel was fast filling, the men were sent into the boats, all crowding into them except six who utterly refused to quit the brig, whether they were under the influence of fright or from some other cause I am wholly unable to conjecture. The men remaining were two Chinese, one Lascar and three Malays. There was no time to save clothes or provisions. I went below and brought up 2 bottles of brandy and 4 of porter—and about a dozen of crackers.

At daylight we landed on the beach about 7 miles I judge from the reef, and where we saw some fires burning. I knew we were not very distant from Fort Ross and hoped to find some Indians to give us information. After going 2 miles inland and seeing no one, we returned to the beach. One of the boats was very leaky and most of the men (we numbered 20) were averse to going in the boats, and wished to travel by land. The officers remained with me and ordering 4 men into the boat, and placing the sick Lascar in her, we began to pull to the SE. We met with delays from a southerly wind and fog and made but very slow progress.

On the 29th at 5 P.M. we reached a Rancho, having on our way slept on the beaches, subsisting on mussels. At the Rancho we procured beef and milk, stayed there all night, and at noon the next day reached the settlement at Ross. Two of the boat's crew ran away on the way down. I arrived at Capt. Smith's house at Bodega on the 31st very much fatigued and sore. Both Mr. Benitz at Ross & Capt. Smith informed me that strong currents had prevailed for a month previous, running to the North. To this I attribute the loss of the *Frolic* and also to my being deceived by the apparent clearness of the weather, while a haze indistinguishable to the observer hung over the coast. Both Capt. Nichels of the *John Q. Adams* and Capt. Johnson of the *Gallego* and others were near losing their vessels, the breakers being only within a mile of them when first seen—and no land distinguishable until close aboard of it. Could we have been set $1/2$ mile more to the SE I think we should have gone all clear or else brought up by our anchors as there was plenty of room had we cleared the extreme of the reef where we struck—and which was bare on the receding of the rollers.

It should also be mentioned—I speak in the authority of others resident at Ross, Bodega and this place—that the coast is very inaccurately laid down from St. Francisco to the Northward, and in some places to the extent of 35 miles. Of my personal loss I have nothing to say. But in justice to myself I wish this letter, if it be thought necessary, to be shown to the underwriters at Canton. I shall I hope soon be present to answer any inquiries they may wish to make although I believe what I have written covers everything. The loss must be classed as one of those ever likely to happen in the ordinary course of navigation and which with all the vigilance, prudence and skill possible to be exercised, do and will continue to occur.

I remain
Very truly Yrs.
E. H. Faucon

The *Frolic* left Lye moon anchorage on the 10th June 8 A.M.

CHAPTER 5

Point Cabrillo, California, 1850

I stood on the bluff looking out at the spot where the *Frolic* had wrecked. Beyond the mouth of the cove, I could see the white foam where waves broke across a mostly submerged rock. Faucon had succeeded in turning the *Frolic* away from the rock, but the water's surge had pushed her backwards. She had struck the rock stern-on, breaking her rudder and staving in her hull. Leaving the *Frolic* lying against that rock, Faucon and his men had launched the two quarter boats and pulled south into the night.

My study of the wreck divers' collections led me to believe that much of the *Frolic*'s cargo had been salvaged soon after she was wrecked. In addition to the pottery fragments I had found at Three Chop Village, I had read eyewitness accounts of Indians wearing silk shawls and of giant China jars in a rude settler's hut. How had those goods come ashore? Had the six men Faucon's letter mentioned as remaining aboard managed to survive and get to shore with some of the cargo? And twelve crewmen had been left barefoot on the beach at Big River the morning after the wreck. Had any of them returned to the ship for salvage? Had the Indians whose fires Faucon had seen gathered flotsam from the wreck along the beach? As I looked out from the windswept bluff, I tried to imagine what had happened the night of the wreck.[1]

❦

Figure 28. The brig *Frolic* approaches the Mendocino Coast, by moonlight, 9:30 P.M., July 25, 1850. Original illustration by S. F. Manning.

"Fifty miles, maybe a little less," said Mr. Deutcher, pointing toward the mountains. Mariano Rosales, head serang of the brig *Frolic*, stood at the binnacle with the first mate. He glanced at the compass. Since the Captain had sighted land, Custodio, the helmsman, had been holding the brig to an east-southeast course. It was a lee coast, and they would follow it at a safe distance south to the straits of Santo Francisco, a hundred miles away. At this rate, they would be there by morning.

Rosales recalled what he had overheard the captain telling Mr. Deutcher. They would need to wait for the tide. No sailing vessel could fight the full current through the straits into Santo Francisco harbor on a falling tide. They might need to take on a pilot before entering the bay.

"Senhor Rosales, I see foam to the north!" Custodio pointed across the black water into a low-hanging haze. Rosales walked to the port rail, shielding his eyes from the moonlit sky. At first he saw nothing. Then, as his eyes adjusted to the black water, he saw it too—a long broken line of whitecaps. Rosales looked at Deutcher. For an instant, the first officer stood frozen.

"Sound the bell!" he shouted.

Rosales untied the clapper and rang out a staccato beat. From down the companionway he heard Deutcher shouting for the captain.

Faucon burst onto the deck, his shirt still unbuttoned.

"Put the helm to port!" he bellowed.

Custodio strained to pull the topmost grip of the wheel. Rosales grabbed for the next. Responding to the bell, Panaji boys staggered up from their quarters before the mast. Slowly, the vessel began to turn. The jib sail billowed with the breeze coming from the direction of the breakers. Now the mainsail and topgallant sails luffed and filled away. Rosales crossed himself. God was sending the offshore breeze to pull them away from danger.

They had almost succeeded in turning the vessel when Rosales heard a low roar. Looking back over his shoulder he saw the rocks. Now he could hear the crash of individual waves. The tidal current was stronger than the wind. Satan was pushing them backwards.

"*Dez*—ten fathoms," shouted Pedro.

Rosales heard the slosh of rushing water, the hiss of foam.

"*Oito*—eight fathoms."

The vessel shuddered. Rosales fell backward against the binnacle. Men were skidding across the deck, grabbing for handholds. The wheel

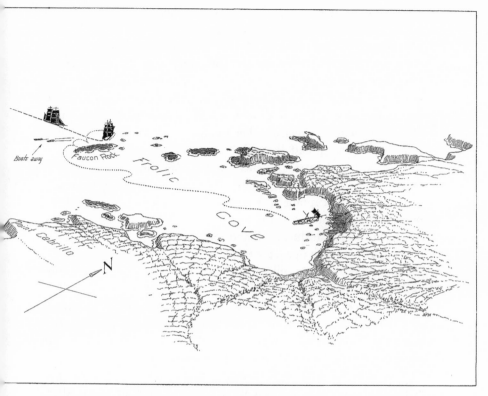

Figure 29. On the night of July 25, 1850, Captain Faucon saw breakers against offshore rocks and attempted to turn the *Frolic*. She struck stern-on and filled with water. Judging the vessel lost, Faucon abandoned ship. After Faucon departed for Fort Ross, his crew probably careened the vessel into the adjacent cove, lodging her near shore, where she was pillaged. Original illustration by S. F. Manning.

spun. Custodio screamed as a grip struck his wrist. There was a sharp crack from below and the wheel ropes fell limp.

For an instant, there was silence. Rosales felt the surge—the grasp of Satan. Slowly, relentlessly, the vessel rotated until she was broadside to a large rock that emerged between the waves, only a few feet above water. The *Frolic* took a blow from the side with an excruciating, grinding screech of stone striking yellow pine planking. With each gouging, grating roll, Rosales felt the deck vibrate beneath his feet as the vessel reverberated like a giant guitar. Now waves washed across the deck and the men clung to the rigging for safety.

"Captain, the hull's holed! Water's up to the cabin floor," gasped Mr. Harrison, as the second officer worked his way aft, clutching the starboard rail.

"Officers, launch the quarter boats!" Faucon's voice was as calm now as if he were going ashore to drink tea with the Bombay harbormaster.

Rosales watched the men clamber into the boats. Mr. Harrison called for his monkey, but it had disappeared.

"Keep clear of the yards," called Captain Faucon.

Rosales looked up. A dangling spar swung wildly across the deck.

"Rosales!" The captain beckoned to him. Together they stumbled down the companionway to the cabin. The oil lamp still burned in its gimbals, but water sloshed back and forth across the floor as the vessel rolled. The captain opened a trunk.

"Take these!" he said, filling Rosales' arms with bottles of liquor and tins of crackers.

Back on deck, Rosales heard loud whimpering. Overhead, men were clinging, terrified, to the mainmast shrouds. He recognized the three Malaymen he had hired in Hong Kong. And there were the Chinese cook and carpenter—and Miguelito, a Panaji boy. The captain ordered the men to come down. The carpenter started first, but he had scarcely reached the deck when a massive wave nearly carried him away. After that, nothing would convince the others to descend. Rosales, his arms full of supplies, looked on helplessly. He hooked one elbow over the rail for support. A bottle slipped from his grasp and bounced across the deck.

Faucon stood perfectly still. Only his lips moved as he counted the intervals between the waves. He motioned Mr. Deutcher's boat toward the stern. The oarsmen fought to hold their boat away as Rosales and the captain jumped aboard. They had scarcely pushed off before the next wave crashed against the *Frolic*'s hull.

They were a hundred yards seaward, well beyond the breakers, before the captain spoke.

"Hold water," he ordered. For a few moments, Faucon watched his vessel, her masts striking arcs across the moonlit sky.

"Captain!" Mr. Harrison's voice had a tone of urgency. "We're taking on water."

Captain Faucon sat rigid and stoic, like the martyr Santo Sebastiano, thought Rosales. The men in Mr. Harrison's boat were bailing with their hands, while Mr. Harrison used his felt cap. Rosales felt sick. The port quarter boat had baked in the afternoon sun from Singapore to Whampoa. He had seen daylight between the dried planks, but he had neglected to mention it. Perhaps it was that dereliction of duty that had brought on God's wrath. In the distance, he could hear one of the abandoned men shrieking in terror. Was it Miguelito? What would he tell the boy's mother? Why hadn't he dragged him down and thrown him into a boat? Why hadn't he—?

"She'll be under water in an hour," said the captain, turning to face the men. "Pull south."

Rosales gazed up at the cliffs—towering bastions to a darkened land, waves crashing at their bases. Wet and shivering, the men pulled at their oars. He looked at their faces. He himself had recruited most of them from Panaji town in Goa. His half-brother Custodio, the steersman, and his nephew Valerio, the sailmaker, were among them. They had always worked well together, each man knowing his job. And they all believed in the one true faith, brought to Panaji by Santo Francisco Xavier himself. No Hindus or Muslims had ever sailed with them—they were too much trouble for the cook. Hindu men ate no beef and Muslims ate no pork. Goa men ate both.

Rosales thought about his first voyage. He had been twelve when Uncle Mateo's sailing dhow arrived from the Malabar coast, carrying a cargo of calico, cardamom, and two freshly cut teak logs for sale as keels. They needed one more man to make a full crew, and Mariano had hardly been able to contain his excitement as they sailed on the ebb tide down the Mondavi, past coconut-laden palms. Below the fort they steered north, and two days later at Bombay they took on ten passengers, Muslims on pilgrimage to Mecca.

They sailed directly for Aden, where the Muslims boarded an Arab vessel for passage up the Red Sea. Meanwhile, Uncle Mateo sold the teak keels and took on Persian carpets. They continued south along the coast of Africa to Mombassa and Mozambique, where they traded the calico, cardamom, and rugs for elephant tusks and rhinoceros horn. Finally, east of Madagascar, they caught the southwest monsoon, which drove them across the Arabian Sea toward home. Uncle Mateo sold the horn and ivory to Goa merchants for shipment to the Chinese in Macao.

Not long after his sixteenth birthday, Rosales had sailed again. That time he went to Macao with his grandfather, head serang on a Portuguese barkentine. As the years passed, Mariano rose from seaman, to helmsman, until finally he, too, became a serang. For fifteen years now, he had sailed on English and American clippers carrying Malwa opium from Bombay to China—down the Malabar coast, across the Bay of Bengal, through the Strait of Malacca, up the China Sea, and then back again. But Rosales had never sailed to California. Though a few of his Panaji boys had refused the voyage, saying it was too long and cold, he had welcomed the adventure. The voyage had gone well, and only forty-six days out of Hong Kong the captain had sighted land.

Now Rosales' stomach growled. To the east, the sky was beginning to redden. It had been hours since they abandoned ship, and more hours since they had last eaten. He wondered when the captain would give them some of the crackers he had helped to salvage. They rounded a headland. The cliffs seemed broken by a cove, and he could make out a low area and two faintly glowing spots on what looked like a beach. Indios, he thought.

"Campfires!"

The captain had seen them, too. The men pulled harder at their oars. Now Rosales could make out brush huts above the beach. But as the boats approached shore, the Indios ran away into the woods. As the men dragged the boats up onto the sandy beach, Rosales saw piles of shells where the Indios had feasted on roasted mussels and sea snails.

Captain Faucon gave each man a biscuit to chew on for breakfast. Now he wanted to find the village of the Indios and ask them how far it was to the old Russian colony of Fort Ross. He put Mr. Harrison in charge of the men, with orders to launch the boats if they were approached by any armed men. Rosales followed the captain and Mr. Deutcher along the path, hiking up onto the bluff and a mile inland. They saw bark houses and dead campfires, but all of the Indios had vanished. The captain called out in English and Spanish, but no one answered.

When they returned to the beach, Valerio was caulking the leaky boat, using Mr. Harrison's knife to force narrow strips of cloth torn from the men's shirtsleeves into the largest cracks between the planks. The captain and the officers walked down the beach to confer. After a few minutes, they called for him. They planned to pull for Ross—sixty miles south was the captain's guess. Rosales gathered the sailors together. They discussed the distance and the leaky boat. The men were unanimous. They wanted to walk.

"There are several rivers between here and Ross," the captain explained to Rosales. "But now is the dry season, and they will be low like this one and easy to cross on sand bars." He gestured at the stream, barely knee-deep as it flowed across the sandy beach.

Rosales thought how the Mondavi, too, became shallow in the hot, dry months before the southwest monsoon.

The captain continued. He would meet them at Ross, or, if they were delayed, he would make arrangements there for their passage to San Francisco, where they should go directly to Macondray & Company to claim their pay and get passage home.

Rosales remembered the Panaji boy, Miguelito, who he had last seen clinging to the rigging. He asked Faucon's permission to go back across the headlands to see if any of the men left on the *Frolic* had survived.

The captain paused for a moment. He chose his words carefully.

"You may check to see if any of the men have reached shore. But, you will remember, the vessel and her cargo are the property of Augustine Heard & Company."

The captain paused again and stared directly into Rosales' eyes.

"Should the vessel have been washed ashore . . . "

Rosales felt their eyes lock. He felt as if the captain could see into his very soul.

"Should the vessel have been washed ashore, you are to take nothing beyond the supplies you need to reach Ross. And when you reach Ross, you will report to me or to the authorities there. Should salvage be possible, I will arrange it."

Captain Faucon needed oarsmen. Rosales asked for volunteers, but no one wanted to go. Finally, he ordered four men into the captain's boat, and within minutes they were gone.

Before the captain had rounded the point, Rosales took charge. He must attempt to rescue Miguelito before they began the trek south. He ordered three men to remain with Valerio to guard the boat. The seven others followed him up onto the bluff, where they found a well-beaten trail leading north across the headlands. By midday they stood at the edge of a cape, looking at the *Frolic* four hundred yards out. Six men shouted and waved from her rigging.

Rosales' mind worked quickly. Buoyed by a pocket of air trapped beneath her deck, the vessel had floated free. The tide was receding, the waves had calmed, and the vessel's topgallant sails had caught a slight offshore breeze. He could save the men and, with luck, salvage enough supplies for their trip to Ross, but he would have to work fast and he needed the boat. He ordered five men to wait. Taking the two youngest with him, he started back across the headlands at a trot. Within minutes, he was winded and had to stop to catch his breath. They resumed at a fast walk. His feet hurt, and he favored the flattened grass near the center of the path.

At the beach, Valerio already had the boat caulked and in the water. They shoved off immediately, and by early evening pulled in over the *Frolic*'s sunken port side and tied up to her mainmast. The wet, weary men clambered down from the rigging and into the boat, and Rosales directed the oarsmen toward a small pocket beach at the head of the adjacent cove. Putting the rescued men ashore, he ordered his six strongest Panaji boys into the boat.

Rosales sent two men aboard the *Frolic* to run a rope from her bowsprit down to the boat. Then, as he called cadence, the four men in the boat pulled at their oars. There was no movement at first, but then, slowly, the ship began to turn. Soon the vessel pointed into the cove and was moving forward. As the tide rose, the surge helped to push them shoreward. Rosales chose a spot on the protected northern side of the cove. As the men rowed, an onshore breeze filled the *Frolic*'s topgallant sails, and within minutes her bow was wedged between two large rocks only fifty yards from shore. As soon as they were safely on land, the men knelt on the beach and prayed.

The rescue had taken most of the day, and now the sun hung heavy on the horizon. Rosales looked at the steep trail that twisted up to the top of the bluff. There, surrounded by broken mussel shells, stood six rude huts. Rosales shuddered. He had heard of shipwrecked men murdered and eaten on the islands off Borneo. As darkness fell, he posted guards at the top of the path. The other men slept huddled at the base of the cliff, shielded from the wind by their upturned boat.

❧

"Senhor Rosales!"

He heard the words, but they seemed to be part of a dream. He snuggled deeper into the clump of sleeping sailors. In the middle of the night, he had joined the boy Miguelito to stand watch on the bluff, and when he returned to the beach he had wriggled his way back into the cluster, like a suckling pig in Panaji town.

"Senhor Rosales!" Carlos shook his shoulder again. "Wake up! *Um Indio!*"

Mariano Rosales crawled reluctantly out from the shared body heat of the crew. It was daylight. Cold dew dripped from the edge of the boat onto his face. He followed Carlos up the path.

The Indio wore an otter-skin cape and a string of blue glass beads around his neck. With dignified formality, he handed Rosales a hollowed-out log full of glowing coals, then stared intently at the silver crucifix that hung around his neck.

"*Cristo?*" the man asked.

"*Cristão!*" replied Rosales, crossing himself.

Rosales tried to talk to the man, but he did not understand. Finally, when Rosales said "Americanos?" the Indio nodded enthusiastically and made signs he would return.

Rosales gave the hot coals to Alok. An hour later, with his back to a crackling driftwood fire, he gazed out at the waves breaking across the *Frolic*. Her bow was elevated and pointed to shore; her stern lay in deeper water. As the tide ebbed, he could see the foredeck rail emerging gradually from the water. By noon, the water had receded almost to the foremast, and he and Valerio launched the boat and rowed to the wreck. They tied to the foremast shrouds and pulled themselves aboard. The bell clanged as each blast of the northwest wind filled the sails and rocked the vessel. Suddenly, Valerio spied his sea chest floating among the jumble of clothing and bedding in the forward companionway. They pulled it up onto the deck. Valerio fumbled for the cord around his neck, and with a broad grin held up the brass key that hung from it. He unlocked his sea chest, poured out the water, and gazed at his soggy belongings.

Still strapped to the rail were the barrels in which Alok had stored food and cooking supplies. Rosales pried the lid off the meat barrel and saw the fresh white pork inside. It was from their last pig, meant to celebrate a successful voyage. Rosales sighed, remembering the crew's excitement when land had been sighted—only yesterday. Now, somberly, they piled the meat into Valerio's sea chest and lifted it into the boat.

SFM

Figure 30. Mariano Rosales and his Panaji boys salvage supplies from the *Frolic* circa July 27, 1850, before their long walk back to civilization. Original illustration by S. F. Manning.

Back on the beach, Alok and the men roasted the pork over an open fire for their midday meal. Rosales watched the falling tide expose more and more of the *Frolic*'s deck.

By mid-afternoon the tide had completely receded—a full six feet— exposing the *Frolic*'s deck as far back as the main cargo hatch. The men needed blankets and shoes for the long walk south. Rosales launched the boat again and moored to the main mast. The men dove down into their flooded quarters, pulled up their possessions, and loaded them into the boat.

Next, they loaded Alok's iron pots and pans, a barrel of salt fish, and three gunny bags of wet rice. While the men searched for more food amid the chaotic mess that had once been the galley, Rosales considered the rest of the cargo.

He hadn't needed Faucon's reminder that the cargo belonged to the company. Rosales was an honest man, and in his two years as head serang on the *Frolic* he had always warned the men against pilferage. But the brig and everything on it would soon be destroyed by the sea, and he and the men might need goods to offer hostile savages—or weapons, if the gifts proved ineffective. Rosales wondered what he could say to the captain. He had a duty as serang to see the men to safety, and of course they would take no more than they could carry on their backs. He called one of the men over and together they loosed the tarpaulins and lifted one of the hatch-cover panels.

Rosales looked down into the flooded hold. The wooden crates were too heavy to lift, but at high tide, when the water was deeper, a few might be floated out. He stopped, overhearing the men's low conversation behind him.

"The boat must have a treasury—Spanish dollars!" said one.

"Yes, they all do! Every boat!" said another.

"It's probably in the captain's cabin," offered someone else.

Rosales frowned. Some of the men had been talking like this all morning. Now, one of the Panaji boys was bragging that he could dive down to find the silver. Rosales glanced aft toward the officers' quarters. Three feet of water still covered the companionway that led down to their cabins. He would call the men together tonight. He must tell them plainly and firmly that no sailor was to enter the officers' cabins without his permission. He had a duty to protect the treasury and the officers' belongings.

It was late afternoon. The men's sea chests were lined up on the beach and their clothes and blankets hung over driftwood branches to dry. The wind was picking up and fog was blowing in. Rosales ordered Valerio to cut canvas from the sails to make a windbreak. Valerio anchored one end of the canvas with rocks and suspended the rest of the fabric over a driftwood crossbar held aloft by poles dug into the beach sand. That evening, dressed in warm, dry clothes, the sailors feasted on shredded stewed pork over rice. Then, wrapped in his own blanket, Rosales lay down beneath the canvas windbreak and slept.

He awakened to the barking of seals. Their sleek black bodies crowded together on the beach just a stone's throw from where he and his men slept, crowded together in their own way. He planned out the day. They still needed supplies for the trip, but he did not want to linger long at this place. The ship's treasury was too much of a temptation and he wanted to get started for Ross.

He had Valerio put the men to work cutting the sail canvas into rectangles twice the length of a man, to make packs. They looked like bullock bags, with a pocket at each end, but with a hole in the center for a man's head. Valerio showed the men how to punch holes with a spike and lace up the pockets with rope cut from the rigging.

The tide was high and the cargo hatch was now totally submerged. It was time to float out the wooden crates. Rosales ordered six boys who could swim into the boat and moored once more to the mainmast. An hour later, they had eased five buoyant crates out of the hatch and towed them to the beach. The men crowded around as Rosales pried loose the lid from the first one. They screamed in laughter as he removed a small painted box, opened it, and spread an ivory-handled silk fan. Soon all the men held fans and were strutting and pirouetting along the beach, striking poses and winking at each other. The next crate contained silk shawls with long, lacy fringes. Rich colors dripped from the silk, staining the men's hands red, green, and blue. The three other boxes contained men's vests, bolts of uncut silk, and ivory-handled umbrellas.

The boys looked like prosperous American merchants in their new vests. Probably, most of the lighter crates remaining aboard also contained clothing and fabrics, thought Rosales. The men had recovered their own shoes and clothing from their sea chests, and they would not need shawls and fans for their hike to Fort Ross. What they needed was food, and weapons for protection against the savages.

Figure 31. The *Frolic* wreck site, August 1850, after the waves had shifted her stern counterclockwise. Original illustration by S. F. Manning.

By mid-afternoon of the second day, the tide had fallen enough so that the deck around the cargo hatch was dry. Rosales rigged the deck winch and ordered the men to pull out crates that were too heavy to float. They ferried these ashore, one crate at a time. Suddenly, as Rosales was helping to off-load a particularly heavy crate onto the beach, he heard loud cheers and hoots from the *Frolic*. When he returned to the vessel, he saw the men had brought up three iron-bound cases of bottled ale. They had broken the corked necks from the green bottles and were drinking from the jagged bases. Rosales ordered the ale into the boat, commanding that the bottles be delivered unopened to Alok. He did not want any drunkenness; it would undermine his authority. He would ration the beer, one bottle for each man in the morning and another in the evening.

At the beach, Rosales directed the men to open the heavier crates.

The first contained sets of brass weights, nested one inside another. The next held the disassembled parts of a black wood table with a marble top. The third revealed quart-size porcelain jars with blue designs. Rosales had seen jars like these, filled with preserved condiments, for sale in the bazaars of Macao and Canton. Cutting the bindings from one, he pried off its ceramic lid to reveal pale green candied citron in a thick sugary paste. The other jars contained yellow ginger and orange kumquats. As the men ate the tart, sticky fruit from the jars, Rosales looked up at the cliff. A row of Indios—men, women, and children—gazed down at them from the top.

Two men were coming down the path. Rosales recognized the younger one by his otter-skin cape. The older man came forward. He looked like an Indio, but he wore a tattered wool vest and broad-rimmed felt hat.

"*Buenos días, señor,*" said the older man, bowing slightly in deference. "*Me llamo Pedrito.*"

Rosales recognized the sounds of Spanish.

"*Bom dia, senhor,*" he replied. "*Meu nome é Rosales.*"

During the next hour, between bites of candied kumquats, Rosales and Pedrito managed a conversation. Pedrito could not lead them to Ross. He had never been there. It was located in the territory of a fierce people called the Kashaya, and Yokayo people like Pedrito never went there without prior permission from their chief. However, Señor Juan Parker, the Americano, was only two days over the hills to the southeast. Pedrito explained that he was a vaquero for Señor Parker, and that his friend wearing the otter-skin cape was Keetana, whose people claimed this part of the coast. Tomorrow he, Pedrito, would lead them to Señor Parker's rancho. Rosales gave Pedrito and Keetana each a silk vest and a jar of preserves and watched them retreat up the trail to the bluff.

Rosales called the men together. They would not be walking to Ross, he explained. Instead, the Indio would take them over an easier trail to Señor Parker's rancho. From there, they would travel to Santo Francisco to meet the captain. They would only have the rest of the afternoon to prepare for their journey. He ordered more boxes of condiments brought ashore—enough for each man to have a jar of candied fruit in his pack. Back on the vessel, the men lifted crates from the hold with greater vigor, anticipating their return to some kind of civilization.

As the men loaded crates, Rosales waded waist-deep down the deck to the companionway that led to the officers' cabins. The men needed weapons, in case the Indios tried to murder them on the trail. The ship's armory was near the cabin, but its heavy oak door was locked. It might be easier to find the officers' swords in their closets. But Rosales was still under Faucon's command, and a sailor never entered an officer's cabin without permission. He tried to balance need against duty and the strict code of conduct upon which he had built his reputation. He imagined how he could answer a potential inquisitor. He would take no personal belongings but the swords, and those he would return at Santo Francisco.

Crossing himself, Rosales took a deep breath and swam down into the darkness. Feeling his way as he went, he pushed open the door to the captain's cabin. As he moved inside, he felt a length of cloth brush against his cheek. He kicked forward and felt it loop around his throat. As he pushed backwards, the cloth caught against something and held him. He was trapped! Panic seized his chest. He tugged at the cloth. It tightened. In terror, he tugged again. Then, miraculously, the entangling noose gave way and he swam free. He pushed upward, his lungs near bursting. As he clenched the mainmast shroud, coughing up sea water, he recognized that he had seen a divine sign. He had almost yielded to temptation, but the Lord had saved him from breaking his compact with Faucon. The men would have to arm themselves with knives and cleavers from Alok's kitchen.

All afternoon, the Indios watched from the bluff. The beach was littered with broken packages and boxes, lacquered tea trays and chessboards, rosewood desks, carved pearl counters, tortoiseshell combs, and clumps of soggy rice-paper paintings. Piles of checked handkerchiefs and bolts of satin lay in the sand. The men filled, emptied, and refilled their packs, trying to decide what to carry away.

Rosales woke the men early the next morning. Pedrito arrived as they were finishing a breakfast of rice, candied kumquats, and a bottle of ale. Alok had boiled the remainder of the rice and tied portions into silk handkerchiefs for the men to stow for the trip. The day before, the Chinese cook had complained bitterly because no one had found his sea chest with his string of cash coins and the pierced Spanish dollar he liked to wear around his neck. Now, as he forced his feet into borrowed shoes, he complained about the loss of his shoehorn. It had

Figure 32. Keetana's band of Mitom Pomo salvage a portion of the *Frolic*'s cargo of China trade goods, August 1850. Original illustration by S. F. Manning.

been marked with a Chinese character inside a ship's wheel—the chop Alok scratched onto all his belongings.

The men followed Pedrito up the path to the bluff. The huts that had been empty a few days before were now occupied, filled with the sounds of children chattering and babies whimpering. Pedrito's nephews hoisted tall conical baskets filled with dried mussel meat onto their backs and adjusted the tumplines across their foreheads. As he lifted his own basket, packed with dried seaweed, Pedrito pointed to the trail and the men followed. Rosales looked back over his shoulder and saw the Indios crowding down the path to the beach.

"*Cinco chagas de Cristo!*" Rosales slapped the top of his head. The mosquitoes here were as ravenous as those at Whampoa. He examined the mashed, bloody insect in the palm of his hand. Valerio always teased him about his bald spot, and now the mosquito added injury to insult.

With Pedrito and his nephews in the lead, Rosales and his men retraced the trail south across the grassy headlands to the river where they had first seen the campfires. For a while, they followed the river, fording it at a shallows; then they ascended the side of a forested ridge. And what a forest! Rosales had never seen such trees, some as big across as the *Frolic* was wide. Pedrito set a steady pace, faster than the sailors could keep up with. Rosales heard their complaints echoing up the path.

At the top of the ridge, they emerged from the fog into summer heat and followed a trail leading southeast along the crest. Now that they were no longer climbing, the trek was easier. Through grassy openings between the trees Rosales could see for miles across parallel ridges to the north and south. To the west, Rosales looked down on a thick fog that blanketed the coast like Bombay cotton.

That evening they reached a clearing. The exhausted sailors had eaten some of their cold rice and quickly fallen asleep. Rosales sat alone, wrapped in his blanket, gazing at the starry sky. They had walked a full day and were no closer to Santo Francisco. After tomorrow, they would have nothing to eat. Would this detour delay them too long from meeting up with Captain Faucon in Santo Francisco? If he was already gone when they arrived, who would pay them their wages? And once they had reached Santo Francisco, they were still two months away from Whampoa, and another six weeks from Bombay. Would they ever get home to Panaji town?

Rosales stared to the south. Just above the horizon twinkled *escorpião*. At home in Panaji town the scorpion ruled the sky. But here in the northern wilderness, only his venomous tail showed above the horizon. Was it an omen? Would they feel his poison sting? He tried to recall whether a scorpion only stung once and then he drifted off into a dream of mangoes and coconut palms.

Rosales awakened hungry. His legs hurt, and he felt blisters on his shoulders from the heavy canvas pack. He divided his remaining rice into two portions. He would eat one slowly, a little at a time, and save the rest for tomorrow. That afternoon, they descended into a deep valley. They passed two boys with willow whips tending a small herd of broad-horned cattle. The boys waved and Pedrito sent his nephews running ahead to warn Parker of their arrival.

The house looked like a poor farmer's sunshade along the Mondavi River: a dirt floor with poles stuck into the ground, filled in with dried clay, and crudely roofed with thatch. Rosales peered inside. A stretched bullock hide separated the space into two rooms. A scythe lay against the wall. In the yard, Parker's Indios were threshing. One pitched the cut wheat over the rail into a corral; another drove horses in a circle to trample loose the seeds. It was the same as Mondavi farmers driving bullocks around their threshing floors, and just as dusty.

Rosales waited for his men to catch up. Pedrito walked ahead to the corral to greet a tall, burly, balding man. Señor Juan Parker approached, dragging a frayed rawhide whip. He eyed Rosales' silk vest and gazed down the line of men with bright handkerchiefs tied round their foreheads, their shoulders padded against the chafing of their packs with embroidered silk shawls. Parker spat a thick brown stream of tobacco juice and gestured toward a split-log bench.

Rosales arranged his pack beside him, on the side away from Parker and out of his line of sight. He pulled out two ale bottles and a jar of candied ginger.

"I wouldn't let them Indians get near your packs," said Parker, craning to see what else might be inside. "They'd kill you in a minute if I wasn't here."

Rosales opened the ginger. Parker pulled an iron nail from his pocket and forced the cork down into one of the ale bottles.

"You're sailors?" Parker asked, unable to conceal his incredulity.

"We sailed from China," said Rosales. "With Capitão Faucon, an Americano. He went to the Fort Ross. We will meet him at Santo Francisco."

But Parker wasn't paying attention. He seemed transfixed as the sailors opened their packs and pawed through fans, lacquered ware, and ivory-handled umbrellas to get to their rice.

Parker turned, with a deluge of questions coming at Rosales faster than he could answer. How large was the boat? Could it be reached from shore? Was it filled with water? Were the ale, the ginger, and the vests part of the cargo? Was there still anything left aboard? The questions made Rosales uneasy. He felt helpless in the face of his dependent situation and Parker's obvious greed. He needed Parker's protection from the Indios, and his assistance to reach Santo Francisco. He was trapped—and each answer he gave felt like a compromise of his integrity. He had promised his captain not to take any cargo beyond what they needed for their trip south, but he was no longer sure he could be responsible for it. It was beyond his control.

"Pedrito!" Parker called.

The old vaquero came forward, bowing deferentially to his employer.

"That boat—*aquel barco*—is it past Buldam?" Parker pointed north.

Pedrito nodded. "Past Coyote's salt well, where the land bends inward." He modeled a narrow cove between his thumb and finger. "*Muy pequeño.*"

"Bring in the horses—all of them!" Parker ordered.

Pedrito squirmed under Parker's gaze, but he did not move to obey. He mumbled something about a fish. Rosales struggled to follow the story. The vaquero slowly explained that he was Yokayo, but the wreck lay in the territory of another people, the Mitom. He had been visiting his sister, who was married to a Mitom man at Buldam village. He had only been allowed to gather shellfish there with the permission of their leader, Keetana, and it was Keetana who had asked him to talk to Rosales at the beach. He was in an awkward position.

Pedrito described the terms of the truce that governed relations between the Yokayo and the Mitom. Once, long ago, Mitom people had found a stranded whale on a beach that belonged to the Yokayo. Not only had they not sent baskets of whale fat, but they had not even sent word of their find. When the Yokayo found out about it, they were incensed. War had been avoided only when the Mitom presented long strands of clamshell beads to pay for their slight. Pedrito could not break the peace by harvesting treasures from the dead boat—it belonged to the Mitom.

Parker roared in laughter, taunting him. "So the Mitom are better men than the Yokayo! The Yokayo are afraid of them!"

The vaquero blushed, but he was firm. He would lead them back to the wreck, but they would have to negotiate with Keetana themselves for the spoils.

"Señor Rosales."

Parker seemed to be looking at him the way a Mondavi mongoose would eye a rat. Rosales watched him carefully.

"If you and two of your men will go with me to the wreck, I'll have Pedrito take you all to Sonoma. My friend there, Señor Black, will send word to your captain in San Francisco."

Rosales considered Parker's offer. He had no weapons, and if he offended Parker, the Indios might murder them all. He remembered the captain's instructions. The goods on the ship were not his to give away. Still, he could hardly be expected, under these circumstances, to protect them for the company. His duty now was to look after his men, and he had no choice but to cooperate. He did not know this country, and he needed Parker's assistance to reach the bay of Santo Francisco and Captain Faucon. Between the sea and the Indios, the cargo would soon be gone anyway. Rosales nodded his assent. He would ask Valerio and Custodio to return with him to the wreck.

Parker slapped his knee and began shouting orders. Rosales felt like a distant spectator. He had only meant a tentative agreement, but now it was too late to turn back. Parker ordered a vaquero to butcher a beef. Later, as more vaqueros stewed the meat in two massive iron kettles, Rosales watched an India with black lines tattooed on her chin as she baked round flat loaves of bread on an iron griddle. They looked, he thought, just like the bread his mother baked in Panaji town.

Early the next morning, the camp was a flurry of activity. Parker, his pistol in his belt, cinched a rifle to the saddle of a black stallion. There were six horses in the corral—one each for Rosales, Valerio, Custodio, Pedrito, and two other vaqueros—but there were only two saddles. The vaqueros tied rawhide straps around the animals' bellies for handholds. Pedrito handed each man a bag of boiled meat and bread. One of the vaqueros threw a loop around the neck of the half-broken horse Rosales would ride. Parker tied the other end to the horn of his saddle and they took off at a trot.

They arrived at Keetana's camp on the bluff before sunset. The Indios had floated more crates ashore, and their village had become a carnival of color, the brush huts hung with bright bolts of drying cloth. Men and women wore fringed shawls and figured vests, and children played with umbrellas and fans. Across a shallow gully, Parker built a fire and tied the horses within its light. All Indios, he said, were horse thieves. Pedrito would be assigned to guard the corral during the day.

For three days Parker and the men unloaded crates. Each day, as tribute to Keetana, they brought ashore several boxes of fabrics and candied fruit. Parker wanted only the most valuable items for himself.

The men searched for heavy crates containing furniture—marble-topped tables, lacquered-ware tea caddies, and small velvet-lined writing desks like those Rosales had seen carried by supercargoes and traveling merchants. They unloaded nested camphor trunks, some of polished wood and others covered in painted leather with shining brass tacks along their edges. Parker was delighted with the matched sets of porcelain, and joyous as the men brought up case after case of ale.

They opened the crates on the beach and hauled the goods Parker wanted up to their camp. One narrow crate contained a tall China jar, big enough to hold a child. Packed tightly inside were porcelain tea pots and sets of cups and saucers. Parker had them wrestle out every similar crate they could find. Lined up on the sand, the eight China jars gleamed in the sunset like the pillars of the Church of the Good Jesus, far away at home where Rosales had seen the mortal remains of Santo Francisco Xavier himself. Surely *O Santo* would protect them as they journeyed to a city bearing his name.

By afternoon, Rosales' men and Parker's vaqueros had already piled up more goods than they could carry back to the rancho. As they ate their cold beef and bread that evening, Parker told Rosales that he wanted to hide the bulkiest items to carry inland later. On the second day, Parker and one of his men rode up onto the ridge and found a spot well off the trail. That afternoon, Pedrito and a vaquero pried mussels from the thick beds covering the rocks. As night fell he roasted them on a bed of seaweed thrown over hot coals.

By the third day, as Parker's vaqueros hauled horseloads of merchandise to the hiding place on the ridge, Rosales began to wonder if there was anything left on the wreck that was small enough to be carried on his back, yet valuable enough to buy food and lodging for the men on their journey. Then Custodio pulled up a small, heavy crate.

Inside were two velvet-lined boxes, each containing a silver dipper and fifty-three forks and spoons.

Rosales gave one set to Parker. He emptied the other into a shawl and tied the corners into a knot. For the rest of the day they dove deep into the hold searching for more, but it was impossible to pass through the hundreds of crates still densely stacked in the dark nether reaches.

As night fell, they ate the last of the beef and bread, and Parker announced his plans. He would arrange a caravan of Yokayo to carry his goods back to the valley. Then he wanted Rosales and the men to come back to the wreck with him with axes, to cut through the deck to get at the rest of the cargo.

Rosales had enough silver now to buy food for the men. He thought again of Captain Faucon. He could not justify taking more from the wreck. Valerio and Custodio were tired of diving into the frigid water. They wanted to go home. And now, more Indios had arrived from the mountains. They walked through camp, brazenly eyeing the horses and watching the men pack the cargo. They reminded Rosales of pirates in the South China Sea. It was not good to be outnumbered by savages.

Rosales was satisfied with the silver. It would stay hidden in his pack until needed. If Faucon had arranged their passage, he would return the silver to him. If not, they could sign on as seamen with some outbound vessel and be in Macao just as quickly.

I walked along the bluff, mussel shells crunching beneath my feet. I could see Rosales, Valerio, and Custodio lifting their packs to begin their final trek across the grassy headlands. I looked again and they were but tiny specks far down the path. A final flash of sunlight on a green silk sash and they were gone.

I wondered what had become of them. There was no record in the Heard company archives that any of the *Frolic*'s crew ever returned to petition the company for their wages. The men might have fought among themselves for the treasure, or they might have been killed by Indians or bandits. Perhaps they had so compromised themselves that they feared punishment by the company. I wondered if they had joined in subsequent salvage efforts, or gone to the gold fields. Had the Lascars and Malaymen remained in California to be merged into a sea of brown faces with Hispanic surnames? Were the *Frolic*'s Chinese crewmen among the founders of California's Chinese-American community? Did their blood still flow, six generations later, in the veins of my students at San Jose State University? I was not yet prepared to leap that far from the meager evidence I had. I needed to turn my attention back to the *Frolic*, for the first raid of her rich cargo—by Parker, the Indians and, perhaps her former sailors—had not by any means been the last.

CHAPTER 6

The Wreck Divers

In July of 1850, as the crippled *Frolic* was foundering, her sailors worked her into a small, nameless cove less than a mile north of Point Cabrillo. There she sank to the bottom and rested for over a century —undiscovered, but not undisturbed. Mountainous waves powered by North Pacific storms thunder and grind against the rocky shoreline of California's North Coast, roiling the shallow waters. For the first few days, the *Frolic* rocked back and forth in the cove. Every ten seconds, a fresh hundred-ton wave pounded against her hull. In time, she rolled onto her starboard side, her cast iron ballast blocks tumbling over the rolls of coarse porcelain bowls that still lay at the bottom of her hold.

The waves were relentless. Each blow bent the *Frolic*'s pine planking inward against her oak frames. The copper bolts and locust treenails that held the vessel together flexed, bent, and finally snapped. Her shattered timbers washed ashore. And while the last traces of the *Frolic* remaining above the water were being torn away by the Mendocino surf, other forces were at work beneath the surface, gradually destroying the wood, fabric, and metal of the vessel and her cargo. Bacteria consumed the organic materials—wood and fabric—digesting the complex carbohydrates they were made of into simple sugars. Fungi attacked the cellulose. The cotton sails and bolts of silk were the first to disintegrate. Ropes treated with tar or creosote lasted longer, and the wood took yet more time to decompose.

Each plank of the *Frolic*'s hull maintained the cellular structure of the southern Appalachian yellow pitch pine tree it had been made from. Now, shipworm larvae (*Bankia setacia*) attached themselves to the planks and matured into tiny mollusks. Each one, crowned with a chisel-sharp shell, bored into the softer wood—the light-colored spring increment of each annual growth ring. Symbiotic microorganisms living in the guts of the larvae digested the cellulose. Growing into long, voracious worms, they tunneled the full length of the planks, leaving only the thin, dark, hard fall and winter portion of each growth ring. Within a decade, most of the pine planking had been consumed. The dense white oak of the *Frolic*'s frames was less vulnerable to borers and lasted longer, but in time the steady barrage of wave-driven sand and pebbles, along with the water itself, eroded away all exposed wood.

The iron objects aboard the *Frolic* were more resistant to abrasion and erosion, but the oxygen in the water reacted with the metal with an equally destructive result. The high conductivity of the salt water accelerated the electrochemical process of corrosion. Thin objects with broad surfaces, such as knives and swords, rusted away first. Massive objects like ballast blocks, cannon, anchors, and chain grew a thick protective coating of rust that slowed further oxidation.

As the piled anchor chains corroded and melded together into a massive mound, the structural wood that had supported them was eaten away, leaving a large cave-like hollow below. The long pile of ballast blocks congealed into a solid mass. The copper that had sheathed the hull was sealed beneath the ballast pile, and the toxic salts released as it slowly corroded killed bacteria and fungi, helping to preserve the keel, the wooden stocks of pistols and muskets, and a few pieces of camphor trunks.

When the hull of the vessel disintegrated, the crushed rolls of porcelain that had been stored deep in her hold fell free. The shards washed toward shore, tumbling in the surf, and their sharp edges were ground smooth by the action of sand and water. Pink-lavender coraline algae and groping anemones overgrew the anchors and the ballast pile. As the years and the decades passed, the remains of the *Frolic* were gradually hidden beneath a canopy of kelp and sea palms.

Seven months before the wreck of the *Frolic*, the legislature of the California Republic created twenty-seven counties, including one named Mendocino that extended fifty-six miles inland from the North Coast.

On September 9, 1850, six weeks after the wreck, President Millard Fillmore signed the bill admitting California to the Union, and rapid settlement by European-Americans followed. Within four years, cattle and sheep were grazing along the bluffs overlooking the *Frolic* wreck site, and less than a mile to the south the town of Pine Grove struggled into existence.[1] In 1857, the Pomo living at Buldam were driven onto the Mendocino Indian Reservation at Fort Bragg, where for almost ten years the men labored for nearby farmers while their wives and daughters were preyed upon by syphilitic soldiers.[2] Many Pomo died of disease, malnutrition, and violence.

In the fall of 1861, a steam-powered sawmill began operating at the mouth of Caspar Creek, two-thirds of a mile northeast of the cove. Meanwhile, on the other edge of the continent, Confederate forces attacked Fort Sumter, South Carolina. And as the mill at Caspar shipped its first schoonerload of lumber to San Francisco, Captain Edward Horatio Faucon—late of the *Frolic*—sailed the U.S.S. *Fearnot* out of Boston Harbor, carrying supplies for the Union squadron blockading the mouth of the Mississippi River.[3]

Woodsmen cut their way up the Caspar Creek drainage to supply timber for the Caspar sawmill. Bull teams dragged the massive redwood logs down the slope to the streambed. Carpenters built dams below the stacked logs to hold the winter rains. When they dynamited the dams, the massive flood of pooled water washed the logs downstream to the mill.[4] By 1870, steam-powered lumber mills like the one at Caspar occupied the mouth of nearly every major stream along the Mendocino Coast. By the summer of 1871, when John Everett returned to California as a tourist to visit the big trees at Yosemite,[5] the Caspar woodsmen had already cut their way upstream and across ridges into adjacent watersheds, from which logs could no longer be floated to the mill.

In 1875, Captain Faucon's son led the Harvard Football Club to a 4–0 victory over Yale in the first Harvard–Yale game,[6] and the Caspar Lumber Company purchased the first steam locomotive on the Mendocino Coast and began laying track to reach the increasingly distant timber.[7] That same year, in Massachusetts, Augustine Heard & Company—the firm that had owned the *Frolic*—declared bankruptcy. Although the Heards accused their Boston agent—John Everett's nephew, Percival Everett—of mismanagement, the causes of the company's failure were far more complex. The China trade had changed, and the old

Figure 33. The Caspar Mill circa 1870s. Collection of Robert J. Lee.

Heard firm was unable to adapt to new business conditions. A bad decision by Percy Everett may have been the last straw, but the camel's back was already broken.[8]

After the Mendocino Indian Reservation was closed in 1868, many of its survivors moved to rancherias in the interior and made annual pilgrimages to the coast to gather seafood. Some would camp at the cove where the *Frolic* lay underwater, the same place their ancestors had stayed. But now the land was private property. In about 1870, Miguel deFreitos, an Azorian sailor aboard a Portuguese whaler, jumped ship in San Francisco. By 1876 he had married and was farming a small acreage near Pine Grove, and not long after 1882, when his son Bill was born, his holdings had grown to include the cove where the wreck of the *Frolic* lay.[9]

Young Bill Freitos (the family progressively Americanized their surname in each successive generation) was a regular visitor to the Indians' camp, and as they sat under strips of dark green seaweed drying on ropes strung over spindly driftwood poles, the Indians told him stories of a wrecked ship filled with treasure. By that time the vessel's name had been forgotten by the European-American settlers, and her story had been distorted beyond recognition as it passed into folklore. Caspar residents who purchased Lyman Palmer's 1880 *History of Mendocino County* read of an unnamed wreck "laden with silk and tea from China and Japan" driven ashore near the mouth of the Noyo River during the winter of 1851–52.[10]

Throughout the 1870s, lumber schooners far out to sea had sighted the white steam plume from the Caspar mill and followed it into Caspar anchorage. By 1889, the numerous electric lights at Caspar lit the steam plume from below, allowing schooners to locate the anchorage by night. The five hundred people living at Caspar now enjoyed a hotel, five saloons, a school, a lodge hall, an indoor roller-skating rink, and a baseball team which provided formidable competition to teams in Fort Bragg and Mendocino.[11] Not to be outdone, Pine Grove boasted of two hotels, a saloon, a brewery, and a circular horseracing track.

In 1909, a lighthouse was completed at the tip of Point Cabrillo, less than half a mile south of the cove. Its thousand-watt beam, flashing at ten-second intervals, could be seen fifteen miles out to sea. Six years later, as Model T Fords replaced horses at the Pine Grove racetrack, the lighthouse was joined by a fog horn. By 1928, all of the Pomo elders who had seen the *Frolic* as children were dead. That year, Captain Faucon's seventy-three-year-old daughter, Catherine, drafted a letter to the Massachusetts Historical Society. "As the last of my family," Miss Faucon wrote, "I feel it incumbent on me to find a home for—or else burn—papers which my father cared for."[12] She donated some of her father's ship's logs, but she destroyed all of the papers relating to the *Frolic* and to the captain's participation in the opium trade.

The Great Depression hit hard on the Mendocino Coast. The Caspar mill operated only at a minimal level, and other mills in the area closed down entirely. Out-of-work men raided the abandoned mills for their heavy equipment and tore up now unused railroad track for scrap metal to sell to Japan. Some dug old-growth redwood logs out of dried-up millponds and split them into shakes. Bill Freitos and his son Louie raised sheep and hogs and ran a butcher shop from their Model T truck. Each week they drove up and down the coast with a quarter of beef and half a hog, stopping at houses and cutting meat to order.

Figure 34. Louie Fratis, Jr., whose great-grandfather purchased the land overlooking the *Frolic* wreck site. Louie discovered the wreck in 1960. Photo by Thomas Layton, 1994.

When World War II broke out and the Japanese were forging the iron from Mendocino logging mills into guns and battleships, Bill and Louie won the contract to haul garbage from Mendocino and Caspar. They picked up two buckets from each house, one with paper, cans, and bottles; the other with slop—discarded food remains. They poured the slop into troughs to feed their hogs and dumped the rest of the trash over the south bluff into the cove. Now, fragments of amber beer bottles, cobalt-blue Phillips' Milk of Magnesia bottles, and white porcelain dishes bearing American and English makers' marks washed toward shore and mixed on the beach with sherds of Chinaware from the *Frolic*.

In 1950, when he was ten years old, Louie Fratis, Jr., knew all of his Grandpa Bill's yarns—how bootleggers had smuggled whiskey ashore during Prohibition, and how he'd buried "excess" barrels of sacramental wine made by Italian neighbors and spent long afternoons with the Irish priest "testing it." But his favorite of Grandpa Bill's stories was the one about a shipwreck in the cove and a split pine tree somewhere in the fields above marking where the ship's treasure was buried. Louie spent many Saturdays scouring the family property, looking for that tree.

Grandpa Bill had always allowed friends and neighbors to cross his fields to the cove to pick abalone from the rocks when the tide was out. On those evenings, the sounds of abalone steaks being pounded to tenderness reverberated from house to house all over Caspar. Louie's father continued the tradition after Grandpa Bill died in 1953, but within a few years, new people with wet suits, masks, and snorkels were crossing the field without asking for permission. Louie's dad drove them off. He wouldn't allow skin divers because he thought it was unfair for them to take the abalone underwater that old-fashioned rock pickers could pry off exposed rocks on a minus tide.

There was one exception. Louie's dad did allow Don Pifer, the disk jockey on KDAC radio in Fort Bragg, to take diving equipment down to the cove. Don, he explained, wasn't after abalone—he was looking for old shipwrecks. Don had learned to dive in the Navy during World War II, and on summer weekends when the water was flat he would carry his strobe lights and cameras, mounted inside homemade Plexiglas boxes, down to the cove. Don was reputed to have dived every wrecked ship along the Mendocino Coast, from Westport to Point Arena. Louie knew Don had found a wrecked lumber schooner in Caspar anchorage, but Don never revealed whether or not he found anything in the cove.

The mid-1950s marked the end of an era. The long-outmoded Caspar sawmill, now the only steam mill on the coast, had become obsolete. Its capacity for giant old-growth redwood trunks was an inefficient liability in a time of spindly second- and third-growth logs. When the mill closed in 1955, Louie and his friends hiked atop the covered flume that had fed fresh water to the five massive steam boilers. Creeping beneath the mill, they climbed the ten-foot, iron flywheel and traced the welter of frayed belts and straps that had transferred power from the main shaft to the mill's saws, planers, edgers, and grinders.[13] A year later, the Caspar mill and most of the company housing was torn down, and suddenly Caspar was little more than a wide spot on the road to Fort Bragg.

In 1958, when Louie's cousin Mike came out to the ranch with a brand new wet suit and a snorkel, Louie decided he wanted to see the bottom of the cove for himself. He ordered a $19 pre-cut "glue-it-together-yourself" wet suit from Montgomery Ward and resolved to find the wreck that Don Pifer had been looking for. He bought *Skin*

Figure 35. Don Pifer (1928–82) in September 1954. During the late 1950s this Fort Bragg disk jockey was the first diver to discover the *Frolic* wreck site. Photo from Pifer's scrapbook, recovered by Layton from the Santa Clara County, California, coroner's office. Photographer unknown.

Diver magazine and studied the pictures to familiarize himself with what an underwater wreck looked like.

Two years later, Louie was snorkeling in twelve feet of water on the north side of the cove when he saw a big, red abalone attached to a long, narrow rock. Taking a deep breath, he dove down and pried it loose. As he stashed the abalone in his inner-tube float, he thought that the rock he had pried it from looked odd. It had an unusual shape, and a hole in the top of it. Louie swam down for another look. He knew a sea urchin could erode its way into a rock and leave a deep pocket, but this hole wasn't smooth like an urchin hole would have been. The more he looked at it, the more the rock looked like a cannon. After catching his breath, Louie swam down once more and broke off some of the encrustation with his pry bar. Underneath it was a well-preserved four-inch muzzle.

Louie didn't tell anyone what he had discovered. That summer, fresh out of high school, he had a part-time job cleaning bathrooms at Van Damme State Park, just down the road, and he was reading the Park Service literature about local history. On his days off, he explored the wreck site. He found stacked iron ballast blocks, three anchors, and a capstan with a winch-like wooden drum. In the center of the wreck, he saw a low mound with a piece of lead sheathing lying on top, and when he pulled back the sheathing he found a stack of dishes with blue designs.

In the fall, Louie got a permanent job with the State Parks Department on Angel Island in San Francisco Bay, and for the next six years all he could do about the wreck was think about it. Meanwhile, more and more people were coming to the cove. By the mid-1960s, inflatable Zodiac boats had made it possible for divers to enter the cove directly from the ocean. The mile and a half of ocean frontage the Fratis family owned above the cove no longer served to protect it against trespassers. Louie's dad capitulated to the inevitable and began allowing several scuba-diving instructors to bring their students across his land to the cove.

Jim Kennon, a police officer from Willows, was one of the diving instructors who had permission from Louie's father to bring students to the cove. On summer weekends, Jim often came to the cove for recreational diving, too, to escape the oppressive heat of the Sacramento Valley. One June day in 1965, he made a discovery—although at first he didn't realize what it was.

The water was almost flat that day, and Jim, breathing from his scuba tank and clutching a spear gun, swam fifteen feet above the bottom, hunting ling cod. As he scanned the rocks below, looking for movement, he had an uneasy feeling, as if something wasn't quite right. He turned and surfaced to look around. He saw nothing unusual, and descended again, but that indefinable, uncomfortable feeling returned. Then he noticed that some of the objects on the bottom that he had first taken to be rocks weren't shaped like rocks. Their shapes were much too regular—some round and cylindrical, others rectangular. As a police officer, Jim had been trained in close observation, and the unnatural shapes looked as if they didn't belong. Perhaps a barge had dumped a load of garbage, or a house had slipped off the cliff.

Several nights later, Jim lay sleepless, trying to make sense of what

Figure 36. Jim Kennon discovered the *Frolic* wreck site in 1965. Photo by Thomas Layton, 1994.

he had seen. He got out his back issues of *Skin Diver* magazine and looked at pictures of shipwrecks, and at 3:30 A.M. he woke his wife. "We're going back to the coast," he said. "I've found a shipwreck." The next morning, Jim phoned his diving buddy, Bill Kosonen, and described what he had seen. "Let's go back over there, and if there's anything in it, we'll go fifty-fifty."

Jim and Bill swam out from the beach, and Jim aligned himself with the landmarks on shore he had noted on his last dive. As he descended to the bottom, he quickly spotted the strange objects he had seen before. He looked more closely and began to decipher their forms, recognizing the flukes of a massive iron anchor. A low rocky mound was a congealed mass of bar-link chain that covered a cave-like hole. Easing his head and shoulders into the opening, Jim looked upward and saw the bottoms of dishes cemented into the rusty conglomerate.

A few yards away, Jim saw something that looked like a stack of bricks almost three feet high, completely crusted over with coraline growth. He followed the pile for fifteen feet, thinking it might be the foundation of a collapsed wall. But these bricks looked strange—each was five inches square at the end and almost two feet long. Pulling a dive knife from his ankle sheath, Jim began to pry one of the bricks loose from the mass. Bill swam over to help. They were able to move one of the bricks away, but it was so heavy Jim could hardly lift one end. He chipped the encrustation off a corner, and saw a silvery gleam that made his heart pound. Bill pulled down for a closer look, raised his head, and mask-to-mask the two men flashed the "OK" sign. The "brick" appeared to be a gigantic silver ingot—and there were hundreds of them.

They struggled to carry the heavy block up to their float, then swam for shore. The next morning, hardly able to contain their excitement, they brought their find to an assayer in Sacramento. As the man behind the counter filled out a work order, he asked where they had found the ingot. Imagining a million dollars resting on the floor of the cove, Jim answered, disingenuously, "In the Pacific Ocean!" But his craftiness was for nothing—the assay came back 79 percent white cast iron.

That fall, Jim traveled to Washington, D.C., for special police training at the FBI. Bill had recently read an article about Mendel Peterson, curator of Armed Forces history at the Smithsonian and a specialist in underwater archaeology. Jim brought along a box of artifacts to show him. Peterson was quite interested in them and promised to fly out to California in the spring to dive the wreck himself and assist in identifying it.

"Pete" arrived in March, and the three men headed for the cove. Big swells were coming in and waves were breaking directly over the wreck. It was too rough to dive. After four days Pete had to return to Washington, but Bill and Jim agreed to send him anything they found that might help him identify the vessel. A short time later, the diving partners discovered a five-foot iron cannon—the same one Louie Fratis had found a few years earlier. Jim and Bill towed a balsa raft equipped with a block and tackle out to the site, hoping to raise the cannon. They were able to loosen it with a pry bar, but when they tried to hoist it up from the bottom they only succeeded in sinking the raft. Diving down again, Jim knocked the encrustation off the cannon's trunnion to look for identifying marks. There, in big capital letters he read "CA&CO." Peterson was delighted when he heard. He wrote back that while Cyrus Alger had begun casting iron cannons in 1828, all the cannons he had seen bearing that particular imprint dated from the 1840s and '50s.

Eventually Jim and Bill sent Peterson over a hundred pounds of artifacts, including green bottles, porcelain bowls, beads, a porthole cover, a sounding lead, a blunderbuss, and a piece of gold-filigree jewelry. While the cannon had helped to date the vessel, Peterson still could not positively identify it. The best candidate, it seemed to him, was the schooner *Susie Merrill*, which had sunk in 1866. He promised to come back out to dive the wreck himself the following year.

To prepare for Peterson's visit, Jim and Bill modified two compressors to operate off the same motor, which would provide enough air for two divers and an air lift dredge. Meanwhile, they tried to research the wreck themselves. They went to the San Francisco Maritime Museum, but no one there seemed very interested in helping them. Jim and Bill felt the staff treated them as if they didn't believe their find was important. Nevertheless, the divers continued to dive the wreck several times during the summer of 1967, launching their boat, with their new compressor and a four-inch air lift aboard, out of Noyo Harbor at Fort Bragg. Most of the ocean floor near and around the wreck site was covered with an impenetrable calcareous growth, as if someone had poured cement over it. But in the sandy areas, the divers could suction away the soft deposit and expose heavier artifacts. In one area they were able to suction down three feet to bedrock, where they found fragments of wood from the bottom of the vessel's hull with copper sheathing still attached.

In 1966, Louie Fratis transferred back home to Van Damme State Park. One of the rangers there was interested in local history and also wanted to learn to dive. He listened eagerly to Louie's stories about the shipwreck in the cove near Caspar, and together they worked out a plan to raise the cannon. Louie and his dad had once run a wrecking yard on the ranch, and they still had a truck with a twenty-five-foot boom that they had used to drop a three-thousand-pound block of concrete on old car bodies to crush them. Now, Louie backed the wrecking truck out to the edge of the south bluff until the boom extended out over the water. He had borrowed a fourteen-foot aluminum rescue boat from the Parks Department and stowed three big truck inner tubes, some chain, and a tank of air aboard. Underwater, Louie and his partner looped the chain around the cannon and tied the loose ends around the deflated inner tubes. Then they began inflating the tubes.

The first time they tried to get the cannon out of the water, they had put too much air into the inner tubes, so the cannon not only rose to the surface, but continued up two feet into the air and nearly capsized the boat. The second time, the cannon broke loose from the chain. Finally, Louie and his buddy were able to float the cannon to the south side of the cove, where they attached it to the winch line from the wrecking truck and hoisted it up onto the bluff. They dove back down, hoping to find something more that would identify the vessel. They brought up a ballast block, a brass rod, and the base of a porcelain bowl with an inscription on the bottom.

Although Jim Kennon and Bill Kosonen also dove the wreck several times during the summer of 1967, they never encountered Louie. They did notice that the cannon they had tried to raise was gone, but they had no idea who might have taken it. Meanwhile, Louie was also trying to research the wreck. He read an article in some Parks Department literature about seven Chinese junks that had sailed across the Pacific. One of these had landed in Monterey and another was said to have landed on the Mendocino Coast. Louie thought the junk in this story, the wrecked silk ship of local legend, and the wreck in the cove in Grandpa Bill's tale from the Indians might all be the same vessel. The artifacts he'd found at the wreck site seemed to confirm his theory —the pottery looked Chinese, and somewhere he'd read that the Chinese had manufactured iron cannons.

Louie felt the authorities should know about his find. He told his supervisors at the Santa Rosa and Sacramento offices of the State Parks Department about the wreck, but they weren't interested. He tried talking to someone at the Maritime Museum in San Francisco, but he was rebuffed there, too. Then Louie read that Edward Von der Porten, a history instructor at Santa Rosa Junior College, was trying to document Sir Francis Drake's arrival at Drakes Bay. Louie made an appointment with Von der Porten and brought over the pottery he'd collected and some photos of the cannon. Based on that scant evidence, Von der Porten agreed with Louie's theory that the vessel was a Chinese junk.

Louie felt he had done his duty. He had contacted the authorities, but if they didn't care about preserving the site, he wasn't going to sit out there and guard it for them. He quit diving the wreck in 1970. Jim and Bill had reached a dead end in their research, too, and they, also, dove the wreck for the last time in 1970. Other obligations kept Mendel Peterson from returning to California, and the artifacts Jim and Bill had loaned him went into dead storage at the Smithsonian.

Ed Von der Porten made one last effort to bring the wreck to the attention of professional archaeologists. In the fall of 1969, he placed a note in the Society for California Archaeology *Newsletter* requesting assistance:

CHINESE JUNK UNDER INVESTIGATION

Edward Von der Porten, marine historian and archaeologist from Santa Rosa Junior College, is investigating the wreck of a Chinese junk recently found by skin divers off the coast of Mendocino County. A cannon and porcelain have been brought up by divers from the wreck, but Von der Porten is discouraging further removals until a systematic investigation can be organized. Advice and assistance from persons or institutions with experience in underwater archaeology are requested.[14]

The notice brought a response from two divers willing to help, but Von der Porten heard from no one with an institutional base sufficient to finance and manage the large-scale underwater project that would be needed to research the wreck.

At the same time, in the fall of 1969, Robert Nash, a graduate student at UCLA, was beginning his research for a doctoral dissertation in cultural geography. He was studying the Chinese fishing industry that had flourished along the California coast during the late nineteenth century, and he was particularly interested in the ocean-going junks the sailors had built to harvest fish and abalone.[15] Although he had collected considerable information on the fishing industry, none of the junks themselves had survived, and he could not find much useful information about them. From the San Francisco Maritime Museum and the Chinese Historical Society of America, Nash heard that skin divers had recently discovered a wrecked junk near Caspar on the Mendocino County coast. Nash made some further inquiries, but as he had no diving experience himself, decided to complete his dissertation with just the data he already had from southern California.

In 1975, after he had completed his degree work, Nash renewed his interest in the wreck at Caspar. The first thing he needed was to find someone knowledgeable who could dive down and determine whether the wreck was indeed a Chinese junk. Nash recruited Larry Pierson, a treasure hunter and member of the Southern California Wreck Divers Club. Larry wasn't working at a regular job, and the offer of an expense-paid trip to a new diving area sounded exciting. He convinced Patrick Gibson, his diving partner, to take some time off from his job,

Figure 37. Larry Pierson dove the *Frolic* from 1975 to 1979. Photo circa early 1970s. Courtesy Larry Pierson.

and the three men drove from Los Angeles to Louie Fratis' house in Caspar in Nash's old brown van. Louie showed them the cannon and ceramics and marked the location of the wreck on their marine map.

It was December. The ocean was rough, and the wind and rain blew continuously for three days. Larry and Pat waited out the first two days researching the Kelley House archives and making inquiries at the local dive shop. By the third day, there was nothing left to do but dive. The seas were still heaving, but Larry and Pat felt sorry for Nash. He didn't seem to have much money and the motel bills were adding up. They owed it to him to get into the water. It was too rough for them to wear tanks—they might be battered against the rocks. They would have to free dive. As they climbed down the bluff to the beach, they saw massive waves breaking over the wreck site. Once they were underwater, each of those waves bounced them up and down fifteen feet. One moment they would be touching bottom, the next they would be lifted so far above the wreck that they could barely see it.

Larry's job was to determine whether the vessel was a Chinese junk or not, and as soon as he saw the ballast pile, the geared capstan, and the three folding stock anchors he knew it was not. He knew that Chinese fishermen in the late nineteenth century carried rocks for ballast, not expensive cast-iron blocks, and they had used a "junkyard collection" of ground tackle, often scavenging old anchors from the bottom. Only a Western trading vessel would have had three matching anchors.

Larry and Pat swam for shore. They had already checked out of the motel room. Cold and battered, they piled their gear into the van and headed back south. Nash was disappointed, but at the same time relieved that he wouldn't have to return again to investigate that particular wreck. Back home in Los Angeles, Larry and Pat typed up their notes, finished their drawings, and sent them to Nash. They never heard from him again.

Two years later, Larry and Pat had become bored with diving the wrecks around Los Angeles. They took a vacation in Mexico, where they shot fish and collected seashells, but it wasn't the same thrill as treasure hunting. They remembered the wreck at Caspar and decided it would be fun to dive there under better conditions than the last time. They returned in December 1977.

This time the water was almost flat and they were able to pick up a few brass objects and some ceramic sherds lying exposed on the bottom. On their second foray, in August 1978, they towed a Zodiac inflatable boat. They tried to launch it over Caspar beach but got both their Land Rovers stuck in the sand. Larry's big find that year was a brass porthole cover. By the end of that trip they had almost completely explored the surface of the wreck.

They made their third trip in September of 1979. By now, they were familiar with the area, the facilities, and the people. They had also realized that if they wanted to find anything worth collecting, they would have to move aside the huge ballast pile. Larry reasoned that as the wooden structure of the vessel had rotted away, objects would have fallen down into the jumble of ballast blocks and been embedded there as the bars corroded and congealed into a solid lump. He thought the rusty mass might well be an oxygen-free environment which would preserve wooden artifacts trapped beneath it.

For their major assault on the wreck, Larry and Pat brought three experienced wreck-diving friends to help. They launched their nineteen-foot boat out of Noyo Harbor, carrying a compressor and "hookah" breathing device to support two divers, bow and stern anchors to maintain position directly over the wreck, and a winch and air bags to lift heavy objects.

They also brought primer cord and dynamite. Carefully, they set charges at specific spots along the ballast pile, aimed to jolt the pile just enough to break the solid mass into its individual blocks. The blast succeeded in separating the blocks from the agglomeration, and also stunned a large fish.

As the men moved the ballast bars aside, the rusty conglomerate that had melded them together revealed its treasures: silver spoons, perfectly preserved wooden pistol stocks, and a junkyard of brass handles, bolts, and screws. When Larry pried loose one of the large bars, he saw a small golden hand protruding above the rusty sediment. He thought he'd found a gold statue, but when he removed the object he could see that the hand formed the upper element of a hinged brass paper holder.

When they reached the bottom of the ballast pile, the divers bagged the loose sediment that lay over the sandstone substrate and air-lifted the bags to the top. They spread the sediment out on the deck of their boat and sorted through the pebbles and sand, picking out the most attractive pieces and throwing the rest overboard. Each sediment bag held scores of tiny objects—nails, beads, and percussion caps for cap-and-ball guns—but time was short and the divers dumped these over the side along with the sediment. At the end of five days, a substantial quantity of artifacts had been recovered, including porthole covers, oil lamps, pistols, muskets, and blunderbusses. There were Mexican dollars, British East India Company half-cent pieces, and Chinese coins with square holes, as well as beads, bottles, ceramics, and gold-filigree jewelry.

Back in Los Angeles, Larry, Pat, and the other divers laid their loot out on the driveway for division. It was an amicable distribution; they made sure each diver got the particular piece he wanted. Larry surprised his friends by asking for some of the finds that had no apparent value. But he had recently enrolled in the anthropology program at the University of San Diego, and suddenly he was interested in objects that might reveal something about the commercial life of the vessel. Instead

Figure 38. Artifacts from the *Frolic* wreck site displayed on a Los Angeles driveway prior to division among the divers, 1979. Photo courtesy Larry Pierson.

of asking for the showy things like sextants, coins, and gold jewelry, Larry wanted broken pottery and the necks and bottoms of bottles. As a beginning archaeologist, those artifacts already meant something more to him.

Larry had read an article about conservation, so he knew that the wood would shrivel and crack if it was allowed to dry. He borrowed all the wooden artifacts, promising to return them. He wanted to soak them in polyethylene glycol to replace the sea water that saturated them. The pistol and musket stocks would soak for years—Larry never got around to returning them. That fall, he wrote a term paper concluding that the wreck was a mid-nineteenth-century trading vessel. Mentored by his archaeology professor, Larry was undergoing a transformation of values. The wreck at Caspar would be the last he looted.

Meanwhile, word of the wreck was traveling through the close-knit southern California wreck-diving community, and by the spring of 1981 the news had come back to northern California as well. Dave Buller and his brother Steve, living near Berkeley, heard through friends that some members of the Southern California Wreck Divers Club had recovered cannon balls, small arms, and a large quantity of Chinese porcelain from a Gold Rush–period wreck on the Mendocino Coast. But their friends had promised not to reveal the wreck's exact location. "All we can tell you," they said, "is that they launch out of Caspar Anchorage, and it's in one of the coves to the south."

Dave and Steve's dive club scheduled an annual Labor Day weekend outing at Van Damme State Beach, less than three miles from Caspar. The Bullers drove north on Friday afternoon and spent Saturday with the club, spearing fish and collecting abalone for the traditional evening cookout. On Sunday morning, they slipped away to look for the wreck site. Thinking the local saloon might be a good source of information, they stopped at the Caspar Inn. A man at the bar confirmed that there was a wreck in a small cove just south of Caspar Anchorage. He called it the "pottery wreck."

Dave and Steve launched their inflatable boat at Caspar Anchorage and headed south. As they came around the first point, they saw a small cove. They'd heard the wreck had a ballast pile of cast-iron blocks, so as soon as they got to the lee side of the outer rocks Dave turned on his magnetometer. Dave assumed the wreck had to be on the south side of the cove, since the prevailing winds came out of the northwest. They zigzagged back and forth in the boat, but the magnetometer monitor was silent.

Dave was disappointed, but before heading on to the next cove he decided to check the less likely north side. Suddenly there was a telltale buzz from the monitor. He dove down and saw pieces of pottery closer to the shore and followed them like a trail of bread crumbs. The pieces got larger and larger, and there were hundreds of them. Then he spotted the ballast pile.

Dave and Steve knew the site had been extensively worked by the divers from southern California, so they hadn't expected to find much. When the fellow at the bar had revealed that the wreck had been known since the 1960s, their expectations were even further reduced. Still, they wanted to look around. The anchors and capstan obviously indicated the bow area of the vessel, so Dave started finning slowly down what he judged to be the keel line.

Figure 39. Dave Buller (*left*) and Steve Buller (*right*), who discovered the *Frolic* wreck site in 1981. Dave holds an 11.085-inch trophy abalone. Photograph circa 1980, courtesy Steven Buller.

Within minutes, he saw an inch-long stub of fine brass chain protruding from a crevice in the rocky bottom. As he pulled on the chain with one hand and fanned the water with the other, he saw a glint of gold through a cloud of sediment, and then a tiny gold-filigree serpent head that looked like a dragon. Dave surfaced, yelled for Steve, then pulled on Steve's hose to bring him up. As they stared at the tiny delicate filigree head, they realized that there were still interesting things to be picked up that had been missed by the other divers.

As they surveyed the wreckage, the Bullers could see the depressions in the sea floor where previous divers had dredged down to the solid rock substrate. Close by were fresh piles of loose sediment—their tailings. But in many places, the surface hadn't been disturbed at all; it was still hard and compact. Dave and Steve had brought a dredge with a hundred-gallon-per-minute pump, powered by the same motor that drove the compressor that supplied their breathing hoses.

They started by looking through the tailings left by the previous divers. As they fanned the deposits with their hands, the loose sediment rose just enough to be caught by the current and drawn into the suction nozzle of the dredge, leaving larger pieces of glass and porcelain exposed on the ocean floor. There were so many glass beads that in some areas, after sucking away the silt and sand, Dave and Steve could reach out and grab them by the handful. Eventually, they fanned the sediment hard enough to suck the beads away, too. The heaviest, most dense artifacts were usually at the very bottom: lead shot, brass spikes, and gold-filigree jewelry.

The Bullers worked slowly and methodically over subsequent weekends. They were proud of their recovery technique, and their efforts were rewarded with a carved crystal stamp for sealing letters, gaming pieces (including checkers fashioned from horn), flatware forks and spoons, and a large number of brass latches, pulls, and hinges. They also found fragments of a wood-framed window with a pane of translucent shell in place of glass.

The brothers moved forward to the chain mound to look through the tailings there. They found a silver tinderbox shaped like a scallop shell, with a flint and a tiny wad of newspaper inside, so well preserved that they could still make out individual letters on the shredded paper. At the base of the chain mound, under an accumulation of green bottle glass, they found pieces of wooden cases with mortised corners, some still bearing fragments of English words stenciled in black.

One afternoon, Steve investigated a mass of conglomerate that lay higher up on a rock. As he tapped it with his pick, he saw the gleam of gold. As he chipped, he broke loose a clump of rock three inches long and two inches thick. It appeared to be a mass of congealed fragments. All along its edge he could see tiny glints of filigree. He took the rock home and poured muriatic acid over it to dissolve the encrustation. As he watched, a gold pendant, two inches long and exquisite in its filigree complexity, emerged from the bubbling bath.

After finding the pendant, the Bullers began looking for more conglomerate that might conceal other valuables. The southern California divers had blasted most of the ballast blocks from the central portion of

Figure 40. Gold-filigree pendant recovered by Steve Buller from the *Frolic* wreck site, after he dissolved away its calcium carbonate encrustation in an acid bath. This 5.2-cm pendant is similar—perhaps identical— to the dangling brooch elements shown in Rachel Larkin's 1849 portrait (see Figure 11).

the pile, but farther forward some of the ballast appeared undisturbed, still covered with concretion. Dave found the tip of a leather shoe protruding from one such mass. Nearby lay a tightly coiled roll of quarter-inch hemp rope, perfectly preserved in its iron conglomerate coating.

Four trips later, the Bullers invited three of the divers who had worked with Larry Pierson to join them. Among them was the man who had supplied the explosives to break up the ballast pile. Dave asked him to set small charges along the forward blocks and detonate them, but no new treasures emerged from the ten large blocks they were able to move.

By now, the Bullers had found many cargo items and pieces of equipment, but Dave thought it strange that they hadn't found any structural wood. Finally, while working a crevice in an area just fore of the main ballast pile, he uncovered a hand-hewn timber twelve inches across. He traced along it for several feet and found an inch-thick brass drift pin protruding from its upper surface and pieces of copper hull sheathing lying nearby.

The wreck still had not been identified when the Bullers first began exploring it. The artifacts they found and the dates on the coins suggested that the wreck was from the early Gold Rush era, and as there was no record of any other vessel from that period lost on that section of the coast, Dave deduced it had to be the *Frolic*, listed in Don Marshall's book, *California Shipwrecks*, as one of many "undiscovered" wrecks on that stretch of coast.[16] When Dave found the *Daily Alta* newspaper article which described the *Frolic*'s cargo from China, he was sure that the Chinese porcelains he had found confirmed his identification.

The Buller brothers made six trips diving the *Frolic*. By the last of these, they were no longer finding gold jewelry or much else of interest, and they concluded that the wreck had been worked out. Meanwhile, Dave had begun volunteering to help National Park Service archaeologists locate historic wrecks in San Francisco Bay and along the Point Reyes National Seashore. As he learned more about archaeology, he—like Larry Pierson—came to see that it was pointless to collect artifacts if they were not studied, and that storing them in a bucket of water in his garage was not making the best use of them.

Dave faced a dilemma. He wanted to contribute some of the *Frolic* artifacts to the Kelley House Museum in Mendocino, but he was ashamed of the way he had collected them. The archaeologists he was working with now condemned the looting of shipwrecks by sport divers, and he didn't want to lose their respect and friendship. He asked a friend to arrange the anonymous donation of some porcelain sherds and a leather shoe. Two years later, an archaeologist would go to the Kelley House seeking information about some Asian ceramics he had excavated from an old Pomo village site just below the crest of Three Chop Ridge.

CHAPTER 7

The Cargo

I was, of course, that archaeologist. And while researching the story of the *Frolic* and her cargo, I had discovered there were many different ways to look at a collection of material objects. The previous chapters of this book have described the final cargo of the *Frolic* from three very different points of view—that of John Hurd Everett, who assembled the cargo in China and dispatched it to California; that of the sailors who salvaged what they could from the wreck; and that of the wreck divers who, 130 years later, collected what the sailors, the Indians, and the forces of the sea had left. Now it was time to look at those objects afresh, as an archaeologist and a scientist.

When I first entered the Kelley House Museum, I felt out of place. My expertise was with the hunting-and-gathering economies of prehistoric North American Indians. From my research on the Mendocino County Coast, I had devised a cultural chronology spanning five thousand years, and within such a long time span I felt quite comfortable with a five-hundred-year margin of error. Here in the museum, the pictures of the Kelley family, their clothing, and furniture all dated from the late nineteenth century. They were modern. My father, now a hale and hearty seventy-year-old, had known and talked to his own great-grandmother, born in 1835—seventeen years before the first European-American had settled on the Mendocino Coast. I was a *scientist*, and I felt mildly embarrassed to be seeking assistance at a repository of memorabilia.

As I waited to meet Dorothy Bear, the Kelley House historian, I assumed she would provide me with all the documentary information I needed to identify the wrecked ship near Caspar—information that I could use to date the final Pomo occupation at Three Chop Village. I never dreamed that the 50 pieces of porcelain and 153 pieces of green bottle glass I had excavated there would add anything new to European-American history.

When I began, I knew precious little about historical archaeology, and, if asked, I would have been hard put to convince anyone that an archaeologist could contribute much to our understanding of the mid–nineteenth century. The events of that time were recent; they had been reported in contemporary newspapers. Professional historians living then had recorded what was going on around them. It seemed to me that the scarce resources available to support archaeology would be better spent researching prehistoric sites, where only the artifacts found could provide information about those times.

My original research goal had been to trace out the Mitom Pomo settlement pattern, using distinctive ceramics from a well-dated shipwreck. I wanted to see what the wreck divers had collected, in order to document the ceramics that the Pomo might have brought from the wreck to their villages and camps. But as time passed, that goal began to seem impractical. Mitom territory was vast, and I slowly realized that searching for pieces of porcelain in it would be like looking for needles in haystacks. Moreover, as Mitom archaeological sites were a non-renewable resource, I couldn't justify digging them just to look for Chinese potsherds. Finding those sherds in ancient Mitom Pomo villages would have to be a long-term project shared with many other archaeologists conducting surveys and excavations over a period of decades.

Meanwhile, the new colleagues I had found in historical archaeology were interested in the *Frolic*'s ceramics. Some were studying Chinese mining camps in the Sierra foothills. Others were analyzing artifacts recovered from salvage excavations at Chinatowns in the downtown redevelopment areas of Sacramento, Riverside, and Ventura. These sites were yielding large amounts of Chinese ceramics and archaeologists were struggling to describe them.[1]

I hoped these colleagues could help me identify the designs painted on the crushed bowls recovered from the *Frolic*. They, in turn, hoped the *Frolic* collection would provide firm dates for some of the styles they were finding. Unfortunately, both they and I were disappointed. Of the six most common types of bowls aboard the *Frolic*, only one—a rice bowl bearing a painted design variously known as "bamboo" or "three circles happiness"—was commonly found in Chinese-occupied sites in California. Only one other *Frolic* type, "Fu," a broad stoneware bowl bearing a central glyph signifying happiness, seemed to have been found in California. And though a few of these sherds had been recovered from Mexican-period sites, there were scarcely any dating from the Gold Rush or later. Furthermore, the styles most commonly found in the nineteenth-century trash pits of California's overseas Chinese—"wintergreen" and "double happiness"—were completely absent from the *Frolic* collection.

I had spent most of an afternoon at the California State Parks and Recreation storage facility, in Sacramento, sorting through Chinese sherds excavated from downtown Sacramento. Pete Schultz, a State Parks archaeologist, was curious about my research and looked at my sherds from the *Frolic*. Pete remembered seeing similar painted designs on Chinese bowls from Southeast Asia. He suggested I consult *Nonya Ware and Kitchen Ch'ing*, a book published by members of the West Malaysia chapter of the Southeast Asian Ceramic Society.[2] Even though the book didn't sound very promising, I was running out of leads, so I ordered it from the publisher. Meanwhile, hoping to find some of the other patterns represented in the *Frolic* collection, I pored over the illustrations in every monograph I could find that described Chinese ceramics from nineteenth-century California archaeological sites.

Two months later I received a small padded mailer, stamped Singapore. The first thing I saw when I tore open the envelope was a huge color photograph—the back side of the dust jacket—showing a "Fu"-style bowl identical to those shipped aboard the *Frolic*. Inside the book were photos of two other common patterns from the *Frolic*—a "peach and fungus" rice bowl, found in Singapore, and a small saucer designated "rocks and bamboo," collected in Malacca.

As I read the book I began to learn something about the cheaper items in the China export trade. Among the illustrations was one of a plate with the Sanskrit syllable "Om" as a central medallion; another bore a design suggesting the Arabic script for "Allah." It seemed that

during the late eighteenth and early nineteenth centuries, Chinese manufacturers had adapted their ceramic decorations to suit different overseas markets. The ceramics aboard the *Frolic* seemed to include a mix
of designs—some common in Southeast Asia and a few known in California. One of my graduate students, Patricia Hagen Jones, began a
research project to trace the distribution of *Frolic* styles around the Pacific Rim.[3]

In 1992, when I found Jacob Leese's scrapbook at the Society of California Pioneers, I saw another indirect way to gain information about
the *Frolic*'s ceramics. The documents in Leese's scrapbook listed virtually every item purchased in China for the *Eveline*, but the only formal
descriptions I had of the *Frolic*'s cargo were sixteen very general entries
on her bill of lading and twenty-one payment chits to various Chinese
suppliers. Except for a detailed list of parts of a prefabricated house,
none of these entries was more specific than "chinaware," "lacquered
ware," or "silks." But since I knew the *Frolic*'s cargo was modeled on
the *Eveline*'s, I could use the *Eveline* documents as a key to decipher-
ing the *Frolic*'s cargo.[4] I also knew that the Heards had decided to buy
for the *Frolic* only those items that had earned at least 75 percent profit
for the *Eveline*, so I made a table of the entries from Leese's scrapbook
by product category, showing purchase cost of each item in China and
its sale price in San Francisco (Appendix A).

The little I knew about the *Frolic*'s ceramics was still more than I
knew about her other cargo items, so I began my analysis with them.[5]
The two specific items on her bill of lading were "676 rolls Chinaware"
and "20 cases Chinaware"—a total of 696 packages. The only other
relevant document was a payment chit ordering the Heards' comprador
to pay Pohing $615.

Most of the chinaware shipped aboard the *Eveline* had also been
supplied by Pohing, and the *Eveline*'s bill of lading listed "689 packages
China Ware." The *Frolic* had carried only 7 packages more. According
to the *Eveline*'s invoices, her packages had contained over twenty-one
thousand individual pieces, and the *Frolic* had apparently carried an
equivalent number. But while the *Eveline*'s invoices had additionally
provided itemized descriptions of her chinaware, those descriptions,
unfortunately, provided a different type of detail than I expected or
wanted. Although the painted surface decorations were vitally important to California archaeologists who wanted to identify and date the

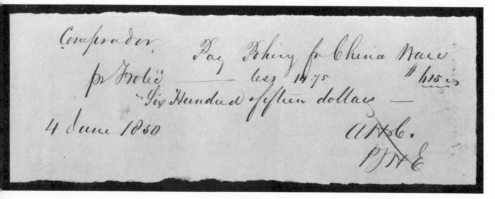

Figure 41. Payment chit authorizing the Heard's Chinese comprador to "Pay Pohing for China Ware pr *Frolic*," initialed "JHE" by John H. Everett. Courtesy Baker Library, Harvard Business School.

sherds they were excavating from nineteenth-century trash pits, the Chinese manufacturers had specified the *Eveline*'s cheap stoneware bowls not by names of patterns but by numbered sizes.

Another problem was that the *Eveline*'s rolls of ceramics were called "plates," though the pieces I had from the *Frolic* had obviously come from shallow bowls. Since true plates of Chinese manufacture were scarce in California archaeological sites, it seemed clear that the term "plate" had been used in a generic sense, and that the items in the *Eveline*'s rolls of stacked ceramics were, like the *Frolic*'s, shallow bowls. And the *Eveline*'s bulk bowls had been cheap! In Canton, the largest common size had cost 3.2 cents each, and the smallest 1.1 cents. And although they had sold cheaply in San Francisco, too—the smallest for 2 cents each—they had still brought in almost 100 percent over invoice.

Cost in China for the *Eveline*'s bowls

large common	150 rolls @ 20/roll = 3,000 pieces	$96.
2nd size	150 rolls @ 20/roll = 3,000 pieces	$72.
3rd size	100 rolls @ 30/roll = 3,000 pieces	$39.
4th size	75 rolls @ 40/roll = 3,000 pieces	$33.

The *Frolic*'s bulk ceramics presented several analytic problems. The collection included six sizes of bowls. There were two sizes of rice bowls in different designs: "peach and fungus," 6 inches in diameter;

Figure 42. Bowls carried in stacked rolls aboard the *Frolic*. Standard bowls from large to small: (*upper to lower left*) Fu, large snail, small snail; and (*lower right*) rocks and bamboo. Rice bowls: peach and fungus (*upper right*), bamboo (*middle right*). Diameter of Fu bowl (*upper left*): 25.6 cm (10 inches). Photo by Tom Liden.

and "bamboo," 4³/4 inches. The four remaining sizes of bowls were in a tight set of size increments with no spaces for intermediate sizes: the 10-inch "Fu" bowl; an 8¹/2-inch large "snail" bowl; a 7-inch small "snail" bowl; and a 6-inch "rocks and bamboo" saucer. I reasoned that the listed bowl sizes #1–4 probably referred to these.

The *Frolic*'s 696 packages of chinaware included 676 rolls, divided into six groups, and it seemed to me that these would neatly accommodate the six different sizes of bowls represented by the sherds in the collection. I tried to confirm this identification by multiplying the groups of parcels, or rolls, by the round number of bowls I thought each roll was likely to contain. Two hundred rolls of size #1 "Fu" bowls at twenty bowls per roll yielded an even 4,000. In similar fashion, 134 rolls of thirty size #2 large "snail" bowls yielded 4,020, and a hundred rolls of forty size #3 small "snail" bowls produced 4,000. Incredibly, the totals all came within one roll of bowls to a target number of 4,000.

My math seemed to break down on the size #4 bowls. Perhaps the 167 rolls I believed to be "rocks and bamboo" were not really size #4. In fact, the "rocks and bamboo" saucers appeared to be from a different "set." The surface finish of these saucers clearly indicated that these were of higher quality. The other styles all had a broad ring of unglazed bisque on the inside surface, showing where they had been stacked one on top of another while being fired, the sign of a mass-production technique for low-end goods. If the "rocks and bamboo" bowls were of a higher grade, they were obviously not size #4 in the same series of stoneware bowls. However, if they had been sold in rolls of thirty, the total would be 5,010—again within one roll of a round multiple of a thousand. The two remaining groups of rolls listed on the *Frolic*'s bill of lading were, I believed, the rice bowls. There were seventy-five rolls of these, which at forty bowls per roll added up to an even 3,000.

But if this explained what had been in the *Frolic*'s 676 rolls of chinaware, what had the twenty cases contained? The *Eveline* had carried a one-hundred-piece "Blue China" dinner set consisting of twenty-four place settings plus serving pieces. She had also loaded aboard fifteen large China sugar jars, variously packed full of jelly jars, vases, toilet bottle holders, and two, sixty-six-piece coffee and tea sets. I had seen few sherds that might have come from such objects. Probably, virtually all of the *Frolic*'s "cases" of chinaware had been removed by her sal-

Figure 43. Fragments of long dish and lid from a dinner set of Canton pattern, with rain and cloud border from the *Frolic*, shown next to a Canton-pattern heirloom piece from a private collection. Upper sherd length: 7 cm.

vagers shortly after the wreck. Indeed, in the spring of 1851 George Gibbs had seen "huge china jars" inside John Parker's wattle-and-daub hovel near modern-day Ukiah.[6] These were probably the sugar jars, packed with the dainty tea sets, that had been aboard the *Frolic*.

It looked as though at least one sugar jar had broken while being manhandled off the wreck. Among the thousands of sherds collected at the *Frolic* wreck site were four that seemed to have come from a jar measuring about a foot in diameter at its base. The outward-curving sides were decorated with a dragon, with a border of breaking waves at the base and billowy clouds above. A single teapot spout from a diver's collection might have come from a tea set the jar had once contained. Two sherds from a "long dish," or serving platter, and a lid, both bearing the "Canton" pattern with "rain and cloud" border, confirmed that the *Frolic*, like the *Eveline*, had carried at least one "Blue China" dinner set.

In addition to the rolls and cases of chinaware listed, other ceramic items were disguised under less obvious headings on the *Frolic*'s bill of lading. For example, there were one hundred boxes of "preserves" supplied by Chyloong for $400 ($4 per box). The jars the preserves had been packed in were most likely represented at the wreck site by the sherds from "ginger jars," the confection-filled crocks which had been the only chinaware carried to Three Chop Village by the Mitom Pomo. The *Eveline* had carried one hundred boxes of "sweetmeats" purchased from the same Chyloong, and fortunately, the *Eveline*'s invoices itemized their contents. Each box had contained six jars—two each of preserved ginger, kumquats, and citron. Six hundred jars of these condiments had been aboard the *Frolic*. The fact that out of six hundred blue-painted stoneware jars only a handful of sherds were left at the wreck site was an indication of how selectively the *Frolic*'s cargo had been plundered in the months following the wreck.

I had been surprised to learn that the most abundant items aboard the *Frolic* were not bowls or jars, but beads. The Bullers had found so many of these that they had eventually just sucked them away by the thousands with dredges. The several hundred beads that the divers had saved were virtually identical: coarse, white, glassy spheres about an eighth-inch in diameter. Their surfaces were so rough and pitted that I could not imagine that they had ever been suitable for jewelry. With my hand lens I could see that they were made of molten blobs of glass wound around a wire, with the spiral seam still visible. But why would the Chinese manufacture so many ugly, rough-surfaced beads? And why would the Heards buy them—paying Lunch cheng, the supplier, $86.50? Once again, Leese's scrapbook provided crucial information. The *Eveline* had carried two piculs (approximately 266 pounds) at $13 each of "white beads" purchased from Yong chong. They had sold for

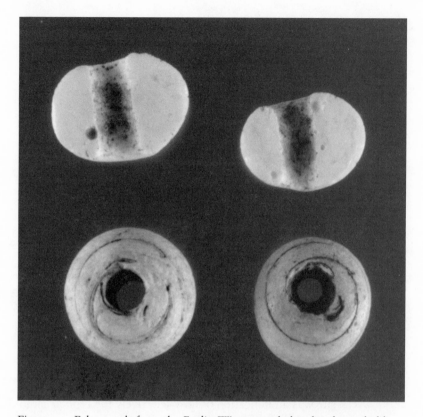

Figure 44. False pearls from the *Frolic*. Wire-wound glass beads, probably originally covered with an iridescent coating of fish glue and macerated fish scales. The two fragmentary upper beads show the stringing hole. Lower left bead diameter: 7.4 mm.

$75 per picul in San Francisco—almost 500 percent over invoice! The nondescript little beads were immensely profitable—but why?

I found out more about the *Frolic*'s ugly beads in an 1863 *Chinese Commercial Guide*.[7] According to the guide, the Chinese cultivated "true pearls" by mixing tiny mud pellets with the juice of camphor seeds and inserting these between the valves of mussels. But halfway down a very long paragraph, the guide's author also described the manufacture of "false pearls." These were produced in Canton by mixing macerated scales of carp with fish glue. Glass beads were heated in the resulting paste, receiving an iridescent coating that made them look like pearls.

These "false pearls" were packed in picul boxes containing a hundred thousand beads each, and exported to India and the Straits. If, as for the *Eveline*, the Heards had paid $13 per picul, the *Frolic* must have carried over six piculs—or six hundred thousand false pearls.

⚜

Artifacts, of course, are not preserved according to their relative market value, but rather by their ability to resist corrosion and decay. Thus the cheap chinaware and beads the *Frolic* carried were preserved because they were inert and impervious to decay, whereas the 243 cases of silks, worth over fifty times more than the chinaware, rotted away without a trace. But there was another reason why little more was left on the wreck of the *Frolic* than broken pieces of cheap dishes and fake pearls.

During the months following her wreck in 1850, the *Frolic* was rapidly and systematically pillaged. Many of her wooden cargo cases were floated ashore so that their contents could be hauled away. Indeed, by the spring of 1851, when Jerome C. Ford came up the coast from Bodega hoping to salvage at least some of the *Frolic*'s cargo, he was already too late. He saw Indian women wearing silk shawls but found virtually nothing remaining at the wreck site.[8] Almost a decade later, local Indians still had bolts of silk to trade to Mrs. Eliza Kelley to fashion dresses for her daughter, Daisy.[9]

If any silks had remained for long on the *Frolic*, there would have been indirect evidence for them. Expensive silk shawls were packed individually in lacquered boxes with brass hinges and clasps such as I had seen at the Peabody Essex Museum, and this hardware would have been preserved. Unfortunately, the recovery techniques used by the wreck divers were such that we do not know for certain whether any of these small objects remained at the wreck site—overlooked and lost.

To the Heards, the silks were the centerpiece of the *Frolic*'s cargo. Though none of these have survived, we can learn about them indirectly, as the *Frolic*'s silks were probably quite similar to those aboard the *Eveline*. The two cargoes of silks had cost almost the same amounts in China—approximately $31,264 for the *Frolic* and $32,917 for the *Eveline*. Moreover, of the five silk merchants who supplied the *Frolic*, three—Lin Hing, Woushing,[10] and Old Yeeshing—had also supplied the *Eveline*. The *Eveline*'s detailed invoices convey visions of opulence,

enumerating sarsnets, satins, velvets, silk gauze, damasks, figured camlets, embroidered crepe shawls, and a score of other fabrics and garments, some in ten choices of color combinations.

❖

Manufactured goods pose a kind of puzzle for archaeologists. These
objects are often complex composites of parts fashioned from different
materials, some of which are preserved while others are not. On the
one hand, we work from preserved pieces with the lofty goal of infer-
ring from them the long-vanished whole article, but, as conservative
scientists, we more often tend to narrow our focus to the individual
pieces themselves. Each corroded brass screw, hinge, handle, and decorative metal garnish recovered by the wreck divers is itself a finished
product which was once part of a larger artifact. But whereas from one
perspective a screw is simply a fastener holding two or more things together, each screw is also a complete artifact in itself, carrying within it
the particular story of its manufacture, along with a history of metal-
lurgy spanning millennia. We archaeologists are on solid ground when
we measure and describe a particular material object, but reconstruct-
ing a complete and finished product from the particularity of screws and
hinges introduces uncertainty, along with weasel words like "maybe,"
"possibly," "probably," and "most likely."

I felt that uncertainty as I laid the *Frolic*'s brass furniture hardware
in neat rows across my lab table. The *Frolic* had carried thirty cases
of camphor trunks and fifty-four cases of furniture. Camphor trunks
were popular export items because their intense odor repelled clothing
moths—valuable in an era when most clothing was made from wool
and silk. I knew also, from an 1848 *Chinese Commercial Guide*, that

Figure 45 *(opposite)*. Typical China-export leather-covered camphor trunks
in graduated sizes, and trunk hardware: *(top)* Bottom trunk brought home
from China by the *Frolic*'s Captain, E. H. Faucon, and donated to *Frolic*
repository by Morris Earle. Upper trunks are heirloom pieces from a private
collection. Length of trunks: upper, 64.5 cm; middle, 77.5 cm; lower, 92.5 cm.
(bottom) The hardware recovered from the *Frolic* for the camphor trunks:
bale handle, end-lugs, backing plates, and corner protectors. The left corner
protector (8.7 cm horizontal) is from a leather-covered trunk; the right
corner protector (8.2 cm) is from the more expensive, varnished wood
trunk. Bale handle length is 11 cm.

camphor-wood trunks were exported in nests of up to five trunks. The best quality were pure camphor wood, simply planed, sanded, and varnished, whereas trunks made of inferior wood were covered with painted leather.[11] As the 1856 edition of the *Guide* warned, the less-expensive leather trunks were sometimes made of cheap pine rubbed with camphor oil which would soon evaporate, leaving expensive clothing vulnerable to hungry moth larvae.[12]

I recognized the trunk hardware I had from what I had seen on complete trunks at the Peabody Essex Museum, and it seemed the *Frolic* had carried both varnished and leather-covered trunks. I had proven this with three brass trunk corner protectors recovered by the wreck divers. One of these had perfectly matched the corner of a large, varnished trunk lid, while the other two matched those on a leather-covered trunk. In order to figure out how many trunks my hardware represented, I considered the different kinds of trunk hardware and how many pieces were attached to each trunk. Since each camphor trunk had four distinctive corner protectors on its lid, and I had three brass corners in two distinct styles, I could see the *Frolic* had carried at least two trunks: one leather-covered and one varnished.

But the *Frolic* had carried more than two trunks! In addition to the corner protectors, I had nine elbow-like brass arms for holding trunk lids open in an upright position. Allowing one arm per trunk yielded nine trunks. Each trunk had two handles, and each handle was an assembly of five parts—a bale handle suspended from two end-lugs, and two oval backing plates to receive the lugs. I had thirty-nine handles, indicating at least twenty trunks—a higher count than the fourteen trunks needed to account for the fifty-three lugs (at two per handle and four per trunk). I had forty-six backing plates of two different kinds. Twenty-four of them had three holes for screws, which would account for six trunks, and twenty-two had four screw holes, accounting for another six. The handles yielded the largest minimum number of trunks, but the two different kinds of backing plates, like the corner protectors, suggested there had been at least two different styles of trunks.

But, the different backing-plate styles did not distinguish the leather trunks from the varnished ones. Both types at the Peabody Essex Museum, judging from the photos I had taken, had four-hole backing plates. Also, since the backing plates I had were all the same size, they did not prove that the *Frolic* had carried nests of trunks in graduated sizes—or more than one size of trunks at all. My hoped-for archaeological tour de force was a flop. I had wanted to figure out the types and sizes of the *Frolic*'s trunks using only the artifacts I had, without the help of written records, but my precious archaeological data were of insufficient resolution even to confirm the size classes I *knew* were there. I could almost hear the historians laughing. Chastened, I got out the *Eveline*'s cargo list.

The *Eveline* had carried twenty-five cases of painted leather trunks supplied by Ashoe in Canton. Each case had contained a nested set of four trunks, in sizes 2, 3, 4, and 5. The sets came in a choice of colors—light blue, green, brown, and red. These had cost $17 per set and sold in San Francisco at 200 percent over invoice! I could see, too, why the Heards had also dispatched a selection of higher-quality varnished trunks aboard the *Frolic*. They would have assumed that the more expensive varnished trunks would bring even more.

When I looked again at the hardware scattered across my lab table, I saw very little that might identify the contents of the *Frolic*'s fifty-four cases of furniture. The divers had recovered only two small pieces of wood with hardware still attached—a ring-style drawer pull and a two-piece recessed handle assembly. They had also brought up a large number of brass rings, but during the initial sort I had tossed them all into a box, assuming they were cringles—metal eyelets or grommets sewn into the corners of sails. Now, in the bottom of the box, beneath a pile of heavy brass rings, I found several tiny ones which exactly matched the drawer pull. But brass ring-pulls were used for small drawers in many different kinds of furniture, so these would not identify any specific furniture type.

The recessed handles gave me more hope. The *Frolic* documents mentioned only one specific type of furniture, in a chit to pay Catchung $88 for writing desks. The *Eveline* had carried a dozen mahogany and a dozen rosewood writing desks supplied by Hechong[13] at $9 and $13 each, plus twenty-one lacquerware writing desks supplied by Soaqua at $6 each. As these prices seemed too low for full-size desks, I concluded that the items must have been traveling desks. These small rectangular cases, meant to be set on a table, were well represented in museum collections. They were generally about two feet wide and seven inches thick, opening to reveal a sloping surface for writing. I looked up "desks" in Carl Crossman's book, *Decorative Arts of the China Trade*, and found a color picture of a traveling desk fitted with recessed handles, identical to those from the *Frolic*.[14]

But that was the most I could do. Although I had keys, keyhole guides, and lock assemblies, these could have come from any of a number of types of furniture. I checked the *Eveline*'s list of furniture. She had carried eight blackwood tables with inset marble tops, supplied by Ushing and Yenchong. I had one four-inch fragment of white marble from the *Frolic*, so she, too, seemed to have carried marble-topped tables.

All of the *Frolic*'s fifty-four cases of furniture had been supplied by Hechung. And, except for the tables, all of the *Eveline*'s fifty-seven cases had come from the same supplier. The Hechung furniture on the *Eveline* had included chintz-covered spring couch bedsteads, wardrobes, and chests of drawers with detachable secretary tops. Perhaps the little ring drawer pulls I had just separated from the *Frolic*'s sail grommets might have come from the drawers in just such a secretary top.

But I felt frustrated. The hardware itself had provided no new information about Chinese export furniture. Even with the help of documents and museum collections, I had only been able to identify a little bit of the furniture the *Frolic* had carried. I could hear archaeologist Jim Deetz muttering, "Why bother digging up artifacts, if they only illustrate what you already know?" Once again, I began sorting through the hardware, looking for something—anything—that might add to our understanding of the China trade. I picked up the two-piece recessed handle assembly I had attributed to a writing desk. Carl Crossman had told me that this kind of assembly was common in "campaign furniture" designed to accompany military men, merchants, and colonial administrators on their travels. The recessed hardware allowed the desk to be stowed without scratching adjacent pieces of luggage.

I turned the assembly over in my hand and looked at its reverse side. A ray of light illuminated an imperfection in the brass. But *was* it an imperfection? I got out my hand lens. There seemed to be a pattern—perhaps a faint Chinese character, not freshly stamped like a chop mark, but part of the casting itself. I examined the whole surface. Near the upper edge was another faint mark, and off to the right were two short, deep scratch marks forming an "X." There were long scratch marks across the smoothly finished front of the assembly too, probably received as the *Frolic*'s timbers twisted and crushed against whatever cargo remained inside. But the short strokes of the "X" and their

Figure 46. China-export portable writing desk, and desk hardware from
the *Frolic*: (*top*) Lap desk with recessed handles (width horizontal: 63.2 cm).
Photo courtesy Carl Crossman. (*bottom*) A recessed handle (rear view) from
a campaign-style portable writing desk (length horizontal: 8.3 cm). Note the
Chinese character at left, Latin letters at top, and "X" at right—all part of
the casting. The two images below the handle are enlarged to better show
the Chinese character and Latin letters (rotated).

placement indicated the mark had been deliberately etched. Then, again, perhaps I was deluding myself—reading imperfections in the metal like tea leaves, projecting meaning onto a random pattern.

There was one way to find out if the markings had been deliberately made. The one other recessed handle assembly I had was still embedded in its hardwood backing. I didn't want to break the wood or damage the assembly, but I had to know if there were markings on the back. I began tapping the assembly with the plastic handle of my screwdriver. I tapped harder, first near one edge, then near the other, being careful not to leave any marks. I felt like a criminal stealthily trying to break into a safe. After two minutes of steady tapping, a tiny crack opened between the assembly and its surrounding wood. I kept tapping until I could rock the assembly back and forth. Finally, holding my breath, I slipped the blade of the screwdriver beneath the edge of the assembly and pried it loose.

I held the corroded lump of brass in my hand, afraid to turn it over. What if there were no markings on the back and the whole exercise had been inspired by an overwrought imagination? I flipped the handle assembly over and slowly opened my eyes. There, to my amazement, were the same two imperfections as on the first handle backing—even, off to the right, the same small scratched "X." I was holding a 147-year-old message from a worker in a brass foundry, but it was a message that I could not read. Perhaps it was a signature—a statement of pride in a well-wrought product—an affirmation of the craftsman's existence, placed on the back side where it would never be seen during the life of the piece of furniture once it had been fastened to it.

I walked across campus to show the strange glyph to my colleague, Dr. Steve Kwan, Professor of Management Information Systems. Steve was Hong Kong born, the grandson of a comprador, and he had earlier translated inscriptions on the bottoms of "bamboo" pattern rice bowls for me. He peered through the hand lens. "I can read it," he said. "But it isn't a common word." The character had two parts, he explained. The left part referred to metal. The right part, a modifier, meant "lance." It might refer to anything—the name of a person, a word of encouragement, or even the name of the part.

My training told me that I should seek meaning in the artifact at hand, not in the vanished piece of furniture I was trying to mentally reconstruct. And so I tried to consider the brass handle assembly only as a product complete in itself. It was clearly based on a European proto-type. I imagined that, years ago, some European customer had brought a piece of "campaign furniture" to a Chinese furniture manufacturer and ordered a copy. The furniture maker had removed a brass handle assembly and sent it to the foundry to have duplicates cast. Once the foundryman had made molds, he would, of course, be able to supply the hardware to any local furniture maker who wanted it. I wondered if I could prove that this particular handle had been cast from a proto-type manufactured elsewhere. If so, all of the non-functional details on the unfinished reverse side would have been exactly reproduced in the casting process. Those marks might be the key to the handle's original incarnation before it had been copied in China.

I got out my hand lens and compared the two recessed handle plates. All three marks—the Chinese character, the illegible smudge, and the "X"—were in the exact same locations, indicating that they had been present on the mold rather than applied afterward. The Chinese char-acter and the "X" were the most distinct; the illegible smudge less so. I rotated one of the units under my lab light, hoping some part of the smudge would project a shadow and reveal a pattern. Suddenly, when I had turned it completely upside down, I saw four Roman let-ters: "imla."

Now I understood how the handle had been produced. The Chinese foundry had received a brass handle assembly with an order to dupli-cate it. The handle bore the "imla" mark of its original manufacturer and a roughly scribed "X." Then, the Chinese foundryman had ham-mered his own chop mark into the assembly before proceeding to make the casting mold. But what was "imla"? Perhaps it was part of a place name, the place where the original had been manufactured. The letters "iml" were clearly visible; the "a" was a guess. The syllables sounded Indian to me. I got out my historical atlas and looked for cities contain-ing those two syllables. I found Simla in the foothills of the Himalayas:

Town and hill resort, NW India . . . summer capital of British Government of India and capital of former provincial government of Punjab . . . First English house built in 1819.[15]

Simla had not become the official summer capital until 1858, but by that time the British had been using it for summer rest and recuperation for almost seventy years. That was certainly long enough for a service industry to develop, which made Simla a likely place to buy a piece of traveling campaign furniture. Was the piece really marked "Simla," or would further research reveal a better explanation? I couldn't be sure, but I had at least found out that the original handle prototype was not cast in China but in a part of the world that used the Roman alphabet. Perhaps the style had traveled to China in the luggage of a British merchant or administrator, and the handle was thus a miniature marker of the spread of Western culture.

But what more could I learn from the handle itself? The Chinese foundryman would have needed brass, an alloy of copper and zinc, to make the handle. In China, however, bronze—a mixture of copper and tin—was the more commonly used alloy. The foundryman would have had to purchase ingots or slabs of copper and zinc and mix them according to a formula to produce brass of a color comparable to the European prototype.

Many visiting Europeans and Americans had described the shops of Chinese merchants engaged in the export trade in the early nineteenth century. Chinese artists had also painted pictures of many of these establishments and sold them as souvenirs to Western merchants. Some artists had documented the thirteen stages of porcelain manufacture, from digging clay to packing finished pots for export. I had also seen pictures depicting the steps in tea production, from farmers cultivating tea trees to barefoot workers stomping leaves into gaily decorated boxes.[16] But, unfortunately, I knew of no pictures documenting the stages of brass handle manufacture in a smoky foundry.

How had this handle been made? I studied it carefully. The recessed assembly comprised two individually cast parts: an escutcheon backing and a bale handle. Under magnification, I could see that the handle had been cast by pouring molten brass into an open one-piece mold. I could see where the liquid metal had spilled over the edge of the mold and then been filed away from the edges so that the handle would fit smoothly into the escutcheon. Once the handle was in place, the unit had been held fast in a vise and drilled from the sides, so that small pins could be inserted on which the handle would swing. I could see marks where the drill had come at the wrong angle on the first try, then quickly corrected. Finally, five nail holes had been drilled through the face of the unit, and the face then ground smooth so that the handle and the backing plate presented a smooth, unbroken surface.

Figure 47. Nine nesting brass weight cups—5 drams to 3 pounds—from the *Frolic*. Diameter of largest cup: 10.8 cm.

Perhaps there were other brass items from the *Frolic*'s cargo that would reveal more about the brass workers. The only brass items specifically mentioned among the *Frolic* documents were nine cases of scales and weights, for which the Heards had paid $215.25. I pulled out a heavy drawer filled with nested brass weight cups. They had been shipped in sets of nine, with cups ranging in weight from five drams to three pounds. I scrutinized the cups for makers' marks, but only the weight designations were inscribed. The only other markings were spiral scars on the inside surface of the cups where they had been turned on a lathe, apparently to trim them to their proper weights, or so they would nest neatly one inside another.

The weight cups were not speaking to me. It seemed that my only message from the foundrymen would be the one on the back of the recessed handle assembly—a message so cryptic that it concealed as much as it revealed. On impulse, I placed a one-pound weight cup on my lab scales, and slid the weights on the balance arms to 453 grams—one pound. The marker arrow fell downward, striking the lower housing of the scale. At first I thought something was wrong with the balance itself, so I carefully adjusted the scale to zero, and began again. The one-pound weight cup weighed 0.819 pounds—18 percent too light. Next, I weighed a three-pound weight cup. It weighed 3.075 pounds—2.5 percent too heavy. Apparently, the Chinese foundrymen had known little about Western weights and measures. Perhaps they had not understood the use for which these brass cups were intended. I could only imagine the difficulties such weights might have caused had they been used in California commerce.

I checked the *Eveline*'s invoices. She, too, had carried scales and weights—seven sets of an expensive version, with eight weights ranging from one ounce to five pounds, and five cheaper seven-piece sets lacking the five-pound weight. The *Eveline*'s eight-piece sets had cost $4.80 each in China and had sold for 500 to 700 percent over invoice in San Francisco. Comparing the cost of the *Eveline*'s weights with the cost of the *Frolic*'s, I calculated the *Frolic* had carried at least forty-five sets. Apparently, when the Heards had seen the profits from the *Eveline*'s weight sets, they had nearly quadrupled their order for the *Frolic*—without, obviously, checking to see if the weights were true.

❧

I studied the *Frolic*'s bill of lading for other items that might tell me something about the metalworking trades. The seventh entry, package #72, was designated "1 case silverware," and the eleventh entry, packages #113–#114, was listed as "2 cases silverware." The two separate entries suggested that the silver had been purchased in two separate transactions—probably from two different shops. I checked the *Eveline*'s invoices. Her silver had been supplied by two silvermakers: Wongshing and Cutshing. I packed up all the brass weight cups and furniture hardware, wiped the table, and got out the silver. I had three tinderboxes, parts of two suspender clasps, and thirty-two pieces of flatware, all donated by the divers. I suspected that there were more pieces hidden in their collections, but as an archaeologist I had learned to work with what I had, and that was rarely all of anything.

My flatware included forks and spoons in five sizes. The first thing I noticed was that it wasn't all silver, and it wasn't all Chinese. For use by the men on board, the *Frolic* had carried a mongrel collection of cheap "white-metal" flatware, made from alloys of copper, nickel, and zinc in several different patterns. Stamped on the backs of the handles were Western manufacturers' marks like "Yates" and "BMFa."

Figure 48. "Plain fiddle"–pattern spoons from the *Frolic*: *left*, unmarked paktong spoon; *right*, Khecheong spoon. Enlarged pseudo-hallmarks: *left*, Wongshing ("W"); *right*, Khecheong ("KHC"). Left spoon length: 21.8 cm.

Almost all of the remaining flatware was of the same pattern, called "fiddle." Each piece had a simple handle shaped like the body of a fiddle, or violin, terminating at a slightly thickened base with a subtly downturned teardrop ridge. Among the twenty fiddle-pattern forks and spoons, I could distinguish three distinct groups. There were fourteen pieces of black-tarnished silver, bearing marks of two different manufacturers, and six minutely wider pieces with a slightly yellow tint, bearing no markings at all. Eleven of the tarnished pieces bore the initials KHC—the mark of Khecheong, a prodigious manufacturer of export silver from about 1830 to the 1870s.[17]

Khecheong's four hand-stamped marks made his silver familiar to his European and American customers. Besides his own "KHC" mark, his other three marks were close copies of British hallmarks: the "lion passant," adopted in 1544 as the official stamp of the Goldsmith's Hall in London; the crowned "leopard's head," or "king's mark," adopted in 1498; and the "sovereign's head," adopted in 1784—originally intended to show the actual profile of the reigning king or queen.[18]

The marks on the two remaining silver forks were perplexing. They were virtually the same as those stamped by Khecheong, but placed in a different order and oriented differently—and in the middle of each was the letter "W." Through my hand lens, I could see the marks were, in fact, subtly different from Khecheong's. The lion passant's right front leg was raised a bit higher, the leopard's crown had three prongs rather than five, and the sovereign's head was turned to the right instead of to the left. Then it struck me. Maybe the "W" stood for Wongshing, who had supplied the *Eveline*'s silver. A telecopy of the marks to Dr. H. A. Crosby Forbes, an expert in China export silver, confirmed that the silver was Wongshing's. Wongshing and Khecheong had operated shops at Nos. 2 and 15 Old China Street—they were neighbors.[19] Khecheong had been almost a generation younger than Wongshing, and I wondered if he might have learned his trade from the older man.

The remaining six pieces of unmarked flatware were virtually identical in shape to the fiddle-pattern items produced by Khecheong and Wongshing, but they were slightly wider, and their corroded surfaces had a slightly brassy tint. They did not appear to be really silver. I put all the forks and spoons into a box and took them downtown to Sal Falcone's coin shop, figuring Sal wouldn't be in business if he couldn't test for silver. I laid the pieces out in a long row on top of his counter, and Sal brought out a small bottle. A drop of nitric acid, he explained, would stay essentially clear or slightly gray when placed on pure silver but would turn blue on copper and bluish-green on brass.

First we tested the forks with Khecheong's and Wongshing's marks. The acid drops remained clear, indicating good silver. Then we tested the otherwise identical pieces that bore no maker's marks. Instantly, the bubbling acid turned a brilliant blue-green. The yellow-tinted metal contained brass. It looked as though either Wongshing or Khecheong had produced a second line of cheap flatware to supply those customers who could not afford real silver. But neither silversmith would have wanted his name associated with such an inferior product, so the shoddy goods bore no maker's mark.

I phoned Crosby Forbes. Did he know of a Chinese silvermaker who produced a lower-quality line of non-silver flatware? Crosby gave me the number of Patricia Grove, a dealer in China export goods. Patricia became quite excited as I described the fork. "I'm almost sure it's *paktong*," she said. "Let me show it to my friend Eldon."

I mailed a fork to Patricia and three weeks later received a letter from Dr. Eldon Worrall, research associate in the Oriental Collection at the Liverpool Museum. The fork, he wrote, was indeed *paktong*—an early form of nickel brass developed in China, "a ternary alloy containing 5–20% nickel; 40–65% copper and 20–50% zinc." Dr. Worrall enclosed an article he had co-authored: *Paktong: The Trade in Chinese Nickel Brass to Europe.*[20] *Paktong* had the advantage of looking almost exactly like silver, but it cost less and it didn't tarnish.

Patricia was unnerved by the discovery that unmarked *paktong* flatware had apparently been produced for export by major silversmiths in China. Chinese *paktong* was considered rare, and thus—at least to knowledgeable modern collectors—more valuable than silver. But if the *Frolic* had carried *paktong* flatware, without makers' marks, who could know how much more was still lying unrecognized in junk shops and flea markets throughout the Western world?

In addition to the flatware, the *Eveline* had carried twenty-four pairs of suspender buckles and thirty-six flint and steel boxes, supplied by Wongshing and Cutshing. There seemed to have been three different grades of flint and steel boxes. Wongshing had sold the Heards six of them at $1.25 each, and another six at $1.90. Cutshing had sold twenty-four at $2.30—almost twice as much as the least expensive ones from Wongshing.

All three of the tinderboxes that survived from the *Frolic* were identical—hinged, silver boxes, each shaped like a scallop-shell less than an inch and a half long. None bore a manufacturer's mark. Each had a slot where a steel striker bar had rusted away, and a ring attachment so the tinderbox could be worn like a locket on a necklace. Two of the little boxes still contained beds of fuzzy tinder and a flake of flint to strike the steel, making a spark that would fall onto the tinder. I could see a bulge near the edge of each flake, radiating outward from the point of impact, where the blow of a hammer had detached it from a lump of flint.

As pieces of jewelry, the tinderboxes were exquisite, but as devices for lighting a fire they were totally impractical. The silver walls of the box were too thin to withstand the repeated impact of stone against steel needed to produce a spark. The piece seemed to be a curiosity of

Figure 49. Two identical silver tinderboxes from the *Frolic*. *Left*: open box showing flint flake on bed of tinder. Note slot for iron striker bar. *Right* (enlarged): a closed box. Horizontal length: 3.6 cm.

conspicuous consumption, never really intended to be used. It was hard to imagine a rough miner trying to use such a bauble to light a camp-fire, but perhaps, after he struck it rich, he might have bought one as a present for a lady.

The three tinderboxes were identical, so I suspected they had all come from the same manufacturer. I did not know, however, which of the two suppliers of silverware on the *Frolic*'s cargo list had made them: Khecheong or Wongshing. Wongshing had supplied silver tinderboxes for the *Eveline*, so the *Frolic*'s tinderboxes had probably come from him as well.

Gold seems to have a motivating power far beyond even its monetary value. The *Frolic*'s wreck divers had certainly been under its spell, for they had taken the trouble to bring up eighty-six tiny fragments from the sediments surrounding the *Frolic*. Altogether, these eighty-six specks of gold weighed less than half an ounce—the weight of an American ten-dollar gold piece minted in the year of the wreck, 1850.

The *Eveline* had carried gold, too. Wongshing had supplied shirt studs, earrings, scent boxes, and breast pins; Cutshing had provided thimbles and bracelets. As I laid out the *Frolic*'s gold, I could recognize pieces that looked like the jewelry supplied the *Eveline* by Wongshing, but nothing that looked like Cutching's thimbles or bracelets. The gold jewelry from the *Frolic* was ornate, most of it fashioned from fine filigree wire. When I examined a piece under ten-power magnification, a whole new universe of complexity emerged, as a drop of pond water under a microscope reveals a world of wriggling, one-celled paramecia. Here, within each piece of jewelry, were the secrets of how it had been made. Under magnification, simple shirt studs and earring fleurettes disclosed the workings of a complex production process involving the assembly of many component parts, each of which was virtually invisible to the naked eye.

From the gold recovered by the divers, it appeared the *Frolic* had carried two styles of earrings. One, based on a Western prototype, had been made from a disk of ivory, girdled with a flat bezel strip of gold and fused to a two-piece hinged hook. The other style was a fleurette built up of fine filigree wire. This was the simplest complete filigree object I could identify in the *Frolic* collection, and analyzing it could help me understand something of the goldsmith's art in mid-nineteenth-century Canton.

The entire fleurette was less than three-eighths of an inch wide. It was composed of a central ball surrounded by a ring of ringlets and centered upon six small petals which were laid upon six larger petals. This assembly was then fused onto a shield-like backing plate. The backing plate bore two tiny hinge tubes to receive between them the single hinge tube on the sharpened wire ear hoop. As I looked at the piece from above, in reverse order of its fabrication, I felt as if I were performing an archaeological excavation.

But time flows forward, and the fleurette had been built up from the bottom. I began my examination where the smith had started, with the shield-like backing plate, a tiny rectangle snipped from flat sheet metal and rounded at one end. The hinged hoop and snap catch assembly

had been put together on the back side of the plate. First the smith had fused a two-piece tube hinge close to one edge of the plate. Then he had pierced a tiny hole into which the sharp tip of the hoop would eventually snap in a closed position, near the other edge. The hoop was made from a single tube hinge fused to the end of a sharpened wire. In the final stage of the earring's assembly, the hinge units on the backing plate were joined to the hoop with a tiny gold hinge pin.

The six-petal fleurette was built up from the front face of the plate. For the first level of filigree, a length of wire, textured like a twisted rope, was coiled clockwise at one end and counterclockwise at the other. A smooth wire was then bent around each coil for a finished outer edging. This edged coil formed two petals. Three two-petal units were then laid on the backing plate, two like an "X" and one crossing, and these were soldered into place to form a six-petaled fleurette. The six smaller petals of the next fleurette were fashioned the same way, and centered and soldered atop the lower petals. Next came a tiny coiled ring, like a Slinky® toy shaped into a circle. To fashion this component, the smith had wrapped the thinnest gauge wire fifty-one times around a mandrel the size of a fine sewing needle, pulled the coil into a circle, and soldered it in place. Finally, a tiny BB-sized ball was applied to the center. Each layer of the little flower was carefully placed so as to hide the soldering of the previous step.

The lady this tiny fleurette earring had been meant for would probably never have known how it had been constructed from twenty separate pieces. I suspected that the piece I was looking at was not the work of a single artisan, but the output of a shop with several goldsmiths, each performing specialized tasks. Some workers would have drawn out hundreds of yards of filigree wire in different thicknesses and finishes, others fashioned hinge assemblies, and still others cut and shaped the wire into filigree designs and assembled the parts into complete pieces.

Among the rest of the gold in my collection I had hooks for eight such earrings, as well as thirteen hinged stickpins for brooches. The brooches had been constructed from equally complex parts, mainly fil-

Figure 50 (*opposite*). Gold jewelry from the *Frolic*: (*top*) Gold earrings with disks of ivory and two-piece hinged hooks (right earring vertical dimension: 2.3 cm). (*bottom*) Gold-filigree fleurette earring, with fleurette enlarged to show detail (fleurette diameter: 1 cm).

igree figures of plants and insects. I looked at a filigree butterfly, part of a breast pin, and marveled at the careful organization necessary to produce such an item. Each separate step was exquisitely simple, yet the result was a finished product of dizzying complexity. This butterfly was much more complicated than the little fleurettes, and I wondered just how its components had been formed and fastened together. But, just as with the facsimile brass handles for campaign furniture, no one had thought to describe step-by-step details for the manufacture of Chinese filigree jewelry.

Among the items listed on the *Frolic*'s bill of lading that might have contained metal pieces was a complete set of parts for a prefabricated house.

1	pkg	contg	4 outside doors
1	"	"	8 Oyster Sh'l windows
3	"	"	12 do [ditto]
17	"	"	74 Planks
3	"	"	24 Beams
1	"	"	16 Boards
10	"	"	40 Planks
10	"	"	40 Beams
9	"	"	40 do
2	"	"	8 Columns
24	"	"	96 Planks
4	"	"	21 Beams
14	"	"	54 do
1	"	"	16 Boards
1	"	"	Ironware

101

By the summer of 1849, large numbers of prefabricated houses were being shipped from China to California to meet the exponentially growing demand for lodging. The *Frolic*'s house had been shipped in 101 packages, divided into fifteen categories, and the last package listed was cryptically identified as "Ironware." I tried to imagine what the finished house would look like from the list of packages, but it was like trying to imagine a model Eiffel Tower given only a list of pieces in a toy Erector Set® with no instructions! I had to find another source of information.

Perhaps I could work out the house plan from reading descriptions of other "China houses." A few months before the *Frolic*'s departure, the Heards had shipped a similar house to California to serve as a store from which to sell her cargo. Dispatched with a crew of Chinese carpenters, the house parts had arrived in San Francisco, where the Heards' agent, J. C. Anthon, had rented a lot and supervised its construction.[21]

Anthon was familiar with China houses. In September of 1849 he had received thirty of them aboard the *Mariposa*, and in December, another twenty-two aboard the *Mary*. These had been sent by Jacob Leese, paid for with the money he had left over after filling the *Eveline*. The houses sent on the *Mariposa* were accompanied by a crew of fifteen Chinese carpenters.[22] A letter of instructions from Bush & Company had introduced them: "Enclosed we hand to you the contracts for the fifteen men who go for us. I beg to advise you that the head man Ating made 30 of the frame houses and is a man capable of doing anything in this line, having been known to us for a series of years. He has built— under contract—many blocks of houses in this colony [Hong Kong]."[23]

Some of the *Mariposa*'s houses, advertised for sale in the *Daily Alta*, were described as "frame houses, with windows, doors, etc., complete . . . 2 rooms each." There was a choice of two sizes—13 x 26 feet or 12^1/$_2$ x 24^1/$_2$ feet.[24] The *Mary*'s houses had come in the same two sizes and were sold at auction in San Francisco for $650 and $700 each.[25] About the same time, Colonel John Frémont and his wife Jessie purchased a China house and had it erected in San Francisco. "Put up," wrote Jessie, "without nails, except for the shingling on the roof, all the pieces fitting in together like a puzzle."[26]

Now I needed to figure out how such a "puzzle" had been put together from the 210 planks, 188 beams, and 32 boards shipped aboard the *Frolic*. I sketched a 13-x-26-foot building and tried to calculate how many planks placed vertically around the sides and flat across the floors would be required to sheath the structure, but try as I might, I could not come up with any design that would employ 188 beams. More distressing, I could not imagine how a house, made of planks, beams, and boards could be assembled as Jessie Frémont had reported—like a puzzle, without nails.

And if the house had been made without nails, I could not imagine what the ironware in package #101 might have been. The house parts on the *Frolic*'s bill of lading were listed as individual pieces of wood that presumably needed fastening, rather than pre-assembled panels, so it was likely that package #101 contained the nails to put those pieces together. But, I could only guess about the ironware—except for her anchors, chains, and ballast blocks, all of the *Frolic*'s iron had long since rusted away without leaving a trace.

The only truly manufactured house components listed on the *Frolic*'s bill of lading were four outside doors and twenty oyster-shell windows, and, fortunately, the wreck-diver collections included both door and window parts. I laid these out on my table. Of the doors, I had one brown-glazed ceramic doorknob and a handful of brass hardware, including two circular, flange-like escutcheons and the parts of a latch assembly. None of these pieces showed any particular evidence of Chinese manufacture—they could have been made anywhere, shipped to China, and then loaded on the *Frolic*.

The windows, however, were obviously Chinese. I had been mystified at first when I saw the thin, flat fragments of shell in several wreck-diver collections, until I discovered the Heard papers and the *Frolic*'s bill of lading. The shell pieces seemed too large and, frankly, too ugly and discolored to have been decorative inlays for furniture. As soon as I found the cargo listing for oyster-shell windows, I contacted the divers with the news. One of them remembered finding such an artifact, and after a thorough search of his garage sent me a crossed piece of wooden sash with an oyster-shell pane still in place. The flat-milled shell formed a triangle with two-inch and three-inch legs meeting at a right angle. Two of these triangular shell elements, placed edge-to-edge along their hypotenuse sides, would have made up one square translucent pane.

The finished window incorporated both Western and Chinese materials and design concepts. It was what archaeologists and anthropologists call "syncretic"—a combination of elements from different cultures. An 1863 *Chinese Commercial Guide* had informed me that the "oyster shells" used in China as window panes were actually "capiz" shells imported from the Philippines, cut square and laid lengthwise, overlapping like tiles.[27] For the *Frolic* house windows, the Chinese carpenters had tried to imitate a Western style with square, wood-framed panes. Nonetheless, the complex triangular mortise joinery employed on the pieces of sash was essentially a Chinese style.

Figure 51. Wooden window sash (or mullion) with capiz-shell pane from Chinese-manufactured prefabricated house carried aboard the *Frolic*. Vertical length of wood sash: 17.6 cm.

I was still at a loss to understand how the house itself had been meant to be constructed. Then Richard Everett phoned. Did I, he asked, want to drive up to Double Springs, near Sonora, and look at a China house? Richard had joined the *Frolic* project three years earlier. He had been an exhibits specialist at the National Maritime Museum in San Francisco, and I had met him when searching for an Everett descendant who might have a portrait of John Hurd Everett. Richard was the great-great-grandson of Rev. Oliver Capen Everett, John's brother, and it was a life-defining experience for him to suddenly discover that he had a family connection to a major focus of his professional work—the maritime history of Gold Rush California. Now promoted to Curator of Exhibits, Richard wanted to mount a major exhibition for the sesquicentennial of the California Gold Rush—and he wanted to build the exhibit around the *Frolic*'s cargo of China trade goods.

Richard knew about the China house that J. C. Anthon had received and assembled in San Francisco for the sale of the *Frolic*'s cargo—a sale which was cancelled when the *Frolic* broke up on the rocks just north of Point Cabrillo. Now Richard wanted to build a similar house to exhibit what remained of the *Frolic*'s cargo. For weeks he had been pestering me for details about the house. He could already visualize soft light passing through the pearly translucent panes of a shell window, but in order to put a whole house together he needed more than a list of planks, beams, and boards. Where, he had pleaded, could he find a China house?

There was one possibility, I told him, but it wasn't a very likely one. In a cloudy, old photo, I had seen what was supposed to be a China house at Double Springs Ranch in the Sierra foothills. In the picture, it looked pretty much like any other miner's shack.[28] There certainly wasn't anything that looked Chinese about it. I didn't think it was a promising lead, but now Richard had talked to the manager of the Double Springs Ranch and made an appointment to look at the structure.

I didn't want to lose a full day of writing, but I did need more information about the China house aboard the *Frolic* than I had so far extracted from a list of parts, a single pane of oyster-shell window, and a ceramic doorknob. The "Chinese house" at Double Springs Ranch was reputedly the remaining one-third of Calaveras County's second courthouse—an improvement, apparently, over the tent that had been used during the spring and summer of 1849. A 1932 article in the California

Figure 52. (*top*) The China house at Double Springs Ranch, erected in 1849: the second courthouse of Calaveras County, California. Note the 3-foot by 8-foot wall panels. A protective shed with a corrugated iron roof stands above the house. House dimensions: 13 by 26 feet. (*bottom*) Chinese character on rafter of China house. Photos courtesy Richard O. Everett.

Historical Society *Quarterly*, citing local townspeople, reported that the building had originally consisted of three 12-x-24-foot China houses placed end to end to make one 72-foot-long building.[29] The author, Ernest Wiltsee, had read back issues of the *Placer Times*, an early Sacramento newspaper, and discovered an August 11, 1849, advertisement for four China houses, 12 x 24 feet, "daily expected on the Schooner *Petrel*." Wiltsee had assumed that China houses were rare and concluded that three of the *Petrel*'s houses had been used for the courthouse.

The house in the photo did not look like a China house, but the construction of the actual building seemed extremely unusual. The frame consisted of sills, plates, posts, and rafters, all joined by wooden tenons fitting into carefully mortised holes. The 36-inch-wide wall panels slid into slots between the posts. There were eight openings for wall panels on each side of the house and four more at each end. Two of the wall panels had been replaced with windowed doors, hinged to posts. Jessie Frémont had been right. A China house was indeed like a puzzle. All of the pieces fitted together without nails, except for the roof boards— which Mrs. Frémont had called "shingles."

My second conclusion was that this China house had not been one of those advertised as coming aboard the *Petrel*. As Richard and his staff swarmed over the building, I measured its length and width— 13 x 26 feet. The *Petrel*'s houses had been 12 x 24. The author of the 1932 article had been so captivated by the specificity of the *Petrel* advertisement that he had never bothered to measure the house. In fact, he had used the measurements of the *Petrel* China houses to describe the original, three-segment courthouse as 72 feet long. Now, simply measuring the length and width of this house had undercut a historical assertion that had stood unchallenged for sixty-five years. I felt pretty proud of myself, and of historical archaeology too, for having done just what we were supposed to do—provide new evidence from the study of material objects, thus demanding a revision of history. I tried to forget that only a week before, I had been willing to dismiss the Double Springs house as irrelevant without even looking at it.

Meanwhile, Richard and his three helpers were busy measuring and sketching the major parts of the house so they could reproduce it for the exhibit. Suddenly, a young man teetering at the top of a ladder shouted down at me: "Tom! I found some Chinese writing." I climbed the ladder, trying not to disturb the nest of mud wasps next to my ear. The Chinese character, scribed in black, shone faintly through an ancient

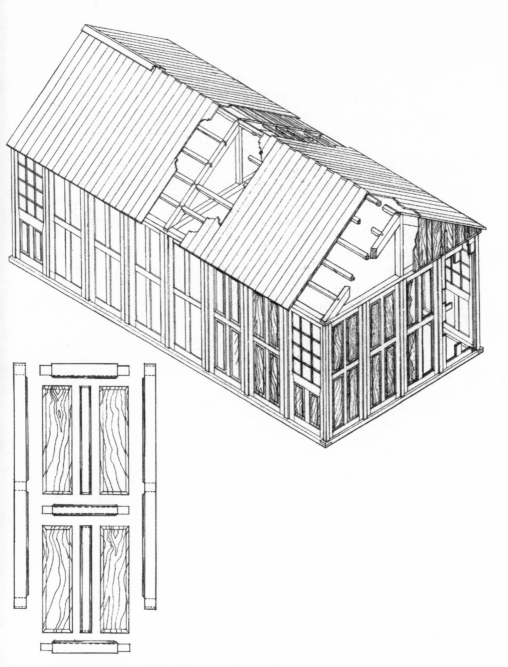

Figure 53. Architect's rendering of the China house at Double Springs Ranch, with exploded wall panel. Exterior dimensions of house: 13 feet by 26 feet; wall panel, 3 feet by 8 feet. Drawn by Peter Gallagher, Jr. Courtesy San Francisco Maritime National Historical Park.

coat of red paint. Next to it, in the same hand, was the number 16. Wrapping my arm around the central support I leaned to the right to see the end of the other rafter. It bore the same Chinese character and the same number 16. The house pieces had been coded for easy assembly. I could almost hear a carpenter from the last century muttering instructions to himself: "Slide rafter #16 into center-post slot #16." For the remainder of the morning, I identified the structural components of the house and counted how many of each there were. I was hoping to match the totals with the numbers of beams, boards, and planks listed in the 101 packages carried aboard the *Frolic*. The next morning, back in San Jose, I compared the two lists. I had counted 403 pieces of wood, less doors and windows, from the Double Springs house. Less doors and windows, the *Frolic*'s packages had contained 438 pieces. The houses semed to have been similar.

One difference was that the *Frolic*'s more numerous windows were made of shell, while those on the Double Springs house were glass. Still, the mortise joinery on the lone surviving pane from the *Frolic* was identical to that on the Double Springs windows. The oyster-shell windows aboard the *Frolic* had been a design option, deliberately chosen, not a cheap substitution for glass. That was implied in a July 31, 1850, auction advertisement in San Francisco's *Daily Alta*, which listed, along with window glass in assorted sizes, "6 cases of pearl shells for verandah windows."[30]

The "oyster"-shell window panes had come from the Philippines, but they were not the only components of the Chinese manufactured goods on the *Frolic* that had been imported into China. I had stored a box of "miscellaneous" artifacts in the uppermost drawer of a fourteen-drawer cabinet towering seven feet above the floor of the lab. As I climbed onto a chair to retrieve them, I felt a twinge of guilt. Had I really tried to relegate these miscellanea to the periphery of my research? But as I lifted the drawer down, it felt empty. Obviously, I had only placed it at the top because it was easier to lift than the heavier trays filled with nested brass weights and mountains of porcelain sherds. It was reassuring to see the bags containing tiny artifacts lying on the bottom of the drawer.

I spread the little pieces out on the table and began to sort them by material: mother-of-pearl, ivory, tortoiseshell, horn, or bone. None of these objects had even been suggested, much less described, in the

Figure 54. Mother-of-pearl gaming piece from the *Frolic* (horizontal length: 2.8 cm), engraved with facing birds, shown above an identical heirloom piece from a private collection.

Frolic's bill of lading. Hidden among the 56 cases listed as "merchandise" and the 174 packages of "sundries," they represented the great miscellanea of the China trade known as "chowchow"—small manufactured items, from fans to combs to toys.

The mother-of-pearl items included fragments of two intricately carved handles. I had seen similar handles, about four inches long, on silver flatware at the Peabody Essex Museum, but these from the *Frolic* had long been separated from any evidence of their working ends. I recognized a tiny, broken, pearlescent sheet engraved with two songbirds face to face, a counter from a box of games. The 1856 *Chinese Commercial Guide* noted that mother-of-pearl came from the islands of the Pacific, especially the Sulu Sea between North Borneo and the Philippines.[31] It had been brought to China in the same vessels which carried dried giant sea slugs, the Chinese culinary delicacy "bicho-de-mar."

"It also comes from California," was the tagline for the mother-of-pearl. Yet, strangely, the *Guide* did not distinguish the pearly white Philippine shell that I had seen in the game counter from the brightly colored abalone shell found in California waters. As I looked at the one piece of abalone shell I had from the *Frolic*, rose-pink at one end, I reflected that this unsung California product had twice traversed the Pacific—first brought to China as a raw shell, and then turned into a decorative garnish, perhaps inlaid in a piece of furniture, and carried back to the California coast.

I sorted through the pieces of worked ivory: eighteen handles, nine fan slats, and an unidentified "mystery object." All were stained black, probably from lying among the *Frolic*'s mound of corroding anchor chain. I had identified them as ivory by their surface textures. The eighteen flatware handles were in five sizes, ranging from $2^{1}/_{2}$ to $5^{1}/_{2}$ inches long, each drilled at one end to receive an iron dowel, the only residue of which was a spot of flaky red rust. The dowel, or tang, had apparently anchored a long-vanished eating utensil made of iron.

One ivory handle had split along the grain to reveal a creamy yellow interior and the full length of the drilled hole. At the bottom of the hole, just beyond the rust, I saw a 1-inch section of gray metal. I felt my stomach knot. Was it silver? I got out a razorblade and scraped at the gray metal. It was soft as butter—or lead solder. Now I could see the production process clearly. First, the workman had drilled the ivory handle to receive the tang of an iron eating utensil. Next, he poured a tiny measure of molten lead solder into the hole and pushed in the iron dowel—a simple and effective technique to bind iron into ivory. But it seemed strange to me that expensive ivory handles would be used on cheap iron flatware. Indeed, I had never even heard of iron flatware.

Then I remembered. My mother's parents had emigrated to the United States in 1940, one step ahead of Hitler, carrying a set of German flatware purchased for the marriage of my great-grandparents in 1879. I had grown up with that set, bending and snapping the soft silver spoons while surreptitiously digging into the hard-frozen ice cream in our freezer. My parents had retired what remained of the collection after finding mangled forks and spoons in our garbage disposal. But now I remembered the knives—the beautiful, hollow silver handles with their ugly, blackened iron blades, their rusted square tangs one by

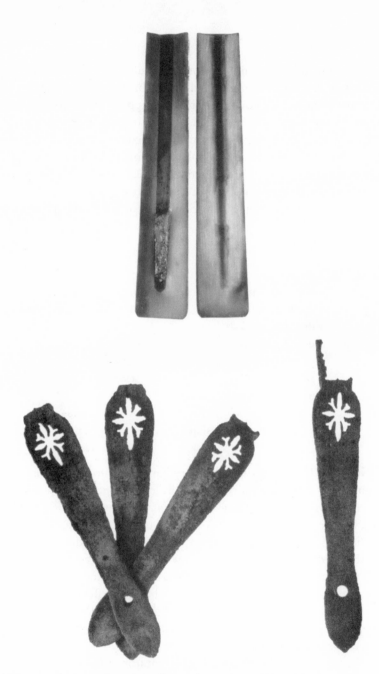

Figure 55. Ivory artifacts from the *Frolic*: (*top*) Knife handle, drilled to receive the tang of an iron blade (length: 9.1 cm); lead-solder binder (also functioning as a counterweight) still fills the bottom of the drilled hole. (*bottom*) Fan slats (length of longest fragment: 8.1 cm).

one working loose and falling from the handles. I searched for the key to my safe-deposit box and headed for the bank, where in the privacy of a small booth next to the vault I unwrapped the bundle of silver. There lay the one surviving iron blade with its rusty tang.

The *Frolic*'s ivory handles seemed to document five sizes of table knives with iron blades, and it looked as though the knives had been separately manufactured and bought. The one detailed itemization of silver flatware from the *Eveline*, a set specially ordered for Rachel Larkin, included a soup ladle and various sizes of forks and spoons, but no knives.

set of silver ware "Rachel Larkin"

1 soup ladle	7.50	
2 gravy spoons	9.75	
1 doz soup spoons	28.94	
1 doz spoons 2d size	22.05	
1 doz tea spoons	11.02	
1 sugar spoon	1.85	
2 salt spoons	1.20	
1 doz forks 2d size	25.35	
cost		107.66
12% for workmanship		12.91
total		120.57

Now that I had explained the ivory handles, I turned to a bag containing nine slats from an ivory fan, drilled all together to produce a lacy, open-work pattern. I knew the *Eveline* had carried "ivory & silk" fans, but the fabric of the *Frolic*'s fans had dissolved long ago in the icy Pacific. I could only imagine the expanse of brightly colored, pleated silk that had once been attached to my blackened stubs.

The mystery object looked like a thin, flattened handle, with each of its faces bearing four recessed circles with holes drilled through their centers. I tried to reproduce it on the Anthropology Department photocopy machine. I traced the blurred outline onto graph paper, added dotted lines to show breakage, and sent the sorry-looking illustration by telecopier to Dr. William Sargent, a curator at the Peabody Essex Museum. Bill's return telecopy included his sketch of a contraption that had once been inside a "Sunday box"—an ivory frame with two sides, four crossbars, and silk strings bearing eight sliding ivory disks. My

Figure 56. The "mystery object": an ivory side-panel of a game recovered from the *Frolic*, shown next to a similar game from an heirloom "Sunday box" containing thirteen games and puzzles. Lacquered wood "Sunday box" courtesy of The Kelton Foundation Collection. Length of fragment: 12.7 cm.; width of box, 35 cm.

mystery object was part of a game from a long-vanished box of toys. Along with other games and puzzles, the Sunday box had probably also carried a set of wafer-thin pearl counters, like the fragment with two facing songbirds recovered from the *Frolic*.

I had searched the 1848 *Chinese Commercial Guide* without finding any entry for ivory. Only several days later, when I was looking up tortoiseshell, did I happen across a listing for "elephant teeth." Ivory, of course, is made from the tusks of elephants—their upper incisors, grown large over millions of years of evolution. Such "teeth," I learned, had been imported into China in large numbers from South Africa, Ceylon, Burma, and Siam.[32]

My box of miscellaneous artifacts also included several pieces of tortoiseshell, the translucent horn-like lamination covering the carapace of turtles. When steamed, it can be easily molded into any shape, and was widely used for combs, ornate boxes, and toys.

An 1856 *Chinese Commercial Guide* reported that the tortoiseshell used in China came from the hawksbill turtle. These were collected from throughout the western Pacific, the best coming from Borneo and New Guinea.[33] Each hawksbill carapace had thirteen inner plates and twenty-five marginal ones, the innermost being the largest, thickest, and most valuable.

I had a tiny section of a fine-toothed comb and a carefully machined two-piece ring assembly, still soaking in the jelly jar of fresh water that the wreck diver had placed it in to preserve it. I fished out the pieces, laid them on a moistened paper towel, and examined them with a magnifying glass. One translucent tortoiseshell ring was threaded to a remnant of a carved ivory cylinder that had formed the ring base. I got out the *Eveline*'s invoices and found one that provided an explanation:

Silk parasols:

tortoise shell staff, ivory handles & lots of chowchow fringe
72 @   2.25 ea
(straw, pink & white, brown, dk lilac, lt blue & lilac, lt green & lilac)

I also had three horn artifacts from the *Frolic*—two checkers and a shoe horn. Horn is the sheaf-like keratin covering over the bony projections on the skulls of cattle and other ungulates. In China the horn probably came from water buffaloes. Like tortoiseshell, it can be softened in steam or hot water and then molded into various shapes. The

Figure 57. Horn and bone artifacts from the *Frolic*: (*above*) Shoehorn with "good fortune" character scratched within ship's wheel (length: 17.8 cm). (*right*) Bone toothbrush (diameter at neck: 8 mm).

checkers were fashioned in three pieces—an outside ring was capped on the top and bottom with molded disks. These checkers, like the mother-of-pearl counters with birds, might have been part of a "Sunday box" of games.

The long, triangular shoe horn had required no shaping after being cut from the side of a cow or buffalo horn. It retained the original curvature of the raw material—an ideal shape and size for sliding the heel of a large foot into the narrow opening of a shoe. A Chinese character was clearly scribed within two concentric rings at the center of the shoe horn's concave face. I took it to Steve Kwan for translation. The inscription, he informed me, had been scratched not by the manufacturer but by the barely literate owner. The shoehorn was, most likely, not part of the cargo at all, but the property of one of the Chinese aboard the *Frolic*, perhaps the cook or the carpenter. Steve translated the inscription as "good fortune" and pointed out that the two concentric circles had knobs, forming a crude picture of a ship's wheel.

The four last items in the drawer were bone artifacts—two identical handles for straight razors and two handles for toothbrushes, also identical. The *Eveline* had carried twenty-four shaving boxes among her lacquered ware, and these razors and toothbrushes could have come from similar boxes. The toothbrushes were cut from long bones—probably from the legs of the same water buffaloes and bullocks whose horns had been transformed into checkers and shoe horns. The craftsman had split the bones open, scraped away their spongy insides, and then cut the toothbrush blanks from their thick outer walls. Five rows of shallow holes, about twelve holes per row, had been drilled partway into one face to hold looped tufts of boars' bristle. Then, from one end, five longer holes were drilled to intersect each row of shallow holes, like a tunnel connecting the bottoms of a row of shallow wells, so that a single strand of wire or bristle could be passed through each loop to anchor it into the handle. Because the toothbrushes and razors I had were identical, I thought they were more likely to have come from the *Frolic*'s cargo, rather than from the toiletry kits of Captain Faucon or his officers—but I could never be certain.

⚜

I replaced the miscellaneous artifacts in their drawer and wiped the table. My few preserved pieces of cargo from the *Frolic* were only a tiny sample of the tens of thousands of items she had carried. As I sat alone in the lab, I thought of John Hurd Everett on Old China Street, visiting the shops of Wongshing, Tingqua, Khecheong, and the many others. He had examined sample items, chosen among them, and ordered what he thought would sell best in San Francisco. The artifacts in my lab represented a few of the things he had selected from a vast array of export products developed by Chinese craftsmen during three hundred years of trade with the West.

In the middle third of the nineteenth century, John Everett had been known as an intrepid merchant, a wit, and a wag, but he had been totally forgotten by the late twentieth century—even by the Everetts themselves. Only one family anecdote memorialized him: Betsey's turning his offensive portrait to the wall. Everett and I had labored over the same cargo: he to assemble it, and I to reconstruct that assemblage almost a century and a half later. I felt a bond with John Everett, and I wanted to do right by him.

I thought about my role as an archaeologist and how the past fourteen years of research had changed me. I had started with the modest goal of identifying and dating the Chinese ceramics aboard a wrecked vessel in order to trace out the Mitom Pomo settlement pattern. The unexpected result of that effort was the delineation of a nineteenth-century commercial venture that spanned the Pacific.

I reflected on the sheer serendipity of the project. Had the *Frolic* sunk in deep water, I would never have made the connection between Three Chop Village and a shipwreck. In deeper water, protected from the crushing North Pacific waves and less accessible to pillagers, much of the vessel as well as her cargo might have been preserved. I might never even have known of the *Frolic*—if she had been studied at all, it would have been by specialists in another field.

Nautical archaeologists would have carefully documented the *Frolic*'s structural remains. Meanwhile, the sheer size of her cargo—21,000 stoneware bowls alone—would have directed the research toward a traditional monograph: the listing of thousands of artifacts, their physical properties, and their placement in the vessel.

Such professional monographs are a necessary and fundamental part of modern archaeology. And while modern historical archaeology uses written records to augment and illustrate information gleaned from material objects, the site and the artifacts themselves are primary in inspiring and directing the research. By placing the artifacts into a cultural context, we are able to see the past afresh, from a different perspective than that provided by the historical record alone. This is what gives historical archaeology its unique power to explain the past.

Yet, as essential as artifacts may be to the enterprise of historical archaeology, their sheer numbers can often subvert a project. A major structural pathology pervading the field is that it takes so much time and effort to describe and analyze a large collection of objects that the archaeologist seldom has enough time left to step back and examine the larger system in which those objects once functioned. Perhaps I was lucky that I had so few artifacts and such poor context. I had been forced to take a wider look.

During my years as a prehistoric archaeologist, the area of my California research had rarely gone beyond Pomo territory, a region extending eighty-five miles north–south and sixty-five miles across. That was the Pomo world. And while the Pomo had engaged in trade with their neighbors, their direct trade relations rarely spread more than twenty-five miles beyond their borders.

Historical archaeology demands a broader approach. During the past five hundred years of the historic period, the peoples of the world have become integrated by the spread of Western culture and capitalism. As a consequence, historic sites can rarely be understood apart from an international context. This truth is as valid for the Pomo in northwestern California as for the native peoples of Australia, Africa, and South America. Thus, as we leave the prehistoric period and follow the Pomo into the first half of the nineteenth century, we must expand our purview far beyond Pomo territory to consider the Spanish colonization of Alta California, Russian settlement at Fort Ross, and the California Gold Rush.

For me, the need to explain the blue-and-white potsherds we had excavated at Three Chop Village opened the door to a bigger story. That story transcended the Pomo, the shipwreck, and the cargo to explain part of a world system: the spread of Western culture through commerce. In this enterprise, the artifacts from Three Chop Village and from the *Frolic* have provided me with the opportunity not only to describe that system but also to connect it to a human scale of people, places, and things. That process of connection is historical archaeology's unique contribution to the study of humanity.

Epilogue

California's Highway 17 snakes its way through the Santa Cruz Mountains, sometimes clinging to steep canyon walls, sometimes following the old trail that links Santa Clara Mission and Pueblo San Jose to the mission and embarcadero at Santa Cruz.

At the summit, I downshifted to pass a freight truck and looked down on the bank of fog blanketing the coast. Neither I nor my colleague, Russell Skowronek, had time for this trip. I was trying to finish a manuscript describing the cargo of the *Frolic*, and Russ was working on a book summarizing his archaeological investigations at Mission Santa Clara. We commiserated about the insatiable demands our respective universities made on the scant time we had for research.

But today, it was not university chores that were taking us from our own work. We were doing public service, responding to a citizen's request that we evaluate the research potential of the Castro adobe, twelve miles south of Santa Cruz. Edna Kimbro, a museum consultant who owned the property, was that citizen. Edna's professional specialty was the restoration and furnishing of nineteenth-century houses, but her first love was pre–Gold Rush adobes.

Russ and I turned east from the Coast Highway onto a country road and within a mile turned into a narrow lane named Old Adobe Road. Russ saw it first—a massive, two-story adobe behind a curtain of green overgrowth. Two hundred yards beyond it, we turned into Edna's driveway.

The sun broke through the fog as Edna led us down the path to the adobe. We stepped over California poppies, their orange petals glowing in the brilliant summer light. As we emerged from the remnants of an abandoned orchard we saw the old building, eighty feet long and thirty feet wide, with a second-story balcony extending along its full length. Edna told us that in 1830, José Joaquín Castro, aged sixty, had taken fourteen-year-old Maria del Rosario Briones as his second wife, and sometime after 1835 he had built this magnificent house.[1] He had modeled it after the adobe that Thomas Larkin had built a few years earlier for his own wife, Rachel, twenty-five miles south in Monterey—the house that would forever after define the Monterey style of California architecture.

Edna had moved into the adobe in 1988, and a year later, on October 17, 1989, the ground began to shake with the first tremors of the Loma Prieta earthquake. She ran into the yard and saw a cloud of brown dust envelop the south end of her house. When the dust cleared she saw that the upper third of the adobe wall beneath the south gable had collapsed into the yard. Now, eleven years later, scraggly weeds grew from the pile of adobe rubble. There were gaping cracks in the walls—one with a six-inch offset. The county had condemned the structure, and for five years, before building a new house next door, Edna and her family had occupied a house trailer parked in the yard.

As we entered a narrow doorway, I measured the thickness of the wall—twenty-seven inches. Unfired adobe walls had to be thick in order to support their own weight, but that same thickness kept the house warm in winter and cool in the summer. Where the plaster had fallen away I could see fourteen-inch gray adobe bricks cemented with thick, reddish-brown mud mortar. The whiskers of straw temper in the mortar still looked fresh after over a century and a half. We followed Edna upstairs to see the fandango room—the ballroom—a full fifty feet long. I could imagine John Everett standing in the corner, watching dancers wearing brightly colored dresses and shirts made from the fabric he had sold them from the *Tasso*. The floor of an adjacent bedroom was still strewn with the Legos® that Edna's sons had been playing with when the earthquake struck. Edna had been so emotionally devastated by the quake's destruction that she had left many of the family's belongings where they had fallen. As we finished the tour, she crawled into a cobweb-draped closet and dragged out a large wicker picnic basket. "Here," she said. "These should interest you!"

Figure 58. Thomas Layton, Charlene Duval, and Edna Kimbro (*left to right*) sorting potsherds from the Castro adobe, July 1999. Photo courtesy Russell Skowronek.

The basket was filled nearly to the top with potsherds. The first to catch my eye bore a pale blue-gray glaze identical to that on thousands of sherds I had cleaned and catalogued from the *Frolic*. When I turned it over in my hand I could see part of the "peach and fungus" design that decorated so many pieces of the *Frolic*'s tableware. I felt a surge of excitement. Suddenly, the visit to the Castro Adobe was no longer an imposition on my time, but a serendipitous opportunity. Russ reached into the basket and pulled out another sherd with bold concentric bands in brown and blue. "English annular pearlware," he said. "Common throughout the early nineteenth century."

Edna told us that Elizabeth Lyman Potter, the previous owner of the adobe, had combed the grounds for twenty-four years looking for sherds. She had collected them to serve as examples to guide her in purchasing complete bowls and dishes from antique shops to decorate the house. After the Loma Prieta quake, an archaeologist at the local community college and his students had scraped the surface around the adobe to recover any additional sherds. Edna promised she would get those back from the college for me to study.

I carried the heavy basket back through the orchard to Edna's patio. She found a piece of wire screen to dump the sherds onto, and we hosed them off. On our hands and knees, we pawed through the broken fragments, sorting them into little piles of similar glazes and designs. Russ immediately began separating out early-nineteenth-century transfer-printed wares. Edna started a pile of 1920s knob-and-tube electrical insulators and another of pastel bathroom tiles from the 1950s. I focused my search on China export wares.[2]

Later that afternoon, as Russ and I drove back to San Jose, we talked about the significance of our finds at the adobe. I noted that the Chinese ceramics from the picnic basket and those from other pre–Gold Rush California sites were quite different from those recovered from sites occupied by Chinese immigrants only a few years later. And Chinese ceramics had virtually disappeared from the assemblages left by European-Americans after the Gold Rush.

Russ offered an explanation. "With the Gold Rush," he said, "everybody in California made a status change. Indians became "Mexicans," Mexicans became "Castilians," and American squatters became "landed gentry." Each group tried to separate itself from those of lesser social status. When large numbers of Chinese laborers arrived in California, they were stuck at the bottom of the social ladder, along with the Indians. This forced a change in the perception of Chinese ceramics. Where these ceramics had formerly been perceived as elegant status symbols, suddenly they became "ethnic" and low-class. "By the mid-1850s," Russ concluded, "the only Californians buying Chinese ceramics were the Chinese themselves!"

A week later, Edna had retrieved the rest of the Castro Adobe collection from the community college and I had all the Chinese sherds arrayed on my lab table. The thirty blue-and-white fragments I had were pieces of eight different dishes or containers: five bowls, two plates, and a cylindrical vase or brush holder. The bowls included two sizes of "peach and fungus." Both of these, and the two bowls with unglazed bisque rings on their inside surfaces that I had pieces of, were forms also recovered from the *Frolic*. There were also two sherds from a "chrysanthemum"-style bowl, a style not among the *Frolic* artifacts but well represented in pre–Gold Rush deposits in San Diego.[3] Finally, there were three sherds from two different sizes of "Canton"-style plates, decorated with a lake scene showing a boat, a pagoda-like pavilion on a rocky island, and distant mountains, all within a "rain and cloud" pattern border. A similar set of tableware with the same "rain and cloud" border had been carried aboard the *Frolic*.

My review of the literature, as well as unpublished collections, confirmed my theory. The Chinese export sherds that came from the *Frolic*, the Castro Adobe, and from virtually all of the archaeologically excavated ranchos, missions, and pueblos in pre–Gold Rush California were clearly distinct from those found in sites occupied by Chinese immigrants after the Gold Rush.[4] Indeed, of the five major styles of tableware carried aboard the *Frolic*, only "bamboo"-style rice bowls were well represented at later sites occupied by California Chinese. The arrival of the *Frolic*'s cargo seemed to mark the end of one era of consumer preference in ceramics, while the arrival of the Chinese themselves marked the beginning of another.

Although Chinese ceramics virtually disappeared from European-American assemblages with the beginning of large-scale Chinese immigration, I wondered what the archaeological record might tell us about this transition. Were there, I wondered, any well-dated archaeological sites that spanned this transition? I contacted my colleague Dr. Adrian Praetzellis of Sonoma State University.

Adrian had created the historical archaeology program at Sonoma State, and he regularly accepted contracts for archaeological survey and excavation to provide training opportunities for his students. He told me how, during the early 1850s, the Chinese of Sacramento had built "Chinadom"—a community of businesses and boarding houses constructed on stilts over "China Lake," a fetid, oxbow meander of the Sacramento River. Unfortunately for the Chinese occupants, but to the lasting benefit of archaeology, the community had burned to the ground in the fire of 1855. The remains had lain relatively undisturbed for over a century, until the construction of the Federal Court Building was planned on the site. Adrian had made an archaeological survey of the land before construction began—as federal law requires.

There were two striking aspects of the ceramic assemblage from Layer 903, the ash layer from the 1855 fire. First, the Chinese had used both Chinese and English tablewares in nearly equal proportion. Secondly, the Chinese portion of this assemblage was far more heterogeneous than the assemblages recovered from Chinatowns dating from the 1860s and later. Although the Sacramento collection included a good representation of ceramic styles also found in later Chinatowns— "bamboo," "celadon," "double happiness," and "four flowers"—there were nine designs unique to the earlier site.[5]

Adrian attributed this heterogeneity of Chinese styles during the 1850s to a poorly developed import trade supplying the Chinese community of that time. By the 1860s, he argued, the lines of supply to Chinese consumers in California had become so well established as to be almost completely ossified. With only a few large suppliers from the 1860s on, there was not much variety in the ceramic styles used throughout the overseas Chinese diaspora. Moreover, Adrian argued that the mixture of English and Chinese ceramics in Layer 903 at Chinadom reflected the fact that earlier California Chinese were more receptive to European-American culture than they would be in the next decade.

Adrian did not know of a California Chinese collection that could be cleanly dated to the 1860s and no later. Most urban Chinatowns occupied in the 1860s continued to be occupied into the 1870s and '80s, and their trash deposits were hopelessly mixed. To find an uncontaminated assemblage from the 1860s, I would need to look for a rural site.

My friend Dr. Paul Chace had been one of the first archaeologists in California to focus his research on Chinese immigrant towns and work camps. Paul told me that the best way to find a Chinese assemblage from the 1860s would be to look for a Chinese work camp located along the Western Pacific Railroad right-of-way through the Sierra Nevada Mountains. Chinese workers had provided the bulk of the labor force for the railroad, and all of their campsites would date from between 1865 and 1869, when the railroad was completed. In fact, back in his undergraduate days, Paul had helped Bill Evans, an archaeologist at Santa Monica Community College, conduct a survey of those camps.

I reached Bill Evans by phone. Bill confided that he was now seventy-seven years old and long retired from research and teaching, but he remembered well how, during the summer of 1961, he and a very young Paul Chace had walked along the railroad right-of-way over the crest of the Sierras near Donner Summit. He recalled that the granite substrate had produced very little soil cover, and the evidences of Chinese occupation were abundantly exposed across the surface of the sites. They had found a great diversity of artifacts. Bill's report listed 154 fragments of opium pipes and 115 parts of opium tins. Bill, too, had been struck by the homogeneity of the tablewares. Looking at his report, he told me that 81.2 percent were of the "double happiness" pattern, 10.2 percent were "bamboo," and less than 4 percent each were of "celadon" and "four seasons."[6] The predominance of one pattern— "double happiness"—suggested to him that the supply from China at that time had been regular and standardized.

I wondered why the tablewares in the late 1860s were more standardized than those in the early 1850s. The Chinese had been mass producing inexpensive tableware for centuries. Paul Chace offered one explanation. In 1850 the T'ai-p'ing Rebellion, the first of a series of civil wars, had erupted in Kwangsi Province, just to the west of Canton. For fourteen years the T'ai-p'ings fought their way north from the Pearl River to the Yangtze, wreaking devastation in their wake. In 1854, the Triad Societies, locally known as the Red Turbans, instigated a series of rebellions that lasted ten years in the Pearl River delta adjacent to Canton. Then, in 1856, the mutual hatred of the Cantonese and their Hakka neighbors devolved into open warfare.[7] When order was finally restored in the mid-1860s, the eastern third of China was devastated, with an estimated twenty million people dead from battle or from starvation.[8]

Paul argued that the massive emigration of Chinese workers to California had been a direct result of this turmoil. Moreover, he attributed the diversity of styles in Adrian's 1855 assemblage not to a poorly organized market of Chinese merchants in California, but to the disruption of normal ceramic production in China.[9] With the re-establishment of order, circa 1865, Paul surmised that normal ceramic production would have resumed. California Chinese merchants would then be able to import the cargoes of standardized ceramics that would later be found in the Chinese work camps along the Western Sierra Railroad right-of-way.[10]

The two scholars were looking at the 1850s from different perspectives. Paul was seeing the period and its assemblages from a China-based, pan-Pacific point of view. On the other hand, Adrian's perspective was local, and he saw a profitable, cooperative interaction between Chinese-American and European-American merchants in one town—

Sacramento, California. The disruption of production in China provided an explanation for one kind of heterogeneity in the 1850s assemblages, but there was still another kind of diversity. Adrian had noted that the mixture of European-American and Chinese wares reflected an initial openness of California Chinese communities to European-American culture.

Chinese immigration into California had grown exponentially during the period we were studying. In 1850, there had been about four thousand Chinese in California. Two years later there were twenty-five thousand, and by 1856 there were forty-five thousand.[11] In 1850, as Adrian described, European-Americans had considered the Chinese merely exotic, and been open to Chinese culture. As the numbers of Chinese immigrants increased, however, European-Americans began to perceive them as an economic threat. By the 1860s, these immigrants were isolated, ghettoized, and persecuted. In response, their communities turned inward—a trend shown archaeologically by the virtual absence of European tablewares in the later sites.

Still, I wondered if the diversity of tableware used by California Chinese during the 1850s could have reflected, in part, a hesitation by Chinese merchants to exploit a new market. Some years earlier, I had asked one of my students, Rikke Giles, to examine cargo manifests from vessels carrying goods from China to San Francisco during the 1850s. She had looked at ten manifests—five from 1850–51 and five from 1859.[12] I got out her data sheets.

What immediately struck me in her tallies was the relatively constant ratio of Chinese and Western surnames among the merchants to whom the cargo was consigned. Of 56 names in 1850–51, 57 percent had been Chinese. Of 128 names in 1859, 68 percent were Chinese. Chinese-American merchants were already the most numerous consignees of China cargoes in 1850–51, and they continued to be well represented throughout the decade. It seemed clear that intrepid Chinese merchants had hurried to Gold Rush California to exploit the new market as quickly as the European-Americans had. Of course, that was to be expected, for Chinese merchants already had centuries of experience supplying overseas markets.

But how successfully had these Chinese merchants competed with European-American merchants for the goods imported from China during that decade? Although in my small sample of ten ships' manifests, the proportions of Chinese and European-American importers remained roughly the same throughout the 1850s, there was a difference over time. In terms of sheer tonnage, it appeared that in 1850–51 imports by Chinese-Americans represented only a fraction of the market, but by 1859 they virtually monopolized it. Their share of the rice imported aboard these vessels from China rose from 17 percent to 97 percent, and their share of sugar imports from 12 percent to 87 percent. In 1850–51, there had been no opium carried aboard any of the cargo ships in our sample, but in 1859 all five vessels had carried the drug, and Chinese consignees controlled 100 percent of the five tons listed.[13]

It appeared that during the decade of the 1850s, the California Chinese community had become progressively more and more isolated from the European-American mainstream. As their number increased exponentially, the Chinese immigrants were segregated and persecuted by the European-Americans. But this ostracism had worked to the benefit of Chinese-American merchants, who had thus gained a virtual monopoly supplying their ghettoized countrymen—and thereby the opportunity to siphon off their income.[14]

I looked out of my office window toward the old plaza of Pueblo San José de Guadalupe. There, in 1844, John Hurd Everett had climbed on his horse and started down the Monterey Road to collect on the overdue notes for the *Tasso*'s cargo of Boston goods shipped round the Horn. Four years later, he would be dispatching the first of two Chinese cargoes to his California friends. I looked across my desk at the morass of notes and chapter drafts—my attempts to tell the story of the *Frolic*'s gifts from the "Celestial Kingdom."

I stared idly at my ruler—"Made in China." I looked at the bottom of my coffee mug—"Made in China." The same for the solar-powered calculator with which I had just calculated proportions of the sugar, rice, and opium trade controlled by California Chinese merchants during the 1850s. I turned over my telephone—"Made in China." I marveled at the diversity of Chinese manufactured goods, all within an arm's reach. Gifts from the Celestial Kingdom have always benefited California, and they continue to do so today.

Appendices

The Cargo of the 'Eveline' as Sold in San Francisco

This appendix brings together the purchase cost in China of the cargo items carried aboard the *Eveline* and the proceeds from their sale in San Francisco. Item costs are from Augustine Heard & Company invoices to Jacob P. Leese and Thomas O. Larkin, dated July 22 and 23, 1849. Proceeds are from the auction in San Francisco that took place November 20–24, 1849. These documents are all in the Leese Scrapbook at the Society of California Pioneers. Although I have supplied the major category headings, such as "Gold" and "Ivory," the terms and spellings for individual items are transcribed as they appear in those documents. Parenthetical references appear as they do on the original documents; bracketed references are my own clarifications. Since some of the items auctioned in San Francisco are not listed in the invoices from China, it seems that at least one invoice may be missing. San Francisco proceeds, when presented as a range, indicate multiple sales of similar items at different prices. I have not listed the names of the eighty-three California merchants who purchased the 368 numbered auction lots of cargo. See Figure 5 for the first page of the fifteen-page auction listing.

ITEMS BY CATEGORY	SUPPLIER	INVOICE COST IN CHINA	AUCTION PRICE IN SAN FRANCISCO
GOLD			
Shirt studs	Wongshing		9.00–10.00 set
6 sets		4.50 set	
3 sets		3.75 set	
2 sets		5.00 set	
1 set		4.50 set	

ITEMS BY CATEGORY	SUPPLIER	INVOICE COST IN CHINA	AUCTION PRICE IN SAN FRANCISCO
Earrings	Wongshing		26.50–30.00 pr
filigree earrings			
1 pr		14.00 pr	
1 pr		13.50 pr	
3 pr		12.00 pr	
1 pr		9.50 pr	
Scent boxes	Wongshing		21.00–23.00 ea
6		10.00 ea	
6		9.00 ea	
Breast pins	Wongshing		12.50–15.00 ea
12		3.25 ea	
Thimbles	Cutshing		
12		4.25 ea	8.75 ea
Bracelets	Cutshing		
5 pr		7.00 pr	22.00 pr
SILVER			
Hair nets	Wongshing		
with silk tassels			
12		3.50 ea	15.50 ea
Hair nets	Wongshing		
without silk tassels			
12		1.25 ea	3.50 ea
Silver flowers for hair		9.50–10.00 ea	
6	Wongshing	4.00 ea	
6	Cutshing	4.50 ea	
Flint & steel boxes			5.00–5.50 ea
6	Wongshing	1.90 ea	
6	Wongshing	1.25 ea	
24	Cutshing	2.30 ea	
Suspender buckles			6.25 pr
12 pr	Wongshing	3.00 pr	
12 pr	Cutshing	3.00 pr	
Silver fans			39.00 ea
washed with gold			
2	Wongshing	12.00 ea	
1	Cutshing	13.00 ea	
Silver fan			
1	Cutshing	12.00 ea	

ITEMS BY CATEGORY	SUPPLIER	INVOICE COST IN CHINA	AUCTION PRICE IN SAN FRANCISCO
Feather painted fans with silver handles			
12	Wongshing	4.00 ea	18.00 ea
Buttons Mexican pattern [1 doz/box]			
12 boxes	Wongshing	3.50/box	9.50/box
Filigree baskets			50.00–62.50 ea
1 pr	Wongshing	21.00 pr	
1 pr	Cutshing	28.00 pr	
Tea strainers			
24	Cutshing	.50 ea	1.75 ea
Wine & liquor labels			
12 gin, 12 brandy, 12 whiskey, 12 claret, 12 port, 12 California	Cutshing	1.15 doz	
Needle cases			
12 pr	Cutshing	2.00 pr	3 @5.00; 8 @4.50 pr
Set of silverware "Rachel Larkin"	Wongshing		[private order]
1 soup ladle		7.50	
2 gravy spoons		9.75	
1 doz soup spoons		28.94	
1 doz spoons 2d size		22.05	
1 doz tea spoons		11.02	
1 sugar spoon		1.85	
2 salt spoons		1.20	
1 doz forks 2d size		25.35	
Cost		107.66	
12% for workmanship [engraving]		12.91	
Total		120.57	
Silverware set [same as above w/o engraving]:		107.66	266.25/set
1 set S.V. [Salvador Vallejo]		123.23	[private order]
1 set D.S.		123.64	[private order]
1 set RVL [Rosalía Vallejo Leese]		121.10	[private order]
1 set MGV [Mariano Guadalupe Vallejo]		121.17	[private order]
1 set DH		122.02	[private order]

ITEMS BY CATEGORY	SUPPLIER	INVOICE COST IN CHINA	AUCTION PRICE IN SAN FRANCISCO
IVORY			
Flower boats			
2	Tim cheong	8.50 ea	
Mandarin boats			
2	Tim cheong	30.00 ea	
Bouquet holders			
6 pr	Yong cheong	1.25 pr	3.50 pr
Flower vases			
2	Yong cheong	3.75 ea	37.50 pr
Checkers			
1 box	Yong cheong	2.75 box	18.50 box
Fans: ivory & silk			
8	Yong cheong	11.00 all	4.50 ea
Tablets			
12	Fock hing	1.20 ea	3.00 ea
Billiard balls	Fock hing		16.00 set
24 white		2.20 ea	
12 pink		2.20 ea	
12 red		2.20 ea	
Back scratchers	Fock hing		
12		.25 ea	1.10 ea
Puzzles	Tonqua		
6		.75 ea	
Dice (2 boxes @100/box)	Tonqua	.58 box	
Checkers & dice	Tonqua		
1 box		1.90 box	
BONE			
Needle cases	Tonqua		
6		.24 ea	
Bone fans	Yong cheong		
1 doz		1.92 doz	16.00 doz
BONE AND IVORY (VARIOUS)			35.00 all
6 ivory puzzles			
1 box ivory checkers			
1 pr dice boxes			
2 boxes 200 dice			
6 bone needle cases			

ITEMS BY CATEGORY	SUPPLIER	INVOICE COST IN CHINA	AUCTION PRICE IN SAN FRANCISCO
PEARL			
Paper cutters	Yong cheong		
6		.75 ea	1.50 ea
Buttons			
plain buttons			
150 gross	Chesing	12.75 all	33.75 all
figured buttons			
150 gross	Chesing	18.00 all	33.75 all
TORTOISE SHELL			
Toilet combs			
1 doz	Yong cheong	6.00 all	13.50 all
Long toilet combs			
72	Fock hing	.70 ea	1.50 ea
Ladies side combs			
108 prs	Fock hing	.18 pr	.50 pr
Large ladies hair combs			
1 doz	Fock hing	9.00 doz	19.50 doz
MEASURING RODS			
24	Hecheong	5.00 ea	
BEADS			
Beads			
25 boxes	Yong cheong	.26 box	1.05 box
25 boxes	Yong cheong	.17 box	1.05 box
White beads			
2 pecul	Yong cheong	13.00 pecul	75.00 case [picul?]
Pearl beads			
(25 boxes; 3 strings @100 beads/box)	Fock hing	.45 box	
PEACOCK FEATHERS			
4 doz	Yong Cheong	9.00 doz	22.00 doz
RICE PAPER PAINTINGS (12 BOOKS OF 12)			
12 books	Fock hing	1.50 book	6.00 book

ITEMS BY CATEGORY	SUPPLIER	INVOICE COST IN CHINA	AUCTION PRICE IN SAN FRANCISCO
BAMBOO			
Hair combs	Fock hing		
300		3.50/100	
Camp. baskets	Fock hing		
48		.95 ea	
TOYS			
12	Fock hing	.75 box	7.75 box
UMBRELLAS	Sun chue	2.00 ea	4.50 ea
12 blue silk			
15 black silk			
9 brown silk			
STRAW TABLE MATS	Tim cheong		
2 doz sets		4.80/doz sets	
CHINESE LANTERNS	Tim cheong		
3 pr		12.00 pr	30.00 pr
PAINTED COPPER	Tim cheong	182.00 for all	
36 wash basins			
36 pitchers			
36 brush boxes			
36 soap boxes			
FURNITURE			
Rosewood writing desks	Hecheong		
12		13.00 ea	27.00 ea
Mahogany writing desks	Hecheong		
12		9.00 ea	24.00 ea
Blackwood tables with marble tops	Ushing		
4		16.00 ea	65.00 ea
Round with marble top	Ushing		
1		38.00 ea	90.00 ea
Round umottd [*sic*] marble top	Yenchong		
1		40.00 ea	
Centre table, marble top	Yenchong		
1		35.00 ea	

ITEMS BY CATEGORY	SUPPLIER	INVOICE COST IN CHINA	AUCTION PRICE IN SAN FRANCISCO
Centre table yellow marble top	Yenchong		
1		35.00 ea	50.00 ea
Spring couch bedsteads, chintz covered	Hecheong		
4		30.00 ea	61.00–63.00 ea
Couches			
5			21.00–25.00 ea
Chest drawers with secretary top	Hecheong		
12		15.00 ea	55.00–65.00 ea
Measuring tables and measuring rods			
24 rods & 30 tables			252.00 all
Wardrobes			
2			40.00–45.00 ea
Chairs			
37			40.00 doz
Rattan Chairs	Fock hing		
12		13.80 doz	62.00–100.00 doz

Camphor trunks
  (25 painted sets of 4:
  size nos. 2, 3, 4, 5)
    6 sets light blue
    6 sets green
    6 sets brown
    7 sets red
	Ashoe	17.00/set	52.50/set

LACQUERED WARE			
Work tables	Tonqua		
4 pr		32.00 pr	45.00
Centre tables			30.00–40.00 ea [probably]
12	Laoqua	7.50 ea	
12	Saoqua	7.50 ea	
Chess tables			
6	Saoqua	8.00 ea	27.00–35.00 ea
Writing desks			
21	Saoqua	6.00 ea	17.00–21.00 ea

ITEMS BY CATEGORY	SUPPLIER	INVOICE COST IN CHINA	AUCTION PRICE IN SAN FRANCISCO
Cabinet with work table complete			
12	Saoqua	20.00 ea	55.00–80.00 ea
Small cabinets			13.50–16.00 ea
8	Laoqua	4.00 ea	
20	Saoqua	4.00 ea	
Work boxes			12.50–17.00 ea
16	Saoqua	4.00 ea	
8	Laoqua	4.00 ea	
Paper boxes (sets of 4)			
24 sets	Saoqua	5.00 set	15.00 set
Card boxes with counters			
12	Saoqua	3.00 ea	
Cigar boxes			
120	Saoqua	.60 ea	1.70–2.00 ea
Shaving boxes			
24	Saoqua	3.00 ea	10.00–13.00 ea
Tea trays (sets of 5)			
6 sets	Saoqua	5.00 set	13.00 set
Teapoys (sets of 4)			
16 sets	Saoqua	4.50 set	9.00–12.00 set
Tea caddies			
30	Saoqua	1.30 ea	2.50 ea
72	Saoqua	1.00 ea	2.25 ea
Plates			5.50–8.00 doz
4 doz	Laoqua	2.00 doz	
2 doz	Saoqua	2.00 doz	
PORCELAIN			
Blue China dinner set	Ushing	17.00 set	
8 large plates			
1 soup tureen			
6 long dishes			
2 salt cellars			
2 sauce bowls			
2 doz large plates			
2 doz 2nd size plates			
2 doz 3rd size plates			
4 side dishes			
3 pud'g			
3 soup			

ITEMS BY CATEGORY	SUPPLIER	INVOICE COST IN CHINA	AUCTION PRICE IN SAN FRANCISCO
China plates, large common 150 rolls of 20 (3,000 total)	Pohing	96.00 all .64/roll	
China plates, 2nd size 150 rolls of 20 (3,000 total)	Pohing	72.00 all .48/roll	1.12/roll
China plates, 3rd size 100 rolls of 30 (3,000 total)	Pohing	39.00 all .39/roll	1.05–1.15/roll
China plates, 4th size 75 rolls of 40 (3,000 total)	Pohing	33.00 all .44/roll	.80/roll
China bowls, common 84 rolls of 36 (3,026 total)	Pohing	72.00 all	
China cups and saucers, common 51 rolls of 60 (3,060 cups) 61 rolls of 50 (3,050 saucers)	Pohing	60.00 all	.85/doz
China sugar jars and contents	Pohing		7 @ 40.00 ea w/contents
China sugar jars 4 each containing 5 small jars and 5 sets ea. 5 barrel jars	Pohing	3.00 ea .50 ea .75/set	
China sugar jars 3 each containing 10 sets of 5 jelly jars	Pohing	3.00 ea .75/set	
China sugar jar 1 containing 30 toilet bottle holders	Pohing	3.00 ea 1.50 doz	27.50 jar & contents

ITEMS BY CATEGORY	SUPPLIER	INVOICE COST IN CHINA	AUCTION PRICE IN SAN FRANCISCO
China sugar jar			
2	Pohing	3.00 ea	32.50 jar & contents
each containing			
1 pr small vases		2.50 pr	
1 pr vases		1.25 pr	
China sugar jars			
2	Pohing	3.00 ea	
each containing			
1 pr small vases		2.50 pr	
China sugar jars			
2	Pohing	22.00 all	
each containing			
1 teaset yellow & gold			
12 2nd size plates			
1 butter plate			
1 teapot			
1 bowl			
1 coffeepot			
1 milkpot			
1 sugar			
12 teacups and saucers			
12 coffee cups and saucers			
China sugar jar containing part of above	Pohing	3.00 ea	
SCALES & WEIGHTS	Comprador		
3 sets No. 1 ea. with the following weights 1 oz, 2 oz, 4 oz, 5 oz, 8 oz, 10 oz, 1-lb, 5-lb		4.80 set	2 @$40.00; 1 @$30.00 set
5 sets No. 3 ea. same as No. 1, excepting 5-lb weight		3.40 set	29.50 set
4 sets No. 2 same weights as No. 1		4.70 set	37.50 set
LOGARITHM TABLES	S. W. Williams		
1 bundle cont'g 30 tables		5.00 bundle	

ITEMS BY CATEGORY	SUPPLIER	INVOICE COST IN CHINA	AUCTION PRICE IN SAN FRANCISCO
WHITE LEAD (DRY)	E. H. Faucon		
25 kegs ea 28 lbs		96.25 all	56.25
GUTTA PERCHA	Bought in Singapore		
Buckets (36 doz)		4.50 doz	12.50 doz
Bowls (5 doz)		2.50 doz	5.50 doz
FOODS			
Preserves 100 boxes (ea. box has 6 jars: 2 jars ea of ginger, kumquat, and citron)	Chy loong	4.00 box	10.00–12.25 box
Raisins (Malaga) 50 boxes	Saoqua	2.00 box	
Rice (50 bags)			7.25 bag
Peas (148 bags)			3.50 bag
Dates (7 kegs)			5.75 keg
Pickles (18 doz)			17.50 doz
Prunes (23 tins)			1.85 tin
Sugar (163 bags @66 lb each equals 10,758 lbs)			.19 per lb
Chocolate 5 cases each w/ 4 tins @25 lb each equals 500 lbs			.60 per lb
10 cases (total 1,000 lbs)			.50 lb
Soy (23 boxes)			6.00 box
Sardines small tins (3 cases @100 tins: total 300 tins or 25 doz)			17.00 doz
large tins (4 cases @50 tins: total 200 tins or 16.66 doz)			29.50 doz
BEVERAGES			
Tea 15.13 piculs Fine Caper Tea Curious Oolong Flowery O. Pekoe Y. Hyson	Zenqua	381.01 all	

ITEMS BY CATEGORY	SUPPLIER	INVOICE COST IN CHINA	AUCTION PRICE IN SAN FRANCISCO
Pale ale			
33.5 cases @6 doz/case equals 201 doz or 2,412 bottles			5.25 doz
Port wine			
4 cases @6 doz/case equals 24 doz or 288 bottles			7.25 doz
Sherry wine			
4 cases @6 doz/case equals 24 doz or 288 bottles			6.25 doz
MATTING (RED CHECK)	Goqua		
50 rolls of 4/4 (1,000 yds)		.11/yd	
50 rolls of 6/4 (1,000 yds)		.14/yd	
SLIPPERS			
Embroidered slippers			
440 prs (blue, black, brown, green, red)	Chuen hing	.80 pr	
Satin slippers			
16 doz (black, dk. blue, lt. blue, coffee)	Chuen hing	5.10 doz	
PATENT LEATHER BOOTS			
52 prs (Nos. 1, 2, 3)	Chuen hing	4.00 pr	
BLANKETS			
30 pr (white, green, scarlet)	R. McGregor	6.75 pr	
25 pr (green, blue, scarlet, white)	R. McGregor	5.00 pr	13.00 pr

ITEMS BY CATEGORY	SUPPLIER	INVOICE COST IN CHINA	AUCTION PRICE IN SAN FRANCISCO
DRESSING GOWNS	Pody		
12 men's (brn fig'd silk, red lined)		10.00 ea	
6 women's (same as above)		10.00 ea	
6 women's (blue, lined with red)		8.00 ea	
12 child's (same as above)		6.50 ea	
12 child's (brn, lined with red)		8.50 ea	
COTTON SHIRTS	Ahoy		
50 doz		7.50 doz	
50 doz (linen collars, bosoms, and cuffs)		15.00 doz	
CAMLET JACKETS	Ahoy		
75 (single breasted, pockets at sides)		3.50 ea	
CAPS	Ahoy		
Chinese caps 2 doz (chowchow gold crape w/ knob on top, bound w/ blk velvet)		.60 ea	
English pattern 8 doz (blue, black)		1.25 ea	
VESTS	Ahoy		
202 vests sizes (No. 1, 2, 3): variously double and single breasted, with straight or rolling collars; variously in black satin; fig'd satin green flower; white satin figured with coffee or blue; spotted coffee col'd silk; black velvet; dark figured velvet; Scotch plaid		1.50–2.00 ea (avg. 1.80 ea)	

ITEMS BY CATEGORY	SUPPLIER	INVOICE COST IN CHINA	AUCTION PRICE IN SAN FRANCISCO
HANDKERCHIEFS	Dong cheong		
Black & blue checked			
satin		12.25 pkg	
10 pkg of 20			
Chowchow col'd women's			
1 pkg of 20		8.00 pkg	
1 pkg of 20		4.50 pkg	
SILK STOCKINGS (WOMEN'S)	Dong cheong		
6 doz		9.00 doz	
ITEMS NOT SOLD			
2 marble top tables, square			
1 long couch			
4 wardrobes			
1 lacquered work table			
5 cases lacquered cabinets with work tables			
2 cases Japanned ware			
2 boxes candles			
1 bag sugar			
47 bags rice			

Invoices for Purchase of the Cargo of the 'Eveline' in China

The Leese Scrapbook contained five itemized invoices (two for silks, three for merchandise) from Augustine Heard & Company, dated August 22 and 23, 1849, to Jacob P. Leese and Thomas O. Larkin for goods shipped aboard the *Eveline*. In parallel columns, these invoices listed the following: marks and number on each cargo box; number of cases per box; number of pieces per case; total number of pieces; length, width, and sometimes weight per piece; description of piece, including colors; seller; price per unit; and total price. I have transcribed three invoices (two for silks and one for merchandise) to provide a more detailed glimpse of the cargo items listed in Appendix A. The original titles for each of these three invoices have been edited. In the table, parenthetical references appear as they do on the original invoices; bracketed references are my own clarifications. I have also deleted some detail for clarity—some colors and most fabric dimensions. For many textile entries it was unclear whether length referred to the individual piece or to the total length of the entire lot. Researchers studying Chinese textiles should consult the originals in the Leese Scrapbook at the Society of California Pioneers.

INVOICE FOR 43 CASES OF SILKS SUPPLIED BY WONGSHING
SHIPPED BY AUGUSTINE HEARD & COMPANY PER BRIG 'EVELINE'
JULY 22, 1849

CHARGES	11,260.50	Silk
	6.93	Freight to Hongkong
	2.25	Shroffage
	450.42	Commissions 4%
	11,720.10	Total

Plain sarsnets	45 prs	6.80 pr
	(scarlet, green, dk blue, black, pink)	
Figured camlets	120	16.75 ea
	(med blue, cinnamon blk, lt lilac,	
	dk coffee, fawn, brown)	
Striped silks	18	18.00 ea
	(lt blue lilac, lt lilac, straw, lt green	
	& silver grey, pink)	
Silk parasols:	72	2.25 ea
tortoise shell staff,	(straw, pink & white, brown, dk lilac,	
ivory handles & lots	lt blue & lilac, lt green & lilac)	
of chowchow fringe		
Velvet	20 pieces	14.00 ea
	(blk, green, crimson, blue, dk blue,	
	claret)	
	10 pieces	24.00 ea
	(crimson, blk, claret)	
Satins	5	1.00 yd
	(96 yds tot.)	
	(blk, brown, coffee, silver grey)	
Embroidered		
crape shawls	10	16.40 ea
	black chowchow flower	
	white white flower	
	coffee white flower	
	coffee chowchow flower	
	white white flower	
Embroidered aprons	3	1.50 ea
	(brown chowchow)	
Silk gause	24	15.00 ea
	black fig'd satin ground,	
	black g'ze stripe	
	lilac fig'd satin ground,	
	white g'ze stripe	
	green fig'd satin ground,	
	lilac g'ze stripe	
	pink fig'd satin ground,	
	lilac g'ze stripe	
	blue fig'd satin ground,	
	white g'ze stripe	
	straw fig'd satin ground,	
	green g'ze stripe	

Striped silks	75 [10 color combinations]	18.00 ea
Plain sarsnets	35 [5 colors]	6.80 ea
Plain black satins	25	10.00 ea
Silk gause	50 [12 color combinations]	15.00 ea
Changeable col'd silk dresses (each in a cartoon)	25 [5 color combinations]	11.00 ea
Satin damask	15 [2 colors]	13.50 ea
Check sarsnets	80	12.50 ea
Damask cr. scarfs	80 bundles of 6 [6 colors/bundle]	12.50 bundle
Check satin neck hdkfs	10 bundles of 20	14.00 bundle
Blk twilled silk hdkfs	20 bundles of 20	7.00 bundle
Col'd chk silk neck hdkfs with fringe	80 bundles of 20	4.60 bundle
Col'd fig'd silk neck hdkfs flowered border with fringe	20 bundles of 20	8.50 bundle
Check fig'd silk neck hdkfs French pattern	20 bundles of 20	14.00 bundle
Wh. fig'd twilled silk pocket hdkfs	10 bundles of 20	8.25 bundle
Damask silk shawl 11 in. fringe [each] one in a cartoon	25 [5 colors]	4.00 ea
Emb'd coverleds 8 in. chowchow col'd fringe	6 [6 color combinations]	45.00 ea
Fig'd camlets changeable colors [9 colors]	75	18.00 ea

INVOICE FOR 60 CASES OF SILKS SUPPLIED BY LIN HING
SHIPPED BY AUGUSTINE HEARD & CO. PER BRIG 'EVELINE'
JULY 22, 1849

CHARGES		
	11,003.26	Silk
	4.80	Freight to Hongkong
	2.20	Shroffage
	440.13	Commissions 4%
	11,450.39	Total

Emb'd crape shawls,	13 [7 color combinations]	60.00 ea
all emb'd opposite	13 [7 color combinations]	50.00 ea
corners, 72 in. wide,		
10 in. fringe, each		
in laq'd box		
Emb'd crape shawls,	26	30.00 ea
63 in. wide,	13	10.00 ea
12 in. fringe, same as		
above in cartoons		
instead of laq'd box		
Emb'd crape shawls,	72 [8 color combinations]	20.00 ea
72 in. wide,		
10 in. fringe, emb'd		
corners & borders,		
plain centres except		
a sprig or flower		
scattered over them,		
each in cartoon		
Crape shawls as above,	72	5.00 ea
54 in. wide,		
8 in. fringe		
Crape shawls as above,	72	10.00 ea
63 in. wide,		
10 in. fringe		
Emb'd crape shawls,	120 [10 color combinations]	5.00 ea
40 in. wide,		
8 in. fringe, emb'd		
ground borders		
& corners		
Emb'd crape shawls	120	3.00 ea
as above, 7 in. fringe		
Dasmask crape shawls,	120 [6 colors]	2.00–2.60 ea
63 in. wide, 7 in. fringe		
[10 per cartoon]		
Damask crape shawls,	240 [200 chowchow, 40 scarlet]	1.50–2.27 ea
63 in wide, like above		
Crape shawls,	360 [5 colors]	1.49 ea
33 in. wide,		
6 in fringe, thin single		
crape, bunch of flowers		
emb'd in each corner in		
floss silk, chowchow		
colors [6 per cartoon]		

Satin aprons, 36 in. long, emb'd chowchow	120 [4 colors per cartoon]	1.90 ea
Officers silk net bandas with silk ball & tassels, each in a cartoon	18 [3 colors]	3.60–3.80 ea
Silk cords and tassels for ladies waists, each in a cartoon	18 [3 colors]	1.15 ea
Crape bandas, 8 in. fringe, damasked with a bunch of flowers emb'd at each end in chowchow colors	432 [6 color combinations]	1.65 ea
Damask crape bandas, 8 in. fringe	432 [6 colors]	.73 ea (approx.)
Fine sewing silk No. 1 assortment of 11 colors per 1 lb grouping	50 lbs	3.35 lb
Same as above but with larger assortment of colors	25 lbs	3.55 lb
Sewing silk No. 3 largest, same as above	25 lbs	3.55 lb
Floss silk, chowchow colors	100 skeens one paper	3.65 skeen
Satin damask	9 @27 yds [3 colors]	26.80–29.80 ea
Ladies changeable silk neck hdkfs	12 doz [4 colors]	11.95 doz
Mens check silk neck hdkfs, 3 different patterns	12 doz	10.20 doz
Gents black lutestring hdkfs, corded border	12 doz	6.60 doz
Same as above	12 doz [lighter weight]	5.25 doz
Ladies fancy silk ball dresses (2 Rose, 2 Nankeen)	4	36.00 ea
Saya saya	12 [2 colors]	5.85–7.65 ea
Plain Canton satins	20 cases @60 each [5 colors]	12.25–13.25 case

| Changeable silks,
two or three
different patterns
all shaded wh. | 30 cases @18.65 ea
[10 items, each a different
color per case] | | 18.65 case |

CHARGES	10,653.36	Goods	
	5.47	Freight to Hongkong	
	2.25	Duties on 2 cases	
	345.00	Insurance on 11,500 @3%	
	2.00	Fee on insurance	
	426.13	Commission 4%	
	11,434.21	Total	

Crimson lutestring neck hdkfs, chowchow col'd borders	25 pkgs of 20	Lin hing	6.85 pkg
White lutestring neck hdkfs, chowchow col'd borders	25 pkgs of 20	Lin hing	5.75 pkg
Black satin neck hdkfs	28 pkgs of 20	Lin hing	11.35 pkg
Blk Synchew hdkfs	25 pkg of 20	Lin hing	8.06 pkg
Crimson fig'd pongee hdkfs	25 pkg of 20	Lin hing	5.00 pkg
Check sarsnets different patterns	50	Lin hing	6.90 ea
Figured satins	8 [2 color patterns]	Lin hing	23.00 ea
Black levantines	25	Lin hing	8.40 ea
Sewing silk in 1 lb bundles	51 lbs [6 colors]	Lin hing	2.96–3.30 lb
Same as above [5 colors]	29 lbs	Lin hing	3.30 lb
Silk gauze (white, white flower; green, green flower)	25	Lin hing	3.75 ea
Flowered satin dresses (white, rose, sky blue, lilac)	7	Lin hing	11.25 ea

Cotton & silk check	24	Lin hing	4.00 ea
Plain satins [approx. 14 colors]	80	Lin hing	11.15–13.35 ea
Striped silk [approx. 10 colors]	60	Wonshing	17.65 ea
Figured camlets [approx. 12 colors]	50	Wonshing	16.40 ea
Damask silk shawls, 11 in. fringe	32	Wonshing	3.75 ea
Silk camlet shawls, 11 in. fringe	60	Wonshing	6.75 ea
Sarsnets hdkfs, blue & white check	5 pkgs of 20	Wonshing	11.00 pkg
Sarsnets hdkfs, chowchow check	93 pkg of 20	Wonshing	3.50–5.40 pkg
Plain scarlet Canton crapes	100	Old Yeeshing	7.40 ea
Crimson crape bandas	1,000 [2 colors]	Old Yeeshing	.76–.78 ea
Emb'd crape shawls, 11 in. fringe, 1 per cartoon	12 [6 color combinations]	Old Yeeshing	25.00 ea
Same as above	12 [5 color combinations]	Old Yeeshing	48.00 ea
Plain satins, assorted colors	25 [4 colors]	Old Yeeshing	23.00 ea
Silk muslin	48 [12 color combinations]	Yeng foong	7.75 ea
Chowchow colored crape scarfs	1,440	A.R.B. Moses	.47 ea
Black satin neck hdkfs	30 pkgs of 20	Linhing	8.60 pkg
Emb'd silk bags with silk fringe, one per cartoon	24	Wonshing	3.25 pkg

Bill of Lading for the Final Cargo of the 'Frolic,' Canton, May 30, 1850

Courtesy Baker Library,
Harvard Business School

Shipped *in good order and condition, by Augustine Heard & Co.*

on board the good Brig *called the* "Frolic" *whereof* E. H. Faucon *is Master for this present voyage, now lying at* Whampoa *and bound for* San Francisco *to say*

F. Nos 1 @ 4	4 cases	Paintings
5 @ 34	30 do	Lacq'd ware
35 @ 43	9 do	Scales & weights
44. 45. 46. 47. 48. 49		
200. 134. 100. 167. 34. 41	676 Rolls	Chinaware
50 @ 69	20 cases	do
70. 71		
1. 5	6 do	Mdse
72	1 do	Silver ware
73. 74. 75. 76. 77		
7. 7. 7. 7. 2	30 do	Camphor trunks
78 @ 86	9 do	Mdse
87 @ 91	5 do	do
92. 93. 94. 95. 96. 97. 98. 99. 100. 101. 102		
3. 2. 2. 2. 3. 1. 2. 2. 2. 3. 2		
103. 104. 105. 106. 107. 108. 109. 110. 111. 112. 115		
2. 2. 2. 2. 3. 2. 2. 2. 3. 5. 10	54 do	Furniture
113 & 114	2 do	Silver ware
116	100 boxes	Sweetmeats
117. 118. 119. 120		
24. 20. 30. 100	174 pkgs	Sundries
121	84 cases	Beer
H. 1. 2		
32. 1	33 pkgs	Mdse
A H & Co. 1 @ 3	3 cases	do
	1240	

One thousand two hundred & forty packages Mdse

being marked and numbered as in the margin, and are to be delivered in the like good order and condition, at the aforesaid Port of San Francisco *the dangers of the seas only excepted, unto* J. C. Anthon Esq. C or E. H. Faucon Esq

or Assigns, he or they paying freight for the said Goods. As per agreement *without Primage and average accustomed.* **In Witness Whereof** *the Master of the said Vessel hath affirmed to* 4 *Bills of Lading, all of this tenor and date, one of which being accomplished, the others to stand void.*

Dated at Canton *this* 30th *day of* May 1850

Measurement:
86 Tons 19 feet
at $
Total $

E. H. Faucon

Shipped *in good order and condition, by Augustine Heard & Co.*

on board the good Brig *called the* "Frolic"
whereof E. H. Faucon *is Master for this
present voyage, now lying at* Whampoa *and bound for*
San Francisco *To say*

M

1	pkg	contg	4 outside doors
1	"	"	8 Oyster sh'd windows
3	"	"	12 do do
17	"	"	74 Planks
3	"	"	24 Beams
1	"	"	16 Boards
10	"	"	40 Planks
10	"	"	40 Beams
9	"	"	40 do
3	"	"	8 Columns
24	"	"	96 Planks
4	"	"	21 Beams
14	"	"	54 do
1	"	"	16 Boards
1	"	"	Ironware

101

One hundred and one packages of Merchandise *being marked and numbered as in the margin, and are to be delivered
in the like good order and condition, at the aforesaid Port of*
San Francisco *the dangers of the seas only
excepted, unto* J. C. Anthon Esq { and or } E. H. Faucon Esq

Measurement
30 Tons feet
at $
Total $

or Assigns, he or they paying freight for the said Goods
as per agreement
without Primage and average accustomed. **In Witness Whereof** *the
Master of the said Vessel hath affirmed to* 4 *Bills of Lading, all
of this tenor and date; one of which being accomplished, the others
to stand void.*
Dated at Canton *this* 30th *day of* May 1850

E. H. Faucon

Shipped *in good order and condition, by Augustine Heard & Co*

on board the good Brig *called the* "Frolic"
whereof E. H. Faucon *is Master for this
present voyage, now lying at* Whampoa *and bound for*
San Francisco *To say:*

7 S Nos.

1.	2.	3.	4.	5.	6.	7.	8.	9.	10
1.	1.	1.	1.	2.	3.	1.	4.	3.	4

11.	12.	13.	14.	15.	16.	17.	18.	19
4.	8.	5.	1.	1.	1.	1.	3.	1

20. 21. 22. 23. 24. 25. 26. 27. 28. 29. 30
1.   1.   1.   1.   1.   1.   1.   3.   1.   1.   1

31. 32. 33. 34. 35. 36. 37. 38. 39. 40. 41
1.   2.   1.   3.   1.   1.   1.   1.   1.   3.   1

42. 43. 44. 45. 46. 47. 48. 49. 50. 51. 64. 65
1.   2.   2.   1.   1.   1.   1.   2.   3.   1.   1.   1   243 cases Silks

66. 67. 68. 69. 70. 71. 72. 73. 74. 75. 76. 77. 78
30. 12. 10. 10. 8. 2. 1. 1. 1. 1. 1. 3. 1

79. 80. 81. 82. 83. 84. 85. 86. 87. 88. 89. 90. 91
1. 1. 1. 1. 1. 1. 1. 4. 2. 1. 6. 2. 2

92. 93. 94. 95. 96. 97. 98. 99. 100. 101. 102. 103
4. 4. 4. 4. 4. 4. 1. 1.   1.   1.   1.   1

104. 105. 106. 107. 108. 109. 110. 111. 112. 113
2.   4.   1.   1.   1.   1.   1.   1.   1.   2

52. 53. 54. 55. 56. 57. 58. 59. 60
1. 1. 4. 4. 1. 1. 1. 1. 1
61. 62. 63
1. 1. 1.   18 cases Grass cloth

                                                            261

Two hundred and Sixty one packages Merchandise

*being marked and numbered as in the margin, and are to be delivered
in the like good order and condition at the aforesaid Port of*
San Francisco *the dangers of the seas only
excepted unto* J. C. Anthon Esq *(and)* E. H. Faucon Esq *or*

Measurement
19 Tons 28 feet
at $

Total $

or Assigns, he or they paying freight for the said Goods,
            as per agreement
without Primage and average accustomed In Witness Whereof *the
Master of the said Vessel hath affirmed to* 4 *Bills of Lading, all
of this tenor and date, one of which being accomplished, the others
to stand void.*
Dated at Canton *this* *day of* May 1850

E. H. Faucon

Reference Matter

Notes

Abbreviations

Heard 1   Heard Collection, Part One
Heard 2   Heard Collection, Part Two

Heard 1 and Heard 2 are archived at Baker Library, Harvard University Graduate School of Business Administration, Boston, Mass.

Prologue

1. I have told the story of the *Frolic*'s construction in 1844 at Fells Point in Baltimore and of her subsequent life in the opium trade in an earlier volume entitled *The Voyage of the 'Frolic.'*

2. Layton, *Western Pomo Prehistory*. This monograph, containing seventy-four tables of artifact measurements and locational data, as well as seventy-five pages of maps, charts, and artifact drawings, was written for a small audience of professional archaeologists and is virtually unavailable to the public. The description of our work at Three Chop Village was confined to chapter 4.

3. Jones.

4. Edward Horatio Faucon (1806–94) served as captain of the *Frolic* throughout her entire life (1844–50). In 1829 he began his career as a ship's officer in the California hide-and-tallow trade, where his skills and character were immortalized by Richard Henry Dana, Jr., in *Two Years Before the Mast*. Faucon entered the China trade in 1838.

5. Edward Faucon (Singapore) to Augustine Heard & Company (Canton), March 2, 1846, Heard 2, S18, F14.

6. John Hurd Everett (1810–89), Captain Faucon's closest friend, began

his career as a merchant in 1829 in the California hide-and-tallow trade—serving on the same vessels as Faucon. Everett remained in the hide-and-tallow trade until 1844. He followed Faucon to China in 1846 to become a fellow employee at Augustine Heard & Company.

7. Thomas Oliver Larkin (1802–58) came to California in 1832 where he became a close friend of fellow trader John H. Everett. By the early 1840s Larkin was northern California's premier merchant and financier. In 1844 he was appointed Consul of the United States to Mexican California.

8. Jacob Primer Leese (1809–90) came to California in 1833. He opened a store in Yerba Buena, now San Francisco, in 1836. Following his 1837 marriage to Rosalía Vallejo, the sister of General Mariano Guadalupe Vallejo, he acquired tracts of land north of the San Francisco Bay. By 1849 he was a wealthy merchant with close ties to Thomas O. Larkin. Rosalía Vallejo Leese's sister, Encarnación, was the wife of Captain John B. R. Cooper, Larkin's half-brother.

Chapter 1

1. Shangraw and Von der Porten.

2. The Jerome B. Ford diary is now lost. These details come to us as remembered by his son Jerome Chester Ford in 1933 and quoted in Bear and Stebbins, p. 9.

3. Augustine Heard & Company, bills of lading for *Frolic* (Canton), May 30, 1850, Heard 2, S18, F12.

4. John H. Everett (Canton), orders to comprador to pay, April–June 1850, Heard 2, S18, F9.

5. George Parker Armstrong was locally known as John Parker. His ranch was situated near the location of modern-day Ukiah. In 1850 it was the northernmost residence of a Euro-American in the Russian River Valley.

6. Heizer, p. 15.

7. John Heard (Canton) to Augustine Heard (Boston), March 23, 1850, Heard 1, EM 5-3.

8. Augustine Heard & Company, bills of lading for *Eveline* (Hong Kong), August 3, 1849, Heard 2, S5.

9. Hammond, vol. 8, pp. 96–97, 138–39.

10. Thomas Larkin (Monterey) to Jacob Leese, February 15, 1849, in Hammond, vol. 8, pp. 149–50.

11. Jacob Leese (Hong Kong) to Thomas Larkin (Monterey), August 4, 1849, in Hammond, vol. 8, p. 253.

12. "Leese Scrapbook," p. 37.

13. Information from the invoices documenting the purchase of the *Eveline*'s cargo in China and the auction sale proceeds in San Francisco are tabulated in Appendix A.

14. See, for example, Forbes, Kernan, and Watkins.

15. Williams, *Chinese Commercial Guide* (1863), p. 148.

16. For biographical information on John Hurd Everett, see Layton, *The Voyage of the Frolic*, pp. 117–27.

17. John H. Everett (Yerba Buena) to Thomas Larkin (Monterey), July 13, 1844, in Hammond, vol. 2, pp. 166–67.

Chapter 2

1. Hammond, vol. 2, pp. 166–67, 173, 178–79.

2. In the fictionalized vignettes presented throughout Chapters 2–5, I have attempted to interpolate between known facts in order to bring life to the commercial relationships surrounding the cargo of the *Frolic* and its loss. For each of these chapters I have written an extended endnote explaining what is fiction and what is not. The vignettes that follow, taking John H. Everett from Monterey to Yerba Buena to Pueblo San José, are based on his correspondence with Thomas O. Larkin, preserved in Hammond's edition of *The Larkin Papers*.

The Monterey vignette takes place at a time when Thomas Larkin and his family were recovering from smallpox. Larkin is believed to have brought smallpox to Monterey on his return from a business trip to Mexico in April of 1844. Larkin, his wife, three children, and four Indian servants were all infected (see letter from Nathan Spear [Yerba Buena] to Larkin, June 1, 1844, in Hammond, vol. 2, pp. 134–35). For the vaccination process, see Charles M. Weber (Pueblo San José) to Talbot H. Green, June 23, 1844, in Hammond, vol. 2, p. 143. Also see Hague and Langum, p. 53.

For the Yerba Buena vignette, I place Everett in the house of Jacob Leese. This seems possible because Everett's July 13 letter from Yerba Buena to Larkin in Monterey mentions that the day before, Jacob Leese had handed him a letter from Larkin. For a description of Everett's problems with Eaton & Company, see Ogden, "Boston Hide Droghers Along California Shores," p. 297.

Everett's trip to Pueblo San José to collect debts is documented in his letters. The vignette is constructed to describe the exchange of New England manufactured goods for hides and tallow. Alcalde Don Antonio María Pico and Thomas Bowen are historical figures, but Everett's meeting with the *alcalde* is fiction, as is his trip down the Monterey Road to collect from Thomas Bowen. John Charles Frémont described Tom Bowen as "a drunken vagabond about Pueblo San José" (Hammond, vol. 5, p. 256). Bowen's distillery is mentioned in Bancroft, p. 66. Everett's contempt for the accuracy of Richard Henry Dana, Jr.'s, descriptions of California in *Two Years Before the Mast* is recorded as marginalia in his personal annotated copy, now owned by the Bancroft Library, University of California, Berkeley (see Bliss, pp. 6–7).

Everett's romantic interest in a Miss Bandini is mentioned by Alfred Robinson (New York) in a letter to Thomas O. Larkin (Monterey), September 28, 1844 (in Hammond, vol. 2, p. 243). This was Ysidora Bandini. During his final visit to California, twenty-nine years later, Everett wrote to Ysidora's husband, "It is something like forty years since I have last seen your wife & as this is probably my last visit to California it would give me much pleasure to renew an old acquaintance & have a chat about los tiempos pasados" (John H. Everett [San Diego] to Col. S. Couts [Guajome], April 1, 1873, in Abel Stearns Collection, Huntington Library, San Marino). For a description of thousands of burrowing squirrels living in the main plaza of Pueblo San José in 1846, see Bryant, p. 316. Everett's deep affection for Pueblo San José is best expressed in his own words: " . . . here the payments are mighty slow & was it not that the Jugado has no force I would sue the whole bunch of them. Excuse this scrawl as neither pen paper nor place is to my liking" (John H. Everett [Pueblo San José] to Thomas O. Larkin [Monterey], July 26, 1844, in Hammond, vol. 2, p. 179).

3. The *Tasso* departed Boston on January 11, 1841, with John H. Everett as supercargo and Samuel J. Hastings, captain. She departed California on January 8, 1844, arriving at Boston on June 1, 1844. Her California-bound cargo of Boston goods was valued at $15,996 at the Monterey customs office. *Tasso's* outbound cargo included 18,000 cowhides, horns, tallow, and otter skins, and 24,000 pounds of whalebone—probably for corset stays. For a summary of the *Tasso's* 1841–44 voyage, see Adele Ogden's magnificent unpublished compendium of California maritime commerce prior to the Gold Rush, "Trading Vessels on the California Coast: 1787–1848," pp. 992–96. For a discussion of the hide-and-tallow trade, including the *Tasso's* 1841–44 venture, see Ogden, "Boston Hide Droghers Along California Shores," p. 279.

Chapter 3

1. John H. Everett (Boston) to Thomas O. Larkin (Monterey), March 23, 1845, in Hammond, vol. 3, pp. 88–90.

2. John H. Everett (Boston) to Thomas O. Larkin (Monterey), September 1, 1845, in Hammond, vol. 3, pp. 333–34.

3. John H. Everett (Boston) to Thomas O. Larkin (Monterey), April 26, 1846, in Hammond, vol. 4, pp. 349–51.

4. John H. Everett (Canton) to Thomas O. Larkin (Monterey), September 16, 1847, in Hammond, vol. 6, pp. 319–20.

5. John Heard (Canton) to Augustine Heard (Boston), May 20, 1849, Heard 1, EM 5-2.

6. Jacob Leese (Honolulu) to Thomas O. Larkin (Monterey), March 20, 1849, in Hammond, vol. 8, pp. 181–82. See also cargo auction advertisements in the *Daily Alta California* (San Francisco): for the *Emmy*, May 24, 1849; for the *Corréo de Cobija*, June 28, 1849; for the *Rhone*, August 4, 1849. For dif-

ficulties in procuring a cargo for the *Eveline*, see Jacob Leese (Hong Kong) to Thomas O. Larkin (Monterey), August 5, 1849, in "Leese Scrapbook," pp. 33–34.

7. For a biography of Capt. Juan Bautista Rogers Cooper, see Bry, pp. 1–12. For a description of Thomas O. Larkin's captivity during the Bear Flag Revolt, see Hague and Langum, pp. 136–55. For a description of Mariano Vallejo's losses during the Bear Flag Revolt, see Mariano G. Vallejo (Sonoma) to Thomas O. Larkin (Monterey), September 15, 1846, in Hammond, vol. 5, pp. 236–37.

8. I discovered Tingqua's picture of his shop in Crossman, p. 186, color plate 64. The picture of Tingqua's shop illustrated here is owned by Richard Kelton, who has generously allowed its reproduction, as Figure 18, in this volume. The fact that Tingqua had supplied "pictures" for the *Frolic*'s cargo in 1850 suggested to me that John Everett may have had earlier dealings with him. It seemed that John Everett's sitting for a portrait by Tingqua would be a good device to introduce a shopping trip with Leese to purchase part of the *Eveline*'s cargo.

9. This conversation between Everett and Tingqua would have been in pidgin (China jargon), the simplified commercial language in which Westerners and Chinese conducted business. China jargon developed following the Portuguese settlement at Macao in the mid–sixteenth century. Since the Portuguese commercial world included India, this pidgin originally comprised words taken from Portuguese, Chinese, and the Indian languages spoken near Portuguese settlements along the west coast of India. The resulting trade language was already well developed by the mid–eighteenth century when the British began active trade with China. By the mid–nineteenth century, the pidgin, or China jargon, spoken by the British and Americans at Canton had English vocabulary as its predominant ingredient. For discussions of pidgin, see "An Old Resident" [William C. Hunter], pp. 36–39, and Spence, p. 8.

Initially, I attempted to write the dialogue between Everett and the various Chinese merchants in pidgin. Not only was this good-faith effort crippled by lack of a word list sufficient to cover the conversation topics, but the resulting dialogue sounded much like the impossibly racist "heathen Chinee" stories of the last century. Moreover, several Chinese-American colleagues found my version of pidgin to be offensive. So, finally, I submitted to the inevitable and translated the words spoken by Everett and Chinese merchants into a slightly awkward English.

10. Although the "Canton system" restricting Westerners to the factories ended with the Treaty of Nanking in 1842, ambiguities in the treaty text and local resistance kept Westerners out of Canton proper. Indeed, on April 14, 1849, the Emperor had instructed his governor-general and governor not to let the British enter the city (Wakeman, *Strangers at the Gate*, pp. 102–3).

11. This particular painting (artist unknown), reproduced by Crossman (p. 434, fig. 22), shows the factories as they appeared between 1847 and 1856. During this period the Heard firm occupied the site of the Old Dutch factory, sharing the building with Jardine Matheson & Company. The patrol boat illustrated has twenty-six oars.

12. John H. Everett (Canton), order for comprador to pay Tinqua $87.50 for pictures a/c *Frolic*, April 9, 1850, Heard 2, S18, F9.

13. That Tingqua drawing of San Francisco is now owned by Richard Kelton, who has allowed its reproduction as Figure 12 in this volume.

14. Everett's meeting with Pohing is my invention, but the items discussed were all supplied by Pohing for the *Eveline*'s cargo. The description of the beggar was taken from Tiffany, pp. 42–43. I have used many details from Tiffany, particularly relating to shopping and life in Canton, to add color to vignettes throughout this book. Although Tiffany was only in Canton for four months during 1844, and did not speak the language, his descriptions are particularly useful, as they were made within five years of the events that I describe.

15. Invoice, N. Gilbert (Canton) to Augustine Heard & Company (Canton), for Edinburgh ale, for bottling, and for packing cases, May 23, 1850, Heard 2, S18, F6.

16. High-quality silks were produced in a district slightly southeast of Shanghai. By the late 1840s, Canton, far from this center of manufacture, was not able to respond quickly to changes in the market. Because of sudden fluctuations in supply and demand, this was an awkward period for both importers and exporters. Indeed, in 1849 members of the Canton textile hong had cut off all trade with the English—the woolen dealers on February 26 and the cotton dealers on March 3 (Wakeman, *Strangers at the Gate*, pp. 100–101).

17. On August 5, 1849, as he prepared to depart China, Leese alluded to his Canton shopping experience in a letter to Thomas Larkin: "You will no doubt be surprised at the length of time which has elapsed since my arrival here and time of departure, but a stranger in this place encounters so many difficulties in procuring a cargo, that I am fortunate in getting off as I have done. Time does not permit of my going into full particulars, but when we meet, I will give you my opinion at length about China and the style of conducting business here. Suffice it to say that my Canton cargo was upwards of 60 days in preparing, being obliged to have everything manufactured" ("Leese Scrapbook," p. 33).

18. The merchants Woushing, Ahoy, and Ashoe are real, and all of the items described were supplied by them for the *Eveline*. However, Everett's visits with these merchants are my invention. The awkward placement of India ink markings by Chinese launderers is taken from Tiffany, pp. 222–23. The description of Ashoe's furniture shop is taken from the illustration of such a shop in Cross-

man, p. 241, color plate 92 (reproduced herein as Fig. 20, courtesy of Cora Ginsburg). The atmosphere of Carpenters' Square is inspired by Tiffany, p. 78.

19. The merchants Laoqua, Gaoqua, Chyloong, and Wongshing supplied all of the items described for the *Eveline*. For a brief description of Chyloong's shop, see Tiffany, p. 77.

20. One partial set of this "plain fiddle"–pattern flatware, manufactured by Wongshing, has been passed down through the Vallejo family. The forks and spoons bear the engraved initials "MGV" for Mariano Guadalupe Vallejo. They are now curated by the California Department of Parks and Recreation at the Vallejo Home State Historic Park in Sonoma, California.

21. Jacob Leese (Hong Kong) to Thomas O. Larkin (Monterey), August 5, 1849; "Leese Scrapbook," pp. 33–34.

22. Although the farewell dinner honoring Leese and Cooper is my invention, such dinners were commonplace among the entertainment-starved merchants in Canton. John Heard's reasoning for loaning Brinley the capital to become a partner of Larkin and Leese is described in John Heard (Canton) to Augustine Heard (Boston), May 20, 1849, in Heard 1, EM 5-2. Brinley subsequently lost the money in bad investments.

Chapter 4

1. Kessressung Khooshalchund Company (Bombay) to Augustine Heard & Company (Canton), October 18, 1847, in Heard 2, LV11, F19.

2. Edward Faucon (Hong Kong), advanced wages for *Frolic* crews paid in 1848, August 10, 1848, in Heard 2, S18, F10.

3. John Heard (Canton) to Augustine Heard (Boston), August 15, 1849, in Heard 1, EM 5-2.

4. As John Heard expressed it, "We have not bought an article that did not pay 75% *clear profit* on the *Eveline*, while the average *profit* on the articles in her cargo that correspond to ours, was nearer 200%" (John Heard [Canton] to Augustine Heard [Boston], March 23, 1850, in Heard 1, EM 5-3).

5. We do not know, in fact, if Everett conceived the idea to send the Chinese-manufactured prefabricated house to San Francisco to receive the *Frolic*'s cargo. The dispatch of the house, the coolies, and J. C. Anthon aboard the *Stockholm* is mentioned in John Heard (Canton) to Augustine Heard (Boston), April 17, 1850, in Heard 1, EM 5-3. The house was delivered to San Francisco and assembled on a rented lot to await the arrival of the *Frolic*. The costs—from lighterage (transport of cargo from ship to shore) to ground rent—are itemized in G. L. Haskell (San Francisco) to Augustine Heard & Company (Canton), September 27, 1850, in Heard 2, Case 26, F9. The shares of investment in the *Frolic*'s cargo and the commissions to J. C. Anthon as supercargo and Faucon as assistant supercargo are detailed in John Heard (Canton) to Augustine

Heard (Boston), March 23, 1850, in Heard 1, EM 5-3. The description of the sale of the *Eveline*'s cargo in San Francisco—down to the details of the champagne, cheese, and crackers—is taken from "Account Sales of Merchandise received per Brig *Eveline*, Cooper Master, from Hong Kong, at Auction, November 20th, 22d, 23d & 24th 1849 by Lovering & Gay for Account of J. P. Leese," in "Leese Scrapbook."

6. Everett's hyperbole was somewhat disingenuous. He was correct in asserting that opium was the essential commodity by which the West balanced its trade with China. However, as Wakeman points out ("The Canton Trade and the Opium War," p. 173), by 1829 a balance of payments had been achieved, and by the time of this imagined conversation China had been a net exporter of silver for twenty years.

7. Everett's visit to Faucon aboard the *Lady Hayes*, the Heard's opium-receiving vessel at Cumsingmun, is my invention, a device to describe the conduct of the opium trade. Everett had ample opportunity to witness such activities during his years in China. The details of this particular shipment of 869 chests—the *Frolic*'s final cargo of opium—are taken from *Freight List of the Brig Frolic*, Capt. E. H. Faucon from Bombay to China, Kessressung Khooshalchund (Bombay) to Augustine Heard & Company (Canton), March 12, 1850, in Heard 2, S18, F13. The opium testing process is taken from Layton, *The Voyage of the 'Frolic,'* pp. 97–102.

8. Everett's trip with Faucon to Whampoa anchorage is my invention to describe the ambience aboard the *Frolic* during preparations for her departure to San Francisco, and to introduce Mariano Rosales, through whose eyes we will later see the wreck of the *Frolic* and the salvage of her cargo. We do not know that Mariano Rosales was the head serang; however, his name, with higher salary, does appear on crew lists. The *Frolic*'s provisions included 6 pigs and 216 birds: capons, fowls, geese, and pigeons. These and the rest of the provisions are listed in Edward Faucon (Canton) to Augustine Heard & Company (Canton), Portage and disbursement a/c of the *Frolic* 1850, November 11, 1850, in Heard 2, S18, F10. Mr. Harrison's monkey is my invention. The description of the glass deck lights illuminating Faucon's cabin are based on the lights recovered at the *Frolic* wreck site. Ahsig, Faucon's cabin boy, is my invention. For a discussion of the two chronometers, see Edward Faucon (San Francisco) to Augustine Heard & Company (Canton), August 5, 1850, in Heard 2, S18, F14. Faucon would marry Martha Weld on May 20, 1852, a year and a day after his return to Boston.

9. Although Everett's ledger of newspaper clippings for sales of China goods in San Francisco is my invention, all of the items mentioned, and all of the references to San Francisco ordinances and local events, were published in the *Daily Alta California* on the dates listed. Faucon's difficulties in replacing part of his crew are mentioned in Bush & Company (Hong Kong) to Augustine

Heard & Company (Canton), June 4 and June 6, 1850, in Heard 2, LV10, F5. The names Ahsing (for Everett's personal servant), Achen (for the Heard's comprador), and Sunkee (for their senior shroff) are all my inventions. For a description of the Canton Regatta and the *Amelia*, see John Heard's Diary, 1891, pp. 54–56. A typed transcription is on file at the Library of the Peabody Essex Museum, Salem, Mass. The Victoria Regatta Club competition of October 9–10, 1850, was announced in the *China Mail*, September 12, 1850. John Heard gave full credit to George Dixwell for developing the strategy in which the Heards used the proceeds from sale of their Indian clients' opium to purchase tea for their clients in the United States. This is described in John Heard (Canton) to Augustine Heard (Boston), November 25, 1846, in Heard 1, EM 4-4. Although the *Europa*'s cargo of teas is well documented, the replacement of her young hyson with oolong is my invention. The *China Mail*, October 31, 1850, reported the departure of the *Europa* from Whampoa for New York on October 20, 1850, carrying 250,000 pounds of tea—138,100 pounds of souchong and congou, 19,300 pounds of pouchong, and 82,600 pounds of oolong. Everett's nephew, Percival L. Everett (1833–1908), joined Augustine Heard & Company in 1853. He remained with the firm for eight years, in Hong Kong and Foochow. On his return to Boston he assumed the duties of special agent for the company. The Heards later claimed that Percy's activities as their Boston agent led to the bankruptcy of the firm in 1874. For an obituary, see the listing under "Percival Lowell Everett" in the New England Historic Genealogical Society *Register*, vol. 64, 1910, p. xlvi. For a full Everett family genealogy, see Edward Franklin Everett, *Descendants of Richard Everett of Dedham, Mass.* John Heard showed no regret on the loss of the *Frolic*. He wrote to his uncle, "The vessel is splendidly sold, as she is insured for $25,000, with freight, and was not worth $15,000" (John Heard [Canton] to Augustine Heard [Boston], October 25, 1850, in Heard 1, EM 5-3). The wreck of the *Frolic* is best described by Capt. Faucon himself, in Edward Faucon (San Francisco) to Augustine Heard & Company (Canton), August 5, 1850, in Heard 2, S18, F14. I have edited this letter for clarity—adding punctuation, spelling out abbreviated words, and deleting a few phrases containing details of sailing directions.

Chapter 5

1. This entire chapter is my invention. Our only description of the wreck is Faucon's letter to the owners and a shorter, notarized version prepared for the insurance companies. Faucon's letter states that he left six men aboard the *Frolic*, and when they landed on the beach they numbered twenty. Faucon, his two officers, four oarsmen, and a sick Lascar then pulled south for Fort Ross in one of the boats, leaving twelve men standing on the beach. Although we do know the names of Faucon's first and second officers for this voyage, we do not

know the names of the crew. I have assumed that the Lascars all came from Panaji in Goa, and that they served under a serang, or native boatswain. The names of Mariano Rosales and the other Lascars are taken from *Frolic* crew lists prior to this final voyage. The name of the Chinese cook, Alok, is taken from an August 10, 1848, listing of advanced wages. This listing also includes M. Rosales (Heard 2, S18, F10). The names that I have assigned to the helmsman and the sailmaker, Custodio and Valerio, are from Custodio Francisco and Valerio Fernandes, found together with Mariano Rosales on a July 28, 1849, listing of advanced wages signed by Captain Faucon (Heard 2, S18, F10). The final portage and disbursement account for the *Frolic* (Heard 2, S18, F10), dated November 11, 1850, specifies three months' advanced wages for one serang, one tindal, four sea cunnies, ten Lascars, one bandany, and one topas. A tindal acts as a deputy to the deck serang. A sea cunny is a helmsman. A bandany is a cook. A topas is employed in cleaning and may attend the livestock carried on board for feeding an Asian crew. Although these categories confirm Faucon's reliance on native crews, we cannot determine with certainty what part of this listing represents the crew dispatched for California. For clarity, I have referred to Panaji by its modern name rather than Panjim, the name used during the mid–nineteenth century. Mariano Rosales' dhow trip from India to Aden and down the coast of Africa is based on Indian Ocean commerce as described by Bowen, pp. 161–202. To reach John Parker's ranch, near modern-day Ukiah, the sailors would probably have crossed the Albion River and followed a trail along Navarro Ridge into the interior. My description of John Parker and "his" ranch (actually then owned by James Black of Sonoma) is based on Alfred Parsell's undated, typed manuscript, "John Parker and the Indians," part of the NYA Project, housed at the Ukiah Library. I infer Parker's participation in the salvage of *Frolic*'s cargo from the China trade goods seen by George Gibbs in Parker's house in 1851 (see "George Gibbs' Journal," in Heizer, p. 15). Pedrito, the Yokayo Pomo, is my invention, as is his discussion of food-gathering rights. Such rights were fiercely defended (see, for example, Loeb, p. 207). For a discussion of Pomo territorial boundaries, see McClendon and Oswalt, 281–85.

Chapter 6

1. For the early history of Pine Grove, Caspar, and the Point Cabrillo lighthouse, see Connor, *Caspar Calling*, and Connor, *The Golden Years of Caspar*.

2. Winn, pp. 16–17.

3. For the *Fearnot*'s log, see Edward H. Faucon, "Journals of Voyages: 1850–63," handwritten notebook, Massachusetts Historical Society, Boston.

4. For a description of this kind of logging, see Jackson. For a more general overview of logging along the Mendocino Coast, see Sullenberger. For a history of the Caspar Lumber Company, see Borden.

5. John H. Everett (San Francisco) to Abel Stearns (Los Angeles), May 24, 1871, in Abel Stearns Collection, Huntington Library, San Marino.

6. For Gorham P. Faucon's football career, see Blanchard, pp. 365–68.

7. Sullenberger, p. 90.

8. For John Heard's accusation of Percival Everett, see his "Diary," 1891, pp. 168–72, typed transcription on file at the Peabody Essex Museum, Salem. For a more balanced analysis of the decline of Augustine Heard & Company, see Lockwood, pp. 108–9.

9. The story of Miguel deFreitos and his descendants is taken from an oral history I took from his great-grandson, Louie Fratis of Fort Bragg, California. The descriptions of the activities of sport divers at the *Frolic* wreck site throughout the remainder of this chapter are derived from oral histories I took from Louie Fratis, Jim Kennon, Larry Pierson, Cliff Craft, David Buller, California Department of Parks and Recreation archaeologist John Foster, and former National Park Service archaeologist James Delgado. Transcripts of these interviews are on file at the Frolic Shipwreck Repository, Mendocino County Museum, Willits, California.

10. Palmer, pp. 398–99.

11. Sullenberger, p. 92.

12. Catherine W. Faucon (Milton, Mass.) to Julius H. Tuttle, librarian, Massachusetts Historical Society (Boston), October 5, 1928, in Faucon Collection, Massachusetts Historical Society, Boston.

13. Wurm, p. 114.

14. Von der Porten, p. 10.

15. Nash.

16. Marshall, p. 98.

Chapter 7

1. For Sacramento, see Praetzellis and Praetzellis, *Archaeological and Historical Studies of the IJ56 Block, Sacramento, California*; for Ventura, see Greenwood; for Riverside, see Great Basin Foundation.

2. Willets and Poh.

3. Patricia Hagen Jones' thesis presents a typology of the Chinese blue-on-white ceramics recovered from the *Frolic* shipwreck and traces similar ceramics around the Pacific Rim. She does not attempt to reconstruct the quantities carried aboard the *Frolic* or their increments of packaging.

4. For the balance of this chapter, I use information from the *Frolic*'s three-page bill of lading (Canton), May 30 1850, in Heard 2, S18, F12; and John H. Everett's orders to the Heard's comprador to pay the merchants who supplied the cargo (Canton) April–June 1850, in Heard 2, S18, F9. For the *Eveline*, I use her bill of lading (Hong Kong), August 3, 1849, in Heard 2, S5, together with

Chinese merchant invoices for purchase of the cargo and the itemized accounting of its auction sale in San Francisco, all from the "Leese Scrapbook."

5. Archaeologists are always concerned with the proper level of specificity to employ in describing large collections of artifacts. Accordingly, I asked my father to read my first-draft attempt at describing the *Frolic*'s ceramics. "Tom," he said, "I've been thinking about your book." He then launched into a parable—a somewhat mangled version of the construction of the Taj Mahal. "You know," he began, "there once was a great prince way over in India. And when his young wife died he decided to build her a memorial. So he put his men to work cutting and fitting marble blocks and laying out a magnificent garden. Many years passed, and it was a much older prince who returned to inspect the building as it reached completion. 'And what is that ugly old box doing there in the corner?' he asked. 'That's your wife's casket,' replied the architect. 'Get it out of here!' said the prince.

"Now Tom," my father concluded, "I think you're spending too much time worrying about a bunch of broken dishes. Get them out of your book. Put them in an appendix."

6. Heizer, p. 15.

7. Williams, *Chinese Commercial Guide* (1863), p. 131.

8. Bear and Stebbins, p. 9.

9. Daisy Kelley McCallum, oral history, Kelley House Museum, Mendocino, California.

10. In the *Eveline* documents, Woushing's name is sometimes rendered as Wongshing. In the *Frolic* documents, it is rendered as Wonshing.

11. Morrison, p. 182.

12. Williams, *Chinese Commercial Guide* (1856), p. 198.

13. In the *Eveline* documents, Hechong is also spelled as Hechung. Among the *Frolic* documents, it is rendered as Hechung.

14. Crossman, p. 248, color plate 96.

15. *Webster's Geographical Dictionary*, p. 1046.

16. See Crossman, pp. 438–39, for these illustrated stages of porcelain production, and pp. 440–41 for the stages of tea production.

17. Crossman, p. 352.

18. Wyler, pp. 8–9.

19. See Crossman, p. 349, and p. 353, plate 224, for Wongshing and Khecheong's addresses at #2 and #15 Old China Street.

20. Gilmour and Worrall. Subsequently, Dr. Worrall arranged for his co-author, Dr. Brian Gilmour, to ascertain the chemical composition of this fork from the *Frolic* (Worrall personal communication to author, March 15, 2001). The scientific assay was done using quantitative, nondestructive, surface analysis, employing energy-dispersive X-ray fluorescence spectrometry (XRF). The following elements, listed by weight percentage, confirm the fork to be *paktong*:

iron (1.3%); cobalt (not detected); nickel (4.7%); copper (47.8%); zinc (44.0%); arsenic (not detected); lead (2.7%); silver (not detected); tin (not detected).

21. G. L. Haskell (San Francisco) to Augustine Heard & Company (Canton), September 27, 1850, in Heard 2, case 26, F9.

22. Jacob Leese (Hong Kong) to Thomas O. Larkin (Monterey), August 5, 1849, in "Leese Scrapbook."

23. Extract from Bush & Company's letter to J. C. Anthon respecting shipment per *Mariposa*, Bush & Company (Hong Kong) to J. C. Anthon (San Francisco), June 8, 1849, in "Leese Scrapbook."

24. "New Goods Per *Mariposa*, from Hong Kong," *Daily Alta California*, September 7, 1849.

25. "Account Sales of Merchandise rec'd Ex. Bark *Mary* from China and sold by order of J. C. Anthon Esq. for Account and risk of the concerned," Williams & Company (San Francisco), December 12, 1849, in "Leese Scrapbook."

26. Frémont, p. 96. In 1849, Bayard Taylor visited the Frémonts in San Francisco and watched a crew of Chinese carpenters at work. "On my way to call upon Colonel Frémont, whom I found located with his family in Happy Valley, I saw a company of Chinese carpenters putting up the frame of a Canton-made house" (Taylor, vol. 1, p. 204).

27. Williams, *Chinese Commercial Guide* (1863), p. 130.

28. California State Department of Parks and Recreation, p. 129.

29. Wiltsee, pp. 176–83.

30. "Auction Sale, By Kendig, Wainwright & Co.," *Daily Alta California*, July 31, 1850.

31. Williams, *Chinese Commercial Guide* (1856), pp. 154–55.

32. Morrison, pp. 151–52.

33. Williams, *Chinese Commercial Guide* (1856), pp. 197–98.

Epilogue

1. Baer and Fink, pp. 36–39.

2. Our visit to the Castro adobe was organized by local historian Charlene Duval, who was down on her knees with the rest of us sorting potsherds—that is, until she discovered the parts of porcelain dolls. I thank Charlene for supplying me with genealogical data on the Castro family and important information regarding the adobe.

3. "Chrysanthemum"-style sherds excavated from the Wrightington adobe, Old Town, San Diego, are illustrated by Mudge, p. 187, fig. 295.

4. For a sampling of pre–Gold Rush assemblages with Chinese ceramics, see Hampson, p. 99–103. See also Benté, pp. 59–63. A large, as yet unpublished collection of Chinese ceramics from the Cooper-Molera adobe, Mon-

terey, California, is curated at the California Department of Parks and Recreation in Sacramento.

5. Praetzellis and Praetzellis, *Historical Archaeology of an Overseas Chinese Community in Sacramento, California,* pp. 100–101, 281–96. See also the dramatic interpretation of the data (Praetzellis and Praetzellis, "A Connecticut Merchant in Chinadom: A Play in One Act," pp. 86–93).

6. Evans, pp. 89–96, table 2.

7. Chinn, pp. 11–12. See also Wakeman, *Strangers at the Gate,* ch. 14. McKeown makes a strong argument that destruction and disorder were not the major causes of Chinese emigration to California. As he puts it: "Unrest and scarcity of local opportunities existed in South China, but . . . emigration as a family strategy depended more on stability, precedent, and opportunity than on disorder and poverty. That the burst of overseas migration during the second half of the nineteenth century should flow through Hong Kong, Xiamen and Shantou, rather than northern treaty ports like Shanghai or Tainjin, was a result of connections and networks established through a long tradition of migration and exchange with non-Chinese that gave people in South China the experience and the means to take advantage of opportunities presented by a changing Pacific economy" (p. 315).

8. Spence, p. xxi.

9. This coarse, blue-on-white porcelaneous stoneware was manufactured at several coastal locations in regions affected by conflict from circa 1850 to 1865. In the fourth edition of his *Chinese Commercial Guide* (1856), Williams neglects to mention California in his description of the market for this inexpensive ware: "The largest part of this ware now exported is of the cheaper sorts. . . . Much of the common blue crockery is made at Pá-kwoh, a village near Shih-má between Amoy and Chángchau fú, for native consumption; this kind is sent to all parts of the Archipelago, to India, Siam, and even finds its way to Central Asia" (p. 170). Williams is here describing a ware produced in Fujian Province and exported from Amoy, 320 miles east-northeast of Canton. Similar wares were being produced in the vicinity of Shantou in Guangdong Province, 110 miles closer to Canton. Swatow, the then-current Western spelling of Shantou, became a widely used generic term for any inexpensive blue-on-white porcelaneous stoneware.

10. This homogeneity of ceramic styles in Western Pacific Railroad work camps was probably intensified through use of company-chosen Chinese and American supply contractors to provision, respectively, the Chinese and American work camps. Workers were forced to purchase their supplies from the contracting company. The Chinese contractors were major firms in San Francisco, such as Tang Wo Gung (Bristol-Kagan, pp. 26–27).

11. Coolidge, 1909.

12. The five cargoes from the period 1850–51 were those from the *Tepic,*

Mohammad Shah, Margaretta, Lebanon, and *Antilope.* Those from 1859 were from the *Black Warrior, Black Prince, Early Bird, Challenge,* and *Boston Light.* The cargo manifests are filed under U.S. Customs House Records, San Francisco. They are curated at the Bancroft Library, University of California, Berkeley. These records include approximately 1,295 cargo lists, mostly dating from 1850 to 1865. Among these there are 144 cargo lists from China. Cargo lists after 1865 may have been destroyed in the earthquake and fire of 1906. Our sample of five vessels from the period 1850–51 was selected from among the twenty vessels from China for those years. Our five cargo lists from 1859 were selected from among the nineteen vessels from China from that year. Clearly, these cargo lists deserve a more thorough analysis.

13. I emphasize that these percentages refer only to the ten vessels in our sample. They are presented here only to suggest the degree to which Chinese merchants came to dominate the trade in rice, sugar, and opium. For a more thorough analysis, it will be necessary to analyze the cargo listings of the other vessels from China in the San Francisco Customs House listings.

14. Management of Chinese laborers occurred at three levels. The family association protected and assisted the individual; district associations representing specific districts in Kwangtung Province resolved differences among businesses or groups; and the Chinese Six Companies resolved differences among businesses or groups from different districts (Chinn, pp. 65–66). The wealthy merchants managing the district associations worked both as organizers of the emigration and as organizers of workers at the mines. In 1852 this power was formalized by the State of California, which conferred upon the district associations the power to collect the foreign miners' tax (four dollars per month for each Chinese miner) for a 15 percent commission (Bristol-Kagan, ch. 3: pp. 1–15). Indeed, the State of California eventually acceded to an agreement between district associations and steamship companies under which Chinese could only purchase a return passage to China through the district association. Chinese workers were thus obliged to pay off their debts before they could return to China (Bristol-Kagan, ch. 3: pp. 17–18). In addition to commissions for collecting the foreign miners' tax, the merchants managing the district associations found other ways to siphon off the income of miners. They collected large sums from operation of gambling houses and brothels. Control over emigration of women for prostitution enabled them to virtually monopolize this industry until 1854 (Bristol-Kagan, ch. 3: pp. 41–42).

Emigration of most Chinese laborers to California was accomplished through the credit-ticket system, whereby merchant brokers in Hong Kong paid for a boat ticket, whereas affiliated Chinese merchant firms in California found employment for the emigrant and collected the debt (Chinn, p. 15). The economic and social power of overseas Chinese merchants has received scant formal treatment. Pomerantz's study of the Chinese merchant class in the United States is an important exception. She shows that by 1875, six firms and fourteen persons—6.2 percent of the Chinese property owners in San Francisco—accounted for 35.4 percent of the total property within that community. She also demonstrates that rice imports paralleled Chinese population growth in the American West. For a description of the growing sophistication of Chinese merchants engaged in international trade, see Hao Yen-p'ing's *The Comprador in Nineteenth Century China*, and *The Commercial Revolution in Nineteenth-Century China*.

Adrian Praetzellis suggests that for the 1850s, the best accounts of the rapacity of Chinese merchants are to be found in contemporary newspaper articles, which, he cautions, "are clearly flavored by prejudice and must be taken as artifacts of their time" (personal communication). See, for example, the *Daily Alta California*, May 31, 1853, for quotes from a San Francisco Grand Jury report describing a Chinese society named the Four Great Houses, established to force trade with their various establishments and to prevent Chinese workers from buying tickets from anyone but themselves.

Bibliography

Baer, Morley, and Augusta Fink. *Adobes in the Sun: Portraits of a Tranquil Era*. San Francisco: Chronicle Books, 1972.

Bancroft, Hubert Howe. *California Pioneer Register and Index: 1542–1848*. Originally published in *History of California*, vol. 2 (San Francisco: The History Company Publisher, 1886). Reprinted for Clearfield Company, Inc., by Genealogical Publishing Co., Baltimore, 1964.

Bear, Dorothy, and Beth Stebbins. *Mendocino: Book Two*. Mendocino, Calif.: Gull Press, 1977.

Benté, Vance. "Analysis of the Ceramic Sub-Assemblage Recovered from the Estrada Adobe." In *Archaeological Investigations at CA-MNT-1243H: The Estrada Adobe in Monterey, California*, ed. Robert Cartier (San Jose: Archaeological Resource Management, 1985).

Blanchard, John A., ed. *The "H" Book of Harvard Athletics, 1852–1922*. Cambridge, Mass.: Harvard University Press, 1923.

Bliss, Anthony. "Damn that Dana!" *Bancroftiana* (magazine of the Friends of the Bancroft Library), no. 109 (1995), pp. 6–7.

Borden, Stanley T. "Caspar Lumber Company: Casper, South Fork, and Eastern Railroad." *The Western Railroader*, nos. 315–16 (1966).

Bowen, Richard LeBaron, Jr. "The Dhow Sailor." *The American Neptune* 11, no. 3 (1951): 161–202.

Bristol-Kagan, Leigh. "Chinese Migration to California, 1851–1882: Selected Industries of Work, the Chinese Institutions, and the Legislative Exclusion of a Temporary Labor Force." Ph.D. diss., Harvard University, 1982.

Bry, Stanleigh. "John Rogers Cooper: New England Merchant in Mexican California." *The Pioneer* (newsletter of the Society of California Pioneers), vol. 18, no. 13 (1985), pp. 1–12.

Bryant, Edward. *What I Saw in California.* 1848. Reprint, with an introduction by Thomas D. Clark, Lincoln: University of Nebraska Press, 1985.

California State Department of Parks and Recreation. *Five Views: An Ethnic Sites Survey for California.* Sacramento: Office of Historic Preservation, 1988.

Cheng, J. C. *Chinese Sources for the Taiping Rebellion, 1850–1864.* Hong Kong: Hong Kong University Press, 1963.

Chinn, Thomas W., ed. *A History of the Chinese in California: A Syllabus.* San Francisco: Chinese Historical Society of America, 1969.

Connor, Ann M. *Caspar Calling.* Santa Rosa, Calif.: Privately printed, 1967.

———, ed. *The Golden Years of Caspar.* Santa Rosa, Calif.: Privately printed, 1976.

Coolidge, Mary R. *Chinese Immigration.* New York: Henry Holt, 1909.

Crossman, Carl L. *The Decorative Arts of the China Trade: Paintings, Furnishings, and Exotic Curiosities.* London: Antique Collectors Club, 1991.

Dana, Richard Henry, Jr. *Two Years Before the Mast: A Personal Narrative.* 1840. Reprint, Cambridge, Mass.: Riverside Press, 1911.

Downs, Jacques M. *The Golden Ghetto: The American Commercial Community at Canton and the Shaping of American China Policy, 1784–1844.* Bethlehem, Penn.: Lehigh University Press, 1997.

Evans, William S., Jr. "Food and Fantasy: Material Culture of the Chinese in California and the West, circa 1850–1900." In *Archaeological Perspectives on Ethnicity in America,* ed. Robert L. Schuyler (Farmingdale, N.Y.: Baywood Publishing, 1980).

Everett, Edward Franklin. *Descendants of Richard Everett of Dedham, Mass.* Boston: Privately printed by T. R. Marvin & Son, Printers, 1860.

Forbes, H. A. Crosby, John Kernan, and Ruth Watkins. *Chinese Export Silver, 1785–1855.* Milton, Mass.: Museum of the American China Trade, 1975.

Frémont, Jessie Benton. *A Year of American Travel.* San Francisco: The Book Club of California, 1960.

Gilmour, Bryan, and Eldon Worrall. "Paktong: The Trade in Chinese Nickel Brass to Europe." In *Trade and Discovery: The Scientific Study of Artifacts from Post-Medieval Europe and Beyond,* Occasional Paper 109, ed. Duncan R. Hook and David R. M. Gaimster (London: British Museum Press, 1995).

Great Basin Foundation. *Wong Ho Leun, An American Chinatown.* 2 vols. San Diego: Privately published by the Great Basin Foundation, 1987.

Greenwood, Roberta S. *The Changing Faces of Main Street.* Buenaventura: Ventura Mission Archaeological Project, Redevelopment Agency, City of San Buenaventura, California, 1976.

Hague, Harlan, and David J. Langum. *Thomas O. Larkin: A Life of Patriotism and Profit in Old California*. Norman: University of Oklahoma Press, 1990.

Hammond, George P., ed. *The Larkin Papers: Personal, Business, and Official Correspondence of Thomas Oliver Larkin, Merchant and United States Consul in California*. 10 vols. Berkeley: University of California Press, 1951–68.

Hampson, R. Paul. *Data Recovery at CA-MNT-461H, Buena Vista Adobe, Spreckels, California*. Pacific Palisades: Greenwood and Associates, 1996.

Hao Yen-p'ing. *The Comprador in Nineteenth Century China: Bridge Between East and West*. Cambridge, Mass.: Harvard University Press, 1970.

———. *The Commercial Revolution in Nineteenth-Century China: The Rise of Sino-Western Mercantile Capitalism*. Berkeley: University of California Press, 1986.

Heizer, Robert F., ed. *George Gibbs' Journal of Redick McKee's Expedition through Northwestern California in 1851*. Berkeley: Archaeological Research Facility, Department of Anthropology, University of California, 1972.

Jackson, W. Francis. *Big River Was Dammed*. Mendocino, Calif.: FMMC Books, 1991.

Jones, Patricia Hagen. "A Comparative Study of Mid-Nineteenth-Century Chinese Blue-and-White Export Ceramics from the *Frolic* Shipwreck, Mendocino County, California." Master's thesis, San Jose State University, 1992. Subsequently published under the same title in *Volumes in Historical Archaeology*, no. 29, ed. Stanley South (Columbia: South Carolina Institute of Archaeology and Anthropology, South Carolina, 1994).

Layton, Thomas N. *Western Pomo Prehistory: Excavations at Albion Head, Nightbirds' Retreat, and Three Chop Village, Mendocino County, California*. Institute of Archaeology, Monograph 32. Los Angeles: University of California, 1990.

———. *The Voyage of the 'Frolic': New England Merchants and the Opium Trade*. Stanford, Calif.: Stanford University Press, 1997.

"Leese Scrapbook." *Quarterly of the Society of California Pioneers* 8, no. 1 (1931): 9–37. Original ms. at Society of California Pioneers.

Lockwood, Stephen C. *Augustine Heard and Company, 1858–1862: American Merchants in China*. Cambridge, Mass.: Harvard University Press, 1971.

Loeb, Edwin M. "Pomo Folkways." *University of California Publications in American Archaeology and Ethnology* 19, no. 2 (1926): 149–405.

Marshall, Don B. *California Shipwrecks: Footsteps in the Sea*. Seattle: Superior Publishing Co., 1978.

McClendon, Sally, and Robert Oswalt. "Pomo: Introduction." In *The Handbook of North American Indians*, vol. 8, *California*, ed. Robert F. Heizer (Washington D.C.: Smithsonian Institution, 1978).

McKeown, Adam. "Conceptualizing Chinese Diasporas, 1842–1949." *Journal of Asian Studies* 58, no. 2 (1999): 306–37.

Morrison, J. R. *A Chinese Commercial Guide.* 3rd ed. Canton: The Chinese Repository, 1848.

Mudge, Jean McClure. *Chinese Export Porcelain in North America.* New York: Clarkson N. Potter, 1986.

Nash, Robert A. "The Chinese Shrimp Fishery in California." Ph.D. diss., University of California at Los Angeles, 1973.

Ogden, Adele. "Boston Hide Droghers Along California Shores." *Quarterly of the California Historical Society* 8, no. 4 (1929): 289–305.

———. "Trading Vessels on the California Coast: 1787–1848." Unpublished manuscript, Bancroft Library, University of California at Berkeley, n.d.

"An Old Resident" [William C. Hunter]. *The 'Fan Kwae' at Canton, Before Treaty Days, 1825–1844* [1882]. Reissued, Shanghai: Kelly and Walsh, Limited, 1911.

Palmer, Lyman L. *History of Mendocino County, California.* San Francisco: Alley, Bowen, 1880.

Pomerantz, Linda. "Chinese Bourgeoisie in the United States." *Amerasia Journal* 11, no. 1 (spring 1984): 1–32.

Praetzellis, Mary, and Adrian Praetzellis. *Archaeological and Historical Studies of the IJ56 Block, Sacramento, California: An Early Chinese Community.* Rohnert Park, Calif.: Cultural Resources Facility, Sonoma State University, 1982.

———. *Historical Archaeology of an Overseas Chinese Community in Sacramento, California.* Rohnert Park, Calif.: Anthropological Studies Center, Sonoma State University, 1997.

———. "A Connecticut Merchant in Chinadom: A Play in One Act." *Historical Archaeology* (special issue entitled *Archaeologists as Storytellers*) 32, no. 1 (1998): 86–93.

Shangraw, Clarence, and Edward P. Von der Porten. *The Drake and Cermeño Expeditions' Chinese Porcelains at Drakes Bay, California, 1579 and 1595.* Santa Rosa, Calif.: Santa Rosa Junior College and the Drake Navigators Guild, 1981.

Spence, Jonathan D. *God's Chinese Son: The Taiping Heavenly Kingdom of Hong Xiuquan.* New York: W. W. Norton, 1996.

Sullenberger, Martha. *Dogholes and Donkey Engines.* Sacramento: California Department of Parks and Recreation, 1980.

Taylor, Bayard. *Eldorado, or, Adventures in the Path of Empire.* 2 vols. New York: G. P. Putnam, 1850.

Tiffany, Osmond, Jr. *The Canton Chinese or the American's Sojourn in the Celestial Empire.* Boston: James Munroe, 1849.

Von der Porten, Edward. "Chinese Junk Wreck Under Investigation." *Newsletter of the Society for California Archaeology* 3, no. 4/5 (1969): 10.

Wakeman, Frederic, Jr. *Strangers at the Gate: Social Disorders in South China, 1839–1861.* Berkeley: University of California Press, 1966.

———. "The Canton Trade and the Opium War." In *The Cambridge History of China,* vol. 10, pt. 1, *Late Ch'ing, 1800–1911,* ed. Denis Twitchet and John K. Fairbank (Cambridge: Cambridge University Press, 1978).

Willets, William, and Lim Suan Poh. *Nonya Ware and Kitchen Ch'ing.* Published for the Southeast Asian Ceramic Society, West Malaysian Chapter, Malaysia. Singapore: Oxford University Press, 1981.

Williams, S. Wells. *A Chinese Commercial Guide.* 4th ed. Canton: The Chinese Repository, 1856.

———. *The Chinese Commercial Guide.* 5th ed. Hong Kong: A. Shortrede & Co., 1863.

Wiltsee, Ernest A. "Double Springs: First County Seat of Calaveras County." *California Historical Society Quarterly* 11, no. 2 (1932): 176–83.

Winn, Robert. *Mendocino Historical Review* (special issue entitled *The Mendocino Indian Reservation*) 12 (1986).

Wurm, Ted. *Mallets on the Mendocino Coast: Caspar Lumber Company Railroads and Steamships.* Hillsboro, Ore.: Timber Times, 1986.

Wyler, Seymour B. *The Book of Old Silver: English, American, Foreign.* New York: Crown Publishers, 1937.

Index

Achen (fictional character), 61, 97, 245n9

advertising fees, for sale of *Eveline* cargo, 79

Ahoy, 64, 242n18

Ahsig (fictional character), 91, 244n8

Ahsing (fictional character), 70, 92, 245n9

alcoholic beverages, as cargo, 63, 97, 220

Alert (ship), 46

Alger, Cyrus, 136

Alok, in fictional vignette about *Frolic* wreck, 113, 246n1

Amelia (ship), 94

anchors, *Frolic*, 5, 134, 144

Anonyma (ship), 87

Anthon, J. C., 79, 179, 182, 243n5

Antilope (ship), 251n12

archaeology: commodity comparisons in historical, 22–27, 151; museum and comparison work in, 19–21; nautical, 195; personal papers in historical, 15–16, 17, 152, 157, 223–29; specificity in, 248n5; traditional methodology of, 7–8; value of historical, 150, 195

Armstrong, George Parker. *See* Parker, John

Ashoe, 163, 242n18

assimilation, of Chinese into American community, 203–5

auction fees, for *Eveline* cargo, 77, 79

Augustine Heard & Company, 4; bankruptcy of, 128–29; China trade and, 54, 70–71, 77; *Eveline* cargo and, 6–7, 53; Everett as accountant for, 52; lack of records on *Frolic* crew and back wages, 124–25; location at Dutch factory, 58, 59, 242n11; on loss of *Frolic*, 97–98; opium trade and, 13, 74 (*see also* opium trade). *See also* Heard, John

back scratchers, ivory, 212

bagged sediment, collected by divers, 142

bale handles, for camphor trunks, 161

ballast blocks: Fratis discovery of, 134; weight and size of, 88, 136, 141; wreckage patterns of, 4–5, 127

"bamboo" design, on porcelain, 5, 151, 154, 155, 201, 202

bamboo objects, 214

bandany, 246n1

Bandini, Juan, 48

Bandini, Ysidora, 48–49, 239–40n2

Bankia setacia (shipworm), 127

Baring Brothers bank, 96

beads, 157–59, 213

Bear, Dorothy, 11–12, 150

Bear Flag Revolt, 55

bedsteads, 215

Bellum Gallicum (Caesar), 92

Benitz, Mr., 100

beverages, 63, 97, 219–20

billiard balls, ivory, 212

bills of lading: *Eveline*, 15–16, 152, 247n4; *Frolic*, 13–14, 16, 170, 178, 187, 230–33, 247n4

Black, James, 246n1

Black Prince (ship), 251n12

Black Warrior (ship), 251n12

blackwood tables, 164, 214

blankets, 220

"Blue China" dinner sets, 155, 216

bolts, brass, 5, 142

bone objects, 193, 194, 212

boots, patent leather, 220

Boston Light (ship), 251n12

bouquet holders, ivory, 212

Bowen, Thomas, 42–45, 239n2

boxes, lacquered ware, 216

bracelets, 68, 175, 210

brass objects: bolts, 5, 142; elbow braces, for camphor trunks, 21;

handles, for camphor trunks, 21, 142; hinges, 146, 159; latches, 146, 159; manufacture of, 168; paper holders, 142; porthole covers, 141; pulls, 146, 163; recessed handles, 163, 165–68; screws, 142; weight cups and scales, 169–70

"breaking waves" design, on porcelain, 23

breast pins, 175, 210

Brinley, C. H., 71, 243n22

brooches, 68, 177–78

brushes, bone, 193

Buller, Dave, 144–48, 247n9

Buller, Steve, 144–48

Bush & Company, 69

buttons, 211, 213

cabinets, 216

California, settlement after statehood, 127–28

"California banknotes," 7

California Shipwrecks (Marshall), 148

camlet jackets, 221

campaign furniture, 164–68. *See also* writing desks

camphor trunks: backing-plate styles of, 162; designs on, European-American style of, 23; in *Eveline* cargo, 66–67, 215; handles for, 21, 142, 161; hardware from *Frolic* for, 161; modern nested, 26; preservation of pieces of, 127; types of on *Eveline*, 163; types of on *Frolic*, 162

cannons, 136, 137–38

Canton factories, 58, 59, 203, 241n10

Canton pattern dinnerware: sets, 156, 157; serving dish, 63

capiz-shell windows, 13, 19, 180, 181, 186

caps, 221

capstan, 134, 144

cargo: *Eveline* cargo as model for *Frolic*, 6–7, 15–16, 53, 152–57; eyewitness account of *Frolic*, 14–15; invoices for *Eveline*, 19, 60, 69, 159–60, 170, 223–29; manifests, 250–51n12; profit from, 243n4; sales of *Eveline*, 17–19, 209–22. *See also* bills of lading; divers: *Frolic* site artifact collections of; *and specific items*

Carlos (fictional character), 111

Caspar (town), 11, 130

Caspar Creek, 128

Caspar Lumber Company, 128, 129, 132

Castro, José Joaquín, 198

Castro adobe, 197–201, 249n2

"celadon" ceramics, 202

ceramics: analytical problem of *Frolic*, 153–55; changes in perception of Chinese, 200; designs on, 5, 23, 201 (*see also specific design names*); *Eveline* and *Frolic* items compared, 152–57; Fratis discovery of, 134; homogeneity of, 250n10; identification of designs on, 150–51, 250n9; manufacture of, 250n9; naming and size problems of plates versus bowls, 153–55; porcelain, 216–18; rolls of, 6, 20; stoneware, 62, 63, 250n9

Cermeño, Sebastián, 11

Chace, Paul, 202, 203

chairs, 215

Chalcedony (ship), 46

Challenge (ship), 251n12

checkers, ivory, 212

chest drawers, 215

Chinadom, 201, 202; ceramic styles associated with, 201–3

Chinatown, San Francisco, 25–26

China trade: definition of, 25; Heard's involvement in, 54, 70–71, 77; inexpensive items in, 151–52; pidgin usage in, 26, 241n9; trends in, 19, 20–21

Chinese Commercial Guide: for 1848, 160, 162, 192; for 1856, 187–88, 192, 250n9; for 1863, 158, 180

Chinese Historical Society of America, 139

Chinese lanterns, 214

Chinese Six Companies, in Chinese culture, 251n14

chocolate, 73, 219

"chowchow," on *Frolic* bill of lading, 187

"chrysanthemum" design, on porcelain, 200

Chyloong, 68, 157

city ordinances, San Francisco, 94

Coast Miwok, 11

coffee and tea sets, 155, 156

coins, 12, 50

combs, 192, 213, 214

compradors: Heard, 61, 78, 97; payment chits and, 14

Cooper, Encarnación Vallejo, 238n8

Cooper, John B. R., 16, 54, 55, 238n8

copper, painted, 214

copper sheathing nails, 12

corner protectors, for camphor trunks, 161

Corréo de Cobija (ship), 53, 93

cotton shirts, 64, 221

couches, 215
Cowasjee Shapoorjee, 96
Craft, Cliff, 247n9
crew members, of *Frolic*, 89, 91,
    124–25. *See also* Faucon,
    Edward Horatio
cringles, 163
Crossman, Carl, 163, 164
crystal stamps, 146
Cutshing, 170, 173, 175

Daily Alta California, 93, 186
Dana, Richard Henry, Jr., 46, 47,
    48, 237n4
David Sassoon & Company, 83
decomposition, of shipwrecks,
    126–27
Decorative Arts of the China Trade
    (Crossman), 163
Deetz, Dr. James, 164
deFreitos, Miguel, 129, 247n9
Delgado, James, 247n9
designs: on camphor trunks, 23;
    identification of porcelain,
    150–51, 250n9; types of on
    porcelain, 5, 23, 201. *See also*
    specific design names
Deutcher, Mr. (*Frolic*'s first mate),
    6, 83, 89, 104
dice, ivory, 212
dinnerware sets, 155, 156, 216–17
district associations, in Chinese
    culture, 251n14
divers: discovery of *Frolic* wreck site
    by, 132, 133, 134–35; *Frolic* site
    artifact collections of, 4, 5, 8, 12,
    19, 136–37, 142, 143, 146, 163;
    gold and, 174–75
Dixwell, George, 83, 95, 96, 245n9
"double happiness" design, on
    porcelain, 202, 203

Double Springs Ranch, 182–86
dragon jars, 24–25
"dragon scales" design, on porce-
    lain, 23–24
Drake, Sir Francis, 11
Drake's Bay, 11
dressing gowns, 221
dried fruits, 73, 219
dried peas, 73, 219
Dutch factory, 58, 59, 242n11
Duval, Charlene, 199, 249n2

Earle, Morris, 160
Early Bird (ship), 251n12
earrings, 68, 175–77, 210
Eaton & Company, 28, 34
"ecofacts," 7–8
eight-real coins, 50
elbow braces, brass, for camphor
    trunks, 21
emigration, Chinese, 250n7,
    251–52n14
Emmy (ship), 53, 93
end-lugs, for camphor trunks, 161
Europa (ship), 95
Evans, Bill, 202–3
Eveline (ship): cargo as model for
    Frolic, 6–7, 15–16, 53, 152–57;
    cargo not sold, 222; cargo sales
    in San Francisco, 209–22; gold
    objects on, 175; invoices for
    cargo of, 19, 60, 69, 159–60,
    170, 223–29; Leese ledgers of
    cargo sales from, 17–19. *See also*
    specific items
Everett, Betsey, 58, 59, 60
Everett, John Hurd: background
    of, 26–27, 46–48, 237–38n6;
    cowhide trade involvement of,
    7; fictional account of *Eveline*
    cargo purchases, 54–73; fictional

account of pre-*Eveline* events, 29–52; *Frolic* payment chits and, 14; joins Heards in China, 52; Larkin letters to, 28; ledgers of, 43; Leese and *Eveline* cargo and, 6–7; portrait of, 7, 29, 56–58; purchase of varnished camphor trunks by, 67; return to California from China, 128; *Tasso* and, 40, 52, 240n3

Everett, Oliver Capen, 58, 60, 182

Everett, Otis, 97

Everett, Percival Lowell, 97, 128–29, 245n9

Everett, Richard, 182

Falcone, Sal, 172

false pearls, 157–59

family associations, in Chinese culture, 251n14

fans: bone, 212; feather painted, 211; ivory and silk, 190, 212; silver, 210–11

farewell dinners, prior to ships sailing, 70–72, 243n22

Faucon, Catherine, 67, 130

Faucon, Edward Horatio: *Alert* and, 46; background of, 161, 237n4; camphor trunks of, 160, 161; *Chalcedony* and, 46; on China trade, to Everett, 52; earlier *Frolic* voyages of, 6; fees and percentage for *Frolic* voyage, 79, 243n5; in fictional vignette about wreck of *Frolic*, 104–9; joins China trade, 47; on loss of *Frolic*, 98–101, 105; opium trade and *Frolic*, 74, 80; opium trade and *Lady Hayes*, 77, 80; papers destroyed by daughter, 130; *Pilgrim* and, 36, 46; portrait of, 47; skills as

captain, 86–87; U.S.S. *Fearnot* and, 128

Fernandes, Valerio, in fictional vignette about *Frolic* wreck, 107, 108, 111, 115, 246n1

fictional vignettes: of *Eveline* cargo purchasing, 54–73; explanations of fiction versus truth in, 239–40n2; of *Frolic* cargo purchasing and preparations, 77–98, 244nn7, 8; of *Frolic* wreck, 104–24, 245–46n1; of pre-*Eveline* events, 29–52

fiddle-pattern spoons, 171, 243n20

filigree items, 68, 146, 147, 175–76, 211

Fillmore, Millard, 128

final voyage, map of *Frolic*'s, iii

flatware, silver, 69, 170–72, 190, 211. *See also* non-silver flatware

flint and steel boxes, 173, 210

flower boats, ivory, 212

Fockhing, 60

Fong, Edsel Ford, 26

foodstuffs, bulk, 73, 157, 219

Forbes, H. A. Crosby, 19–20, 172–73

Forbes, Robert Bennet, 21

Ford, J. B., 12, 238n2

Ford, Jerome C., 159, 238n2

Fort Bragg, 128

Fort Ross, 100, 105

Foster, John, 247n9

"four flowers" design, on porcelain, 202

Four Great Houses, 252n14

Francisco, Custodio, in fictional vignette about *Frolic* wreck, 104, 246n1

Fratis, Louie, Jr., 131–34, 137–38, 247n9

Freitas, Louie, 130, 131
Freitos, Bill, 129–31, 132
Frémont, Jessie, 179, 184
Frémont, John Charles, 37, 55, 179, 239n2
Frolic (ship): anchors, 5, 134, 144; bill of lading, 13–14, 16, 170, 178, 187, 230–33, 247n4; cargo loading of, 90; crew members of, 89, 91, 124–25 (*see also* Faucon, Edward Horatio); decomposition of, 126–27; *Eveline* cargo as model for cargo of, 6–7, 15–16, 53, 152–57; map of final voyage, iii; map of wreck site, 2; opium trade and, 6, 13, 74, 75, 82; salvage of, 102, 104–24, 159 (*see also* divers); wreck site of (*see* wreck site, of *Frolic*)
Frolic Shipwreck Repository, 12, 160
"Fu" design, on porcelain, 151, 154, 155
furniture: in *Eveline* cargo, 64, 66, 163–64, 214; in *Frolic* cargo, 163–64. *See also specific types of furniture*

Gallego (ship), 101
gaming pieces, 146, 187, 191, 194, 212
Gaoqua, 68
Gardner Brothers shipyard, 5
General Chart of the North Pacific (Norrie), 92
Gibbs, George, 14–15, 156
Gibson, Patrick, 139–41
Giles, Rikke, 204
Gilmour, Brian, 248n20
ginger jars, from wreck site versus Three Chop Village, 11, 157

gold objects, 145, 146, 174–75, 209–10
Goqua, 77
grass matting, 68, 220
Great Wall, Chinese Antique Furniture, 22–23
Grove, Patricia, 173
Gulf of Canton, map of, 76
gutta percha, 219

hair nets with silk tassels, 210
Hakka, 203
handkerchiefs, 222
handles: for camphor trunks, 21, 142, 161; recessed, 163, 165–68
Harrison, Mr., 106, 107
Hastings, Samuel J., 240n3
hawksbill turtles, tortoiseshell from, 192
Heard, Augustine, the elder, 95
Heard, Augustine, the younger, 96–97
Heard, John, 71, 83, 84, 86–87, 94
Hecheong (Hechong/Hechung), 77, 91, 163, 248n13
Hedrick, Mr. (fictional character), 95
hinges, brass, 146, 159
historical archaeology, methodology in. *See* archaeology
History of Mendocino County (Palmer), 130
Honolulu (ship), 53
horn objects, 192–94
House I, Three Chop Village, 10
house servants, Chinese, as cargo, 69
Hugh Walker (ship), 93

imported, non-Chinese manufactured goods, 71–73, 168, 186–88